W9-CMQ-972

Stalin's Keys to Victory

Stalin's Keys to Victory

The Rebirth of the Red Army

WALTER S. DUNN, JR.

PRAEGER SECURITY INTERNATIONAL
Westport, Connecticut • London

Library of Congress Cataloging-in-Publication Data

Dunn, Walter S. (Walter Scott), 1928–
    Stalin's keys to victory : the rebirth of the Red Army / Walter S. Dunn, Jr.
        p. cm.
    Includes bibliographical references and index.
    ISBN 0-275-99067-2 (alk. paper)
    1. Soviet Union. Raboche-Krest'ianskaia Krasnaia Armiia—History—World War,
1939–1945.   2. World War, 1939–1945—Campaigns—Eastern Front.   I. Title.
    D764.D7995   2006
    940.54'147—dc22   2006001237

British Library Cataloguing in Publication Data is available.

Library of Congress Catalog Card Number: 2006001237
ISBN: 0-275-99067-2

First published in 2006

Praeger Security International, 88 Post Road West, Westport, CT 06881
An imprint of Greenwood Publishing Group, Inc.
www.praeger.com

Printed in the United States of America

The paper used in this book complies with the
Permanent Paper Standard issued by the National
Information Standards Organization (Z39.48-1984).

10 9 8 7 6 5 4 3 2 1

Contents

Preface

Many have difficulty comprehending the miracle that took place in late 1941 and early 1942 in the Soviet Union. In the summer of 1941, the German Army routed the Red Army as it had routed the Polish, British, French, and other armies in 1939, 1940, and early 1941. None had been able to withstand German might more than a few weeks. When Hitler invaded the Soviet Union in June 1941, it appeared to most that Hitler would succeed as he had before. A major portion of the prewar Red Army was completely annihilated, millions of prisoners taken, and the most populous and developed provinces of the Soviet Union were occupied by the Germans and their allies.

The purpose of this work is to detail how the Soviet Union was able to create a new army in late 1941 and early 1942 and how the new rifle divisions and brigades and new tank brigades were formed and deployed. The deployment of the new unit reveals the true strategic objectives of Stalin and his generals. Soviet histories tend to dismiss as diversions operations that did not succeed, but some of these operations received major reinforcements of new units before beginning to attack. One does not invest major assets in a venture that does not have a significant objective.

The assignment of the new units is of special importance because of the logistical nightmare faced by the Soviet high command from June 1941 to the summer of 1944. The only practical way to move large formations in the Soviet Union was by rail. There were comparatively few good roads and far from enough trucks to spare for strategic as opposed to tactical troop movements. Marching the troops and carrying their equipment and supplies with horse-drawn wagons was painfully slow. Therefore, once committed to a front, that unit would remain there for some time.

The Soviet rail network generally served the large cities. Few lines were available to the Russians after December 1941. The single rail line east of Leningrad was cut by the Germans. A few rail lines led south from Moscow and east to the Siberian military districts. Lateral north-south movement by rail was extremely difficult, usually accomplished by sending the trains first to Moscow and then from Moscow to the front. Therefore, once a division was ready for combat, it moved by rail to an army on the front and, for the most part, there it remained. When a decision was made to send a division to the Moscow area or to the south, that was tantamount to a final commitment for that division. The Soviets could not move large numbers of divisions laterally as did the German Army. Once committed, the Soviet division remained in the general area.

To make this study more palatable, I have limited the examination to rifle and motorized divisions, rifle brigades, and tank brigades. These units were the building blocks of the armies and tank corps. The number of divisions alone is staggering when one considers that the United States employed less than 100 divisions and Great Britain less than that in campaigns against Germany, Italy, and Japan. While Soviet divisions had fewer men, they had comparable firepower.

Listing the individual units with numbers indicating their lineage is necessary because otherwise the message would not be clear. Simply stating that 84 rifle divisions were formed in two months not only fails to make an impression, but is passed off as an exaggeration not based on any existing document.

More than 9,000 Soviet units of battalion size or greater are included in my computer database, which gives a month-by-month history of each unit and its components. Because the Russians used the same number as many as four times to designate units, I have created a simplified lineage for each rifle division, rifle brigade, and tank brigade. This new designation includes the various numbers used by each unit.

Many of the divisions were originally created as rifle brigades, then built up into rifle divisions, then renumbered with the designation of a division that had been destroyed, and finally renumbered as guard divisions. A large block of divisions were formed with 400 series numbers and then renumbered with the numbers of destroyed divisions or those that had been designated guard divisions. In 1941, some rifle brigades and divisions were in combat a few months after they were formed, but this practice quickly gave way to longer periods of training. Popular myth has it that many Russian divisions were sent into battle with a few weeks or months of training and were slaughtered by the Germans, because the number had recently appeared in the order of battle even though the unit had been in existence for months under a different designation.

Where these new units would be committed was determined by the Soviet strategic plans. Often the German intelligence maps would include a notation of the existence of 60 or so unidentified and unlocated rifle divisions. The German task of identifying these units was made immeasurably more complicated by the Soviet practice of using the same numbers repeatedly.

Although this rebirth of the Red Army has been described in general terms, the exact details have been difficult to extract. Soviet reluctance to release details has been a major obstacle. The Soviet decision in late 1941 to give the numbers of destroyed divisions to the new divisions has caused some confusion. Stalin's decision to disguise some of the new divisions as volunteer divisions similar to those created in Leningrad by his political rival added to the mystery. The practice of creating a rifle brigade, a comparatively simple organization, first and then transforming it into a full-fledged division was significant in concealing the length of time taken to train the division. After 40 years of study, I have not resolved that problem completely—rifle brigades disappear from the order of battle and divisions appear for the first time, but I have not established all of the links. Lack of agreement between Soviet orders of battle and other documents add to the confusion. German intelligence reports often provide useful clues to resolve some problems.

The Red Army identified different divisions with the same number by adding a roman numeral in parentheses; for example, 34(II) was the second formation bearing the number 34. The different divisions were identified in some Russian documents as 137th Rifle Division (I), 137th (II), and so on. However, the roman numerals do not appear in the Russian orders of battle. German intelligence continued to collect data on the various divisions with the same number on the same card but in published lists did identify the new versions of each division. A common German error was to designate a unit as a new division when it simply had been withdrawn from combat for rest and rehabilitation and then returned to combat with the same leadership. Such errors continue to obscure the picture for historians and readers.

In this work, I have simplified the designation using capital letters, 34B being the second formation of a division bearing the number 34. To indicate the lineage of a unit, I have placed slashes between the various designations. For example, 34rb/345/101B/34G designates the 34th Brigade, which became the 345th Rifle Division, which became the 101(II) Rifle Division, which in turn became the 34th Guard Division. The significance of establishing this relationship is that the unit was formed in September 1941 as a brigade and trained for several months. Conversion of brigades to divisions was accomplished either by combining two brigades and adding some replacements or adding a replacement regiment and forming new battalions with cadres drawn from the existing four battalions in the brigade. The same alternatives were used for the artillery, engineers, and so on. The new division received the number of a destroyed division, and perhaps later in the war it was awarded guard status. However, it remained the same unit, in most cases commanded by the same general. The essential personnel provided cohesion regardless of expansion or replacement of losses. For this reason, when these divisions entered combat they generally performed quite well. They were not the masses of untrained men portrayed in some accounts.

Unit integrity was as significant in the Red Army as in other armies. Intimate knowledge of the character and abilities of the regimental, battalion, and company commanders was essential for a division commander. Similar knowledge was essential to the lieutenants and sergeants who led the companies. Men are not robotic clones, and each has strengths and weaknesses. Knowing these led to unit integrity and success on the battlefield. Without unit integrity, ad hoc units soon dissolved on the battlefield. Therefore, tracing the formation and commitment to battle of Soviet units regardless of the changes of designation is crucial to understanding the success and failure of Soviet operations. Knowing whether a division was experienced but low on manpower or whether it was a fresh fully manned division with no prior combat was essential to predict its performance in a coming battle.

Therefore, the identification of truly new units and the way they were committed provides a valuable clue to the true intentions of the Soviet leadership. As Col. David Glantz has remarked, Russian military historians ignore or mention only in passing as diversions operations that ended in defeat and portray the victories as the significant operations. However, a study of the investment of new units will clearly identify those operations considered significant, as the Russians seldom reinforced a sector that had no immediate strategic importance.

The book does not have notes, only an extensive select bibliography. The source of most of the data is my personal database, which is derived from a wide range of sources. To annotate a single list would require more than a hundred references. My earlier books on the Red Army that refer to many of the topics discussed are fully documented, although more recent Soviet materials were not included.

Over the years, I have been helped in my research by many individuals. Among them are James Goff, David Glantz, David McNamara, and Tom Johnson. My wife, Jean, has patiently read this manuscript many times, offering suggestions and deciphering what I meant to say.

Key to Abbreviations

The following abbreviations are used in the tables to identify divisions and brigades. Capital A, B, or C following a division number indicates which formation of that division is listed. Letter A is the first formation, and so on.

b	brigade
cav	cavalry
cdno	Crimea Division of Volunteers
cog	Coastal Operating Group
east	Eastern
G	Guard
Gb	Guard brigade
Gd	Guard division
ir	infantry regiment
ldno	Leningrad Division of Volunteers
lrb	light rifle brigade
mb	mechnized brigade
mdno	Moscow Division of Volunteers
mtn	mountain division
mtr	motorized division
nkvd	NKVD, Soviet internal security
sh	shock
skib	ski brigade
rb	rifle brigade
rd	rifle division

tb	tank brigade
td	tank division
tr	tank regiment
UR	fortified sector

Chapter 1

Introduction

THE ACHIEVEMENTS of the Red Army in World War II surpass those of any other army in history. Facing invasion by the German Army at the peak of its performance in the summer of 1941, the Red Army was all but annihilated, losing more than 3 million killed and missing. The Russian reaction was to create a second Red Army during the summer of 1941, 157 rifle divisions, which the Germans again all but destroyed by December 1941. The Red Army lost 154 rifle divisions in the first six months of the war. However, the Russians began the creation of a third Red Army in August 1941 and by November 1941 had formed an additional 148 rifle divisions and 88 rifle brigades, which stopped the Germans at Moscow and drove them back. Beginning in December 1941, the Russians formed a fourth Red Army, some of which were lost in Ukraine in the spring of 1942, but the majority completed their training by the fall of 1942 and stopped the Germans at Stalingrad.

No other nation has lost one-third of its population and its prewar army and then replaced it three times in the course of 18 months, all the while fighting one of the most highly trained and experienced armies the world has ever seen. This achievement was made possible not only by an authoritarian government that had complete control of its people, but also by a skillful propaganda campaign which convinced many Soviet citizens that they should fight for Mother Russia, as the alternative of German rule would be so much worse. Hitler assisted that campaign by condoning horrible atrocities in the territory occupied by the German Army in the summer of 1941. Had the Germans behaved more humanely, as they did in France and the other countries taken from 1939 to 1941, there is some doubt that the Russian people would have been willing to make the sacrifices. In Ukraine and other regions, the Germans were greeted as liberators in the early months of the war. Later, millions of Russians and other nationalities volunteered to serve the Germans as service and combat soldiers.

The true magnitude of the Russian sacrifices and their accomplishments was obscured after the war by the reluctance of the Communist rulers to reveal the extent of the losses sustained by the Soviet Union in the Great Patriotic War. Doing so would imply that the loss of 28 million people had seriously weakened the nation. Sixty years later, many details concerning the Red Army in World War II are still classified. However, by piecing together data from a wide variety of sources, a partial picture emerges of the massive mobilization of men and weapons.

A careful study of events on the eastern front raises many questions about politics, strategy, and resources. The accepted interpretation of a Red Army composed of masses of poorly armed and poorly led peasants that overwhelmed the Germans does not jibe with details concerning manpower, leadership, and the equipment of the Red Army. One should not stop at merely recording who, what, when, and where (the operational history), but continue on to reveal how (logistics and resources), and why (strategy and politics). The following chapters examine closely these factors, Stalin's keys to victory, which led to the Soviet defeat of the German Army.

First, where did the Russians find the men to replace the divisions lost in 1941 and 1942? One-third of the population of the Soviet Union was in German hands by December 1941, reducing the annual intake of recruits by at least a third. Yet the Red Army had 6 million men on the front in 1942 and 4 million in other areas.

Second, how did the Russians equip the new divisions, not once, but three times after the greater part of the armament factories were either destroyed by the Germans or in the process of moving to the eastern republics? Were there enough weapons to arm the new divisions, or were they just large gangs of poorly armed men?

Third, how did the Russians maintain the strength of the Red Army in the face of horrendous casualties? Were the losses really that severe and how did the Russians maintain the firepower of the rifle companies?

Fourth, why didn't the Russians give up in 1941 as everyone expected? Their losses in men and territory were far more serious than the French experienced in 1940. Given that the Soviet Union was in a desperate state in late 1941, how was it able to rebuild the army and defeat the Germans at Moscow?

Fifth, why did the Russians make such a mess at Izyum in Ukraine in the summer of 1942? More important, what were the changes in November 1942 at Stalingrad?

Sixth, why were the Germans not as successful at Kursk in the summer of 1943 as they had been in the two previous summers, inasmuch as the common belief was that the Russians could win battles only in winter?

Seventh, what were the causes of the sudden shifts of policy in 1944 and the mind-boggling defeat of German Army Group Center in Russia, as well as the collapse in France in June and July 1944? Why were the German defeats catastrophic?

Eighth, were the Russians reaching the point of exhaustion in 1945? The number of men in the rifle companies had dwindled to less than 100, but the total number of men at the front increased from 6 million to 6.5 million. Why did the Russians discharge more than 300,000 technicians to begin rebuilding the formerly occupied area? Why did the Russians reduce the production of weapons in 1944 and 1945?

The prevailing image of the Red Army during World War II is a mass army, poorly trained and inadequately equipped, with a few exceptions, such as the T-34 tank. The general interpretation has been that this inexhaustible mass of men had overwhelmed the German Army through sheer numbers while absorbing huge losses. The true picture is more complex and deserves a closer look.

Once the Germans unleashed their panzer divisions, the Polish, French, British, Yugoslav, and other armies had collapsed within weeks. The English Channel and the Royal Air Force saved Britain, but all the others surrendered.

The eastern front in World War II was a bloodbath of gigantic proportions for both soldiers and civilians on both sides of the conflict. More than 28 million Soviet citizens died, most of them civilians. More than 6 million soldiers were killed in action or died of wounds, another 4.5 million were missing or prisoners of war, and another half million died of sickness or accidents, for a total of 11 million military dead or missing. In addition, 22 million were wounded or sick, including 1.4 million who died later and 3.8 million who were permanently disabled. These totals are beyond comprehension when compared to the losses suffered by other nations. The Germans and their allies lost only 4 million soldiers who were killed or died of wounds during the war.

To grasp the dramatic events that occurred in the Soviet Union in the fall of 1941, one must review the events of the previous 24 years. In 1917, following a series of defeats by the German army and revolution at home, the Russian government was overthrown, and the new government made peace with Germany. The Russian army was defeated by less than half of the German army, most of which was engaged on the western front with France, Britain, and the United States. Following the Treaty of Brest-Litovsk, the Germans occupied large tracts of Russia.

The Versailles Treaty in 1919 forced the new Soviet Union to surrender much of what is now Poland, the three Baltic states, Finland, and Bessarabia, which was given to Romania. There followed a bitter civil war in the Soviet Union, which devastated the country. Britain, France, and the United States sent troops to Russia to assist the rebels, but in the end the Communists prevailed despite enormous losses.

The Soviet government launched a series of programs to rebuild the country and by 1939 had assembled a formidable army. With the help of technicians from the United States, Britain, Germany, France, and other countries, a giant industrial complex was created to manufacture railroad rolling stock, tractors, and many other products. These factories, some designed by experts from the Ford Motor Company in Detroit, were converted during World War II to the mass production of tanks and other weapons.

In 1939, Stalin signed a pact with Hitler, agreeing to provide the Germans with raw materials in exchange for weapons. In a cooperative effort when Hitler took Poland, the Red Army took the eastern half of Poland and in the same year occupied Estonia, Latvia, and Lithuania. In 1940, the Soviets attacked Finland with disastrous results in the beginning, as the Finns ambushed the Red Army columns. Eventually the Soviets launched a massive attack in the south and the Finns agreed to surrender some strategic territory. However, the reputation of the Red Army was badly soiled. After Hitler had defeated the Western powers in 1940 and had taken the Balkans in early 1941, he unexpectedly turned to the Soviet Union. Based on the Red Army's experience in the war against Finland and Hitler's remarkable successes in the West, most authorities believed in June 1941 that the Soviets would be crushed by the massive forces Hitler had concentrated on the eastern front. After all, half of the German army was able to defeat the Russians in World War I, and little Finland had bloodied the nose of the Red Army in 1940. The only question seemed to be how long it would take.

In the summer and fall of 1941, the predictions of the experts seemed to be fulfilled. The Red Army suffered catastrophic losses in the first five months after the German invasion but, unlike the others, did not surrender. The Germans were at the gates of Leningrad and Moscow and had gobbled up Ukraine. Millions of Soviet soldiers had been captured and were depicted in the newsreels in endless columns being shepherded back to Germany. However, the Germans were stopped, and in the winter offensive that followed, the German Army suffered its first defeat in World War II. After the Germans surrounded and captured a huge bag of divisions east of Kiev in September, they were surprised to encounter a flood of new Red Army divisions when they redirected their intentions toward Moscow. In short order, the Wehrmacht broke through this line and approached within sight of the outskirts of Moscow, only to be surprised by a massive offensive mounted in December by even more new divisions. While other countries had surrendered after losing one army, let alone two, the Soviets came back with a third that sent the Germans reeling to the rear.

The enormous distances gave the Russians some breathing space to gather hastily assembled divisions to halt the Germans at Leningrad and drive them back from Moscow and Ukraine in December 1941. Soviet divisions, not cold weather, stopped the Germans.

The actual reason the Soviets were able to stop the Germans in late 1941 was an unbelievable mobilization of men and weapons beginning in September 1941, which created a new Red Army. The Soviets formed and sent into combat in a few months more new divisions than the United States formed in the entire war.

Commonly reported by German veterans who served on the eastern front was the constant appearance of new Soviet units. German intelligence records continued to note the appearance of new Soviet units that were committed to the front, usually in the spring and fall of each year thereafter.

Beginning in the summer of 1941, an incredible effort was made not only to form new divisions and other units to replace those destroyed by the Germans, but also to equip them with modern weapons capable of matching German weapons. The herculean effort culminated in the defeat of the German Army at the gates of Moscow, the first defeat inflicted on Germany during World War II.

Tracing the introduction of new units to battle will answer questions concerning the capability of the Red Army to develop efficient divisions in a relatively short time. Winston Churchill derided Gen. Marshall for his plan to create combat-ready divisions in six months. In comparison, the Russians used divisions formed only a few months earlier to deal the German Army its first defeat at Moscow in the winter of 1941 and divisions existing usually less than six months in the year that followed. A major difference between the United States and the Soviet Union was that the Russians had millions of men with combat experience in World War I and the Civil War that followed. In addition, the Soviet Union had compulsory military service between the wars, providing a vast pool of trained men.

Assembling men from the same area into regiments was eased by the fact that most had experience, training, and knowledge of one another. A Soviet rifle platoon described in a captured Soviet document still retained its integrity after two years of combat and heavy casualties. It was commanded by a lieutenant and a sergeant who had been with the platoon since its creation in Asia years earlier.

During World War II, the Red Army created more than 10,000 combat regiments, brigades, and divisions. Professor James Goff made a pioneer study of the formation in the winter of 1941–42 of the group of 54 rifle divisions that received numbers in the 400 range, but then were assigned numbers of destroyed divisions, which has confused both German intelligence experts and historians. When and where the various groups of divisions were formed and where they were assigned will point up the strategic planning of the Red Army as well as revealing their true intentions.

In the early years, men were drained excessively from the economy and replaced by women and children. In the later years of the war, skilled men were returned to the economy to begin the enormous task of reconstructing the nation. A detailed examination of the replacement system of the Red Army will show that far from carelessly throwing thousands of disorganized, untrained men into battle, the Soviets wisely used the resources at hand to resist and drive back the invaders when the initial shock had been absorbed. Once the Red Army was stabilized in 1942, the replacement command and Soviet industry continued to strengthen the Red Army, maintaining a force of 6 million men on the eastern front equipped with ever more powerful weapons. By the end of 1942, the Germans were not only outnumbered but also outgunned. As the war progressed, the crushing weight of the new weapons, not numbers of riflemen, led to German defeats at Stalingrad, Kursk, Belarus, and finally Berlin. As the war evolved,

Soviet rifle formations increased in number but with fewer riflemen. More and more men were used in armored units and artillery brigades. In the battle of Berlin, 76 mm guns were attached to platoons of 20 men attacking pockets of German defenders while tanks and self-propelled assault guns were everywhere. The fanatical resistance of the Germans was reduced by overwhelming firepower.

Chapter 2

Creating a New Red Army

THE MAJOR FACTOR in the resurgence of the Red Army in the fall of 1941 was the multitude of trained reservists, many of whom had combat experience in World War I and the following Civil War. These men did not require basic training and were quickly formed into rifle divisions and brigades able to defend Moscow and Leningrad. By December 1941, a new Red Army had replaced the divisions destroyed in the summer and fall of 1941.

The heavy losses in the opening months of the war and the occupation of the most populous regions of the country by the Germans deprived the Red Army of one-third of its potential manpower after 1941. Because of the demand for labor, farms and factories competed with the army for the available men. The shortage of men compared to the tasks required forced the Soviet Union to adopt cost-effective uses of manpower. Women and children replaced men in the factories and on the farms. By early 1943, the Soviet Union had over 6 million well-equipped and trained men in the field against the Germans. The sacrifices to attain that goal were greater than those demanded in any other nation.

Four factors determine the potential of a nation in a war of attrition such as the Russo-German War: first, the industrial capacity to manufacture weapons and other equipment; second, the labor force; third, raw materials; and fourth, the skills to employ and manage the first three. Given time, industrial capacity to manufacture weapons could be expanded as the United States and Britain did during World War II. Another factor, managerial skills, could be learned.

However, the other components, labor force and raw materials, were relatively inflexible and required sacrifices, placing women and children in dangerous occupations and depriving the civilian economy of food, clothing, shelter, fuel, and more. Additional manpower could be acquired by occupying countries as the

Germans did between 1938 and 1941, but although the Germans successfully absorbed the Austrians and the ethnic Germans in Czechoslovakia and Poland, the French, Polish, Soviet, and other nationalities were of limited use to the German war effort. In 1943, Albert Speer instituted a program to employ the French, Dutch, Belgians, and others in the production of nonmilitary goods, freeing up German factories and workers to produce war material. Additional raw materials could also be acquired by conquest as well as cooperation from allies, for example, oil from Romania and nickle from Finland.

The Soviets were in a strong position in all four areas before the war. They had an incredible industrial base as a result of their Five-Year Plans, as well as unlimited supplies of raw materials needed for military production. However, German advances deprived the Russians of a significant portion of their industry and raw materials. This led to shortages, which were made up at the expense of the civilian economy. The German advances also created problems in extracting raw materials and moving them, which often created shortages. In 1942, the Germans captured the farmlands and coal mines in Ukraine and the oil in the Caucasus.

In the third area, the Russians excelled. They had learned managerial skill from the Americans in the 1930s, when major American corporations such as Ford established factories in Russia. The Russian factories were built with mass production in mind and were directed by managers familiar with the concept.

The supply of manpower was the most critical factor. Although there were about 200 million people in the Soviet Union in June 1941, the Germans occupied the heavily populated western area, depriving Stalin of 60 million people. Faced with a reduced population base, the Red Army had to replace millions of men killed and captured in 1941 and form new divisions and brigades to fight the Germans. Millions of additional workers had to be found to work in factories, when their equipment was moved with some of the workers from the German-occupied territory.

Military mobilization of manpower can be scheduled in four stages. The first easy stage is taking unemployed men and those not fully employed and adding them to the workforce. In the second stage, people are moved from leisure and consumer-oriented activity, for example domestic service and entertainment, to war-related activity. In both the first and second stages, the military could take great numbers of men from nonessential activity. However, in the third stage, having exhausted the surplus in the civilian economy, the government was left with hard choices, balancing the needs of industry for workers with the army's need for recruits. The Soviet solution was employing women, children, and handicapped men both in the factories and in the service elements of the armed forces. The fourth stage, which the Russians did not resort to, was removing workers from essential weapons production for the military, with a subsequent loss of production. In contrast, in 1944 the Red Army began releasing men to return to civilian occupations and cut military production as well, because they had achieved mastery over the German Army.

The Russians began preparations for war in 1939. They occupied eastern Poland and Bessarabia on the Romanian border to create buffer zones. A similar buffer zone was acquired from Finland after a badly executed war. By June 1941, surplus manpower had been absorbed and the Soviet Union was in the second stage of drafting workers for military service or converting them from civilian production to military production. In 1942 the Russian position moved to the third stage, where priority decisions had to be made concerning the labor force. In comparison, the Germans also reached the third stage, but because of their high regard for women and family life made little use of women in military production. However, the Germans did recruit thousands of children to man antiaircraft guns and, in 1945, to serve in combat units. The *faustniki*, as the Russians called them, were teenage boys given a Panzerfaust antitank rocket and ordered to get within a few yards of a Soviet tank and destroy it. Most of them were killed, either before or after they attacked the tanks. In 1945, light antiaircraft units with teenage girl crews were placed in the front lines.

A major loss of Soviet manpower occurred in 1941 when the Germans destroyed the Red Army on the border and occupied the western regions of the Soviet Union. Some adult males in the occupied area were evacuated along with the factory machinery, others joined the partisans, and others simply fled eastward. The occupied area was home to 40 percent of the population, about 80 million persons. Perhaps 20 million escaped. According to German estimates, 66 million lived in the occupied zone.

The loss of these 66 million persons had a devastating impact on the Soviet economy. The number of farmers dropped from 35.4 to 15.1 million; industrial workers fell from 11.0 to 7.2 million; and the number employed in all other types of work declined from 20.2 to 11.2 million. The total number of persons in farming, industry, and other occupations fell from 70.8 million in 1940 to 44.4 million in 1942, a net loss of 26.4 million. Approximately 20 million workers were lost, nearly one-third of the work force, as the result of the German occupation of the western provinces. Another 15 million were inducted into the armed forces. At least 9 million women and children were added to the workforce. As the war progressed, more and more Russian women and children entered the workforce to increase the production of weapons and supplies. After 1942, the army took only young men reaching draft age and men from the liberated areas.

The Red Army lost 4,473,000 men in the last six months of 1941. More than 10 million new soldiers were needed immediately to replace the casualties and to create new units to replace those destroyed by the Germans. These new men came from three sources: (1) older men who had received training in the 1930s; (2) the annual class of young men reaching 18 years of age in 1941 and 1942; and (3) men who had been wounded and returned to active service.

In 1941, most of the additions to the army were older men who had trained in previous years and were called back to duty. In one instance in late 1941, an older reserve soldier was called back, given an armband, a World War I rifle, and five rounds of ammunition. In a few days he was assigned to a rifle division without a uniform (none were available) nor any other equipment. However, his previous military training enabled him to carry out his duties.

After the crisis passed in December 1941, the demand for new men decreased and the primary source of military replacements was the class of young men who turned 18 each year. A class consisted of physically fit men born in a specific year and eligible for induction into the army. Men born in 1920 (19 years of age in 1939) formed the class of 1920. Because of the increased birthrate in the 1920s, the number of men in the annual classes of recruits increased steadily during the war. The Germans estimated the annual recruit intake at 1.9 to 2.2 million men.

By 1941, the total Soviet population had increased to 198 million. The Soviet Union had a high proportion of young people in its population: males under 20 years of age, 43.0 million (45.0%); 20 to 39 years of age, 31.5 million (33.0%); 40 to 59 years of age, 14.7 million (15.4%); 60 and over, 6.2 million (6.6%). Additional men came from the population of eastern Poland, the Baltic States, and Bessarabia, areas that had been acquired in 1939 and 1940. However, the Germans occupied these areas by 1941 as well as prewar Soviet territory.

The number of men in a class was directly related to the birthrate. According to German estimates, which were low, the class of 1923 would have had about 1.6 million men minus any deaths. With improved conditions after the Civil War, the birthrate had increased dramatically. Beginning at a low point of 23.9 births per thousand in 1917, the Soviet birthrate climbed steadily to 44.2 per thousand by 1927. The classes of 1921 and 1922 (men reaching age 18 in 1939 and 1940) were probably a little more than 2 million each year. The classes of 1923 through 1927 increased to nearly 3 million annually from the area of pre-1939 Russia. However, German occupation reduced the number of available men to about 2 million annually from 1941 to 1943. Based on a population of 147 million persons in 1926, there would have been about 6.5 million children and 3.25 million males in the class of 1928. Of these, 90 percent were fit for service under Soviet rules, producing a class of nearly 3 million 17-year-olds in 1945. The liberation of the occupied area in 1944 made an additional 1 million youths available each year in 1944 and 1945.

Not all of the Soviet recruits made good soldiers. Even before the war, the men drafted from the recently acquired areas of the Soviet Union were not always reliable. The 22 million added to the Russian population by the acquisitions of 1939 and 1940 did not translate into many additional troops. The Germans were able to recruit hundreds of thousands of pro-German Lithuanians, Estonians, and Latvians to serve in security units of the German Army. Romania and Finland, active allies of Germany, reincorporated the captured area into their homelands and conscripted the men into their armies. Few of these men would have made desirable Soviet soldiers. Some men previously under Communist control were not good prospects, including Lapplanders from the far north, Mongolians from the Far East, the disaffected nationalities of the Caucasus, and some central Asian nationalities.

Most Soviet men between the ages of 18 and 50 had prewar military training, and many had combat experience in World War I and the Civil War that followed in Russia. New recruits passed through a well-established replacement training system. The recovered wounded men were a valuable source of experienced replacements and were returned to their original units if possible. If their parent unit did not need additional men or if other fronts urgently needed replacements, the returning wounded entered the replacement pool and later joined other units. Severely wounded men who were no longer fit for combat, including those who had lost arms or legs, trained recruits in the replacement units, relieving men fit for combat. Men from the liberated areas, "booty soldiers," included former partisans, men taken prisoner by the Germans in 1941, and young men who had reached military age. A boy in Belarus who was 14 years old in 1941, when the Germans occupied his town, was 17 in 1944 and old enough for military service by the time the Red Army returned.

Most of the booty troops required very little further training. Unlike Germany, Great Britain, and the United States, the Soviets had continuous compulsory military training between the wars. However, in the 1930s the Soviets disqualified one-third of the 1.5 million men in each annual class for health and other reasons. The training structure could absorb only 650,000 of the inducted men, and the other 350,000 received only a minimum amount of training. Many men of the classes of 1896 through 1904 had combat experience in World War I and the Civil War. These men, in their late thirties and early forties in 1941 and 1942, formed a large pool of trained soldiers and combat-experienced noncommissioned officers.

Determining the number of potential Soviet soldiers was a matter of prime concern to Fremde Heer Ost (Foreign Armies East, the German intelligence service). In October 1941, a civilian demographer compared available Russian statistics to similar German statistics to estimate Soviet manpower resources. He assumed that the Russians had twice as many men of military age as Germany and therefore could mobilize and maintain twice as many divisions (426 divisions compared to 213 German divisions). This number was very near the number active from 1942 on.

As of June 1942, the Germans had occupied Russian territory with about 66 million people, reducing the Russian base to 133.5 million. Lt. Col. Reinhardt Gehlen also introduced another significant factor: The average Russian was younger than the average German. Half of the Russians were under 20 years old, whereas only one-third of the Germans were under 20. The difference was the result of heavy Russian losses during World War I, the Civil War, and to a lesser extent the Russo-Japanese War of 1905, along with the influenza epidemic of 1918 and a famine in the 1920s that killed off the older people. Another effect of the combat deaths was that 52 percent of the older population were female. Being younger, the Russian population had more combat-age men. Gehlen concluded that 17 million additional Russians were available for military service in 1942.

The Germans analyzed the Soviet population again in 1943. The study increased the potential number of men of military age to 40.3 million in June 1941, but reduced the total by half a million lost in the Finnish war and a further 12.4 million in permanent casualties since June 1941. The report concluded that as of June 1, 1943, the Russians had 12.9 million in the armed forces. The navy and the air force absorbed some men and the Far East diverted others, leaving 5.8 million on the eastern front. These studies produced totals that were very close to the mark. A study made in September 1944 listed the permanent losses since the beginning of the war:

Prisoners of war	5.8 million
Evacuated to Germany	1.7 million
Killed and invalids	6.6 million
Total	14.1 million

However, in September 1944, another German study concluded that there were 10.6 million in the Soviet armed forces, of which 5,154,000 were in units on the eastern front. The conclusion of the study was off by more than a million men, as the Russians had more than 6 million on the eastern front in 1944. In the closing weeks of the war, the Germans estimated that the permanent losses had risen from 14.5 million in September 1944 to 20.5 million in February 1945, including men evacuated to Germany to prevent their employment by the Red Army.

The total potential men of military age, including those born between 1888 and 1927, was 50.4 million. Permanent losses and unfit men subtracted 28 million. An estimated 12.5 million were in the armed forces, of which at least 6.5 million were in the army. The German studies showed that despite heavy Soviet losses, the Red Army maintained its strength, confirming the Soviet sources (table 2.1).

These German studies underestimated the Russian presence on the eastern front by about a million troops. The cumulative losses for February 1945 were high and likely included many men evacuated from the liberated regions. Fremde Heer Ost made other studies with slightly different totals, but the general conclusion was the same: The Russians were able to replace losses and add to their strength. All of the German studies after 1942 underestimated the number of Russian troops facing the Germans.

Table 2.1 Soviet Losses

Date	Cumulative	Total Armed Forces	Eastern Front
October 1941	5,500,000	14,260,000	6,260,000
March 1942	Not available	17,000,000	5,000,000
June 1943	12,400,000	12,900,000	5,800,000
September 1944	14,500,000	10,600,000	5,154,000
February 1945	20,500,000	12,500,000	5,500,000

Russian published data for the period from 1942 on reveal a stable position from June 1943 on the eastern front:

November 1942	6,100,000
June 1943	6,400,000
January 1944	6,200,000
June 1944	6,400,000
January 1945	6,500,000

A Soviet study compared the degree of mobilization of Russia and Germany. At its peak, the Soviet armed forces had 11 million men, representing 6 percent of the population of 194 million. Soviet military losses were 6.9 million dead, 4.5 million missing, and up to 4 million invalids. Adding these to the active troops in 1945, the total is 26.4 million, 13.6 percent of the population of 194 million. The Germans mobilized 13 million, including their losses, of a population of 80 million, or 16 percent, which was partially offset by the availability of foreign labor. The rate of mobilization for both countries was almost identical.

Over and above the enormous contribution made by women in industry, many women served in a wide range of military tasks. Women provided a large portion of personnel in the medical units, the communications units, and traffic control. Women served as military police, directing traffic and guarding prisoners and installations. Rifle companies had at least one or two women. The divisional signal company had 10 women, and at the army level, the signal regiment had up to 200 women radio and telegraph operators. Women were part of the rifle regiment medical unit, placing them directly on the battlefield. In February 1944, the 176th Guard Rifle Regiment had women serving as medical aides and as telephone operators in the signal units.

Women also assumed combat roles. The major contribution by women was manning the antiaircraft guns that defended Russian cities and factories. In March 1942, 100,000 women were serving in the home air defense organization (PVO); 20,000 in Moscow, 9,000 in Leningrad, 8,000 in Stalingrad, and 6,000 in Baku. In 1945, women made up 74 percent of the home defense antiaircraft regiments, freeing over 100,000 men for other service. They also flew transport and combat aircraft and drove trucks and tanks. In March 1943, the artillery division had an entire battalion of trucks with women drivers. Women tank drivers were especially valuable to the armored force. With prior experience in operating tractors on collectives, farm women could quickly learn to drive a tank. Training time for a tank driver, longer than any other position in a tank crew, was reduced considerably if the student had prior experience with tractors. The need for more than 20,000 tank drivers each year to replace losses was a staggering training burden.

A unique role that women played in the Red Army was sniping. Sniping was as much a psychological weapon as a means of killing Germans. Every soldier who served in the front line in World War II shared a fear and intense hatred for enemy snipers. The Soviet snipers caused severe emotional pressure on the German frontline soldier, who knew that momentarily raising his head above the ground would subject him to Soviet sniper fire. Sniping demanded enormous patience, remaining motionless for hours, waiting for a German to show himself. Any movement would reveal the Soviet sniper's position to German countersnipers. Sniping also called for the emotional intensity to deliberately kill an unsuspecting person, as opposed to killing an enemy by firing a howitzer that might kill someone miles away or dropping a bomb. Women, especially those who had been raped or abused by Germans, were among the most successful snipers in the Red Army. In 1943, there were 1,061 women snipers and 407 sniper instructors. During the war, women snipers were credited with killing 12,000 Germans. More than 2 million women served in the Russian armed services by 1945, 400,000 in the PVO and 1,600,000 in the army and the NKVD (the security service).

Women also replaced men in industry, allowing more men to serve in the armed forces. In 1941, half a million housewives entered the workforce. The percentage of women in industry increased from 41 percent in 1940 to 53 percent in October 1942. In the rural workforce, the proportion changed from 52 percent in 1939 to 71 percent in early 1943. The factories and farms were being run by women, older men, and youngsters, as the military-age men left for the army.

The returning wounded made up many of the replacements for the army. Comments concerning the care of wounded men vary. Alexander Werth, writing during the war, described the death of a Russian soldier in an overcrowded field hospital where giving the individual attention and care needed was physically impossible. Only the seriously wounded men were sent to the rear. Walking wounded returned to their units immediately after treatment in field hospitals. There was no evacuation for psychological reasons. The commissars (political officers) dealt with chronic complainers.

Given the large classes of incoming recruits, as well as the booty soldiers and the returning wounded, the Soviets did not exhaust their manpower in 1945. The Red Army received more than 2 million recruits in 1943 and 3 million in 1944 and 1945, more than enough to replace losses. The Red Army lost 2.3 million killed and missing in 1943, 1,760,000 in 1944, and 800,000 in 1945, far fewer than the number of new recruits.

Soviet military strength on the eastern front was more than 6 million men from 1942 on. The reduction of men at the front in 1945 resulted from a partial demobilization. Because some men were not urgently needed to fight the collapsing German Army, the Red Army discharged them to begin rebuilding the civilian economy.

Determining the extent of the losses incurred by the Soviet Union is difficult. The changes in boundaries complicate the matter. The official figure for many years was 20 million military and civilian dead. In an article in *Pravda* on April 6, 1966, Kosygin said that the loss was more than 20 million. A Soviet demographer in 1967 estimated the wartime deaths at 21 million. In 1989, Gorbachev raised the total to 27 million killed during World War II. Other computations estimated a loss of 19.6 million men and 6.1 million women.

Nearly 2 million Russian prisoners of war died during the war. In 1993, military losses were published:

Killed and died of wounds	6,885,000
Missing that did not return	1,783,000
Total dead and missing	8,668,000
Prisoners that returned	2,775,000
Total dead and returnees	11,443,000

After the war, 5,458,000 former prisoners and civilians returned to the Soviet Union. Many persons chose not to return, especially those from the Baltic states and Ukraine. An estimated 45 million fewer people lived in the Soviet Union in 1959 than would have been expected had the birth and death rates of 1940 continued. The estimated loss included 10 million military deaths, 15 million civilian deaths, 10 million children who were not conceived because of dead potential parents, and 10 million prisoners and civilians who left the Soviet Union and either died or chose not to return.

As important as the number of men in the army was their physical and emotional condition. The improved living conditions in the Soviet Union in the 1930s made dramatic improvements in the health of the population, specifically in the health of potential soldiers. During World War I, 30 percent of the men called up were rejected for medical reasons. By 1933, improvement in health was already evident. Of the men examined prior to induction in Moscow in 1926, 3.8 percent had tuberculosis. Seven years later in 1933, only .057 percent had it. The rate of heart disease dropped from 78 per 1,000 to 18.6; and those with "poor physical development" dropped from 25.7 per 1,000 to 4.4 per 1,000 from 1926 to 1933. Similar improvements in the health of those called up were recorded for other regions: For example, heart disease in Ukraine dropped from 73.5 per 1,000 to 5.1 per 1,000.

The Germans estimated that of the 50.4 million Russians in the classes of 1888 through 1927, 7 percent were unfit for service. The classes of 1926 and 1927 were called up in the last two years of the war. Of the class of 1926, 90 percent were inducted; 5 percent were considered unfit; and 5 percent had been evacuated to Germany before the Russians liberated the area. Of the class of 1927, 90 percent were inducted; 5 percent were unfit; 2 percent had been sent to Germany; and the remaining 3 percent were unknown under the Soviet criteria. The health of the average Russian citizen was good enough for him to qualify as a soldier.

Of great significance was the age of the combat soldier. In the first six months of the war, the Red Army included the regular army professionals, the class of 1923 that was undergoing their regular training, and several million older reserves. In 1942, Stalin had to dip more deeply into the reserves to replace the losses of 1941. Reservists 32 to 36 years of age made up most of the 358th

Division in January 1942. The 360th Division had 35- to 45-year-olds. Most men of the 21st Rifle Brigade were about 30 years old. In August 1942, the 1st Guard Army, the 24th Army, and the 66th Army had many older reservists. A Russian general told the correspondent Alexander Werth that during the Battle of Stalingrad in late 1942, the replacements were pathetic, either old men of 50 or 55, or youngsters of 18 or 19. On the other hand, the general commented that those that survived the first few days quickly became hardened soldiers. The ages of the replacements were in keeping with the conditions in 1942. No amount of training can equal combat experience, which many of the older men possessed. Young replacements were the same in every army. Even at the end of the war, men as old as 52 years were in combat formations, but these were the exceptions. The manpower position improved in 1943 because of fewer losses and larger classes of recruits. The 226th Rifle Division was formed in June and July 1943 in Lgov with men aged 21 to 46. More than 70 percent were 21 to 27 and 90 percent were Russian.

The morale of the troops is always of utmost importance. Napoleon stated that morale was twice as important as material factors. Because most of the Russian infantry had been farmers accustomed to hard physical labor and the outdoors, Soviet soldiers were sturdy and able to endure hardships that would have sapped the energy of troops in other countries. In 1937, the population was 57.9 percent collective farmers and craftsmen who had worked on cooperative farms; 5.9 percent were individual peasants; and 36.2 percent were factory and office workers. In 1940, 68.4 percent of the population lived in rural areas and only 31.6 percent in urban centers. With a farm background, the average Russian soldier was strong enough to dig trenches without complaining.

The Russians were not robots but individuals with dissimilar emotions. The Germans considered the Soviet riflemen very cruel. Men from Russia and the Asian republics were considered the best soldiers. The Belarusians, Ukrainians, and the various Caucasian nationalities were not as reliable and were the major source of Hiwis and Ost troops that served in the German Army. The forced collectivization of agricultural land in Ukraine and Belarus left many farmers with a lingering hatred of the Communist regime, and they greeted the Germans as liberators. The Muslims in the Caucasus resisted Communist rule. Early in the war, Stalin realized that the Soviet soldiers would fight harder for their country than for the Communist Party. Therefore the propaganda directed at the troops stressed fighting for Mother Russia, national patriotism, and hatred of the Nazis. Ilya Ehrenburg was the major spokesman for the campaign of anti-German hatred.

Nevertheless, the Communist Party had considerable influence in the army. In the early years of the war, the commissars served as cocommanders of units and maintained discipline. The party considered the commissars great contributors to the success of the army. The commissars were expected to build self-confidence and foster love of country among the troops, as well as indoctrinate the men with Communist ideology. They encouraged soldiers to join the Communist Party, which would give them valuable perquisites in the postwar world. By the end of the war, there were 3 million members of the party in the armed forces. The army consisted of 25 percent Communists and 20 percent Komsomols (members of the Young Communist League) in May 1945. The highest award, Hero of the Soviet Union, was given to 6,437 Communists, 74 percent of the recipients of the award. Many of the Communists were in the elite units, the tank and mechanized units, and the airborne divisions. In September 1943, 54 men in the mortar company (almost all) of the 1st Battalion of the 3rd Guard Parachute Brigade were Komsomols. Toward the end of the war, Hitler emulated the commissar system with an order that units appoint officers to be charged with political indoctrination.

The morale of the Red Army was still uncertain in 1942 despite the official propaganda and evidence of German atrocities in recaptured villages. In July and August 1942 in the Don Bend entire units disintegrated, while others fought to the last man. The causes of disintegration were poor leadership, insufficient training, and lack of unit cohesion. Some new divisions formed in 1941 were sent into battle before they were ready, and they were unable to withstand the German attacks. However, by the fall of 1942 the next group of divisions formed in early 1942 were fully trained and experienced. These divisions made up the armies that stopped the Germans at Stalingrad.

Soviet morale improved in 1943 and 1944, as detailed in a German report on the average daily number of men deserting from the Red Army. In July 1943 the average number of desertions was 209; in December 1943 only 28; in July 1944 only 12. Tenacity grew from good leadership and harsh punishment of deserters by the NKVD guarding the rear. After the Russian victory at Kursk and the offensives that followed, the troops knew that the Germans were beaten. Nothing helped morale more than defeating the enemy.

A careful analysis of a paper found by the Germans on the body of an unidentified Russian officer produced a case study for comparison to the generalizations concerning the Red Army. The document listed the names and ranks of 15 men, presumably in that officer's platoon. The document listed the military specialty, year of induction in the army, membership in the Communist Party, civilian occupation, previous combat experience, any criminal record, date of birth, birthplace, nationality, education, and whether they had lived in the occupied zone. The document was a microcosm of the composition of the Red Army.

The platoon was a mixture of many nationalities speaking a variety of languages. Achmetov, the sergeant, was from Fergana in Uzbek. Saarkalov, the sniper, was from Tashkent, also in Uzbek, where the language resembled Turkish. Kibayev came from Dzhambul, about 125 miles northeast of Tashkent in Kazakh. Vassilyev, Kvatschow, Lavrenov, Gonscharov, and another (the name was illegible in the document) came from Mogilev in Belarus and spoke a Slavic language. Gremev and Avilov spoke Russian and came from Ryazan. Uchanov, Amyankov, and Stepezov came from central Asia. Uchanov was Russian but came from the Tatar Republic. His language was related to Turkish, and he may have been bilingual. Amyankov was a Chuvash whose language was related to Finnish. Stepezov was a Russian born in Moscow. Smimyagin was a Russian from Sverdlovsk. Romazov was also a Russian, probably from Berdyansk.

Although the platoon represented a broad spectrum of nationalities and languages, the men came from three distinct areas: the south around Tashkent, the area east of Moscow, and Mogilev. The ethnic makeup of the platoon was six Russians, five Belarusians, two Uzbeks, one Chuvash, and one Kazakh, an unusually high percentage of non-Russians and Belarusians. Mogilev, the home of five men, was retaken in June 1944 by the 49th Army of the 2nd Belarus Front. The five Belarusians probably were taken into the platoon after that time.

The platoon had two soldiers ages 50 and 51. Only four of the men were under 24 years of age and eight were over 35. Two birth dates were illegible. Of the six men drafted in 1941, one was 51, and the others were 43, 46, and 37, although they were three years younger when drafted. The 37-year-old was trained in the artillery but had been reassigned to a rifle platoon. As riflemen became scarce, divisions were ordered to reduce the number of men in the artillery gun crews and retrain the younger artillery men as riflemen. Four of the older men were Belarusians born in the Mogilev area, which been occupied for three years. Presumably they had been left behind the lines in 1941 and had returned to their homes around Mogilev on the western edge of the Pripet Marshes, an area that harbored many partisans during the German occupation.

The other two 1941 draftees, both young Russians, were submachine gunners and presumably the best soldiers in the platoon, based on the weapon assigned and experience. There was another Belarusian from Mogilev, age 44, who had been drafted in 1943. He had also lived in the Mogilev area during the German occupation but had no combat experience. Of the 15 men in the platoon, 6 were identified as booty troops, given a few days training, issued parts of a uniform and a rifle, and assigned to a rifle company. The Germans realized that the Red Army would recruit all available men when it retook a district. The Germans shipped as many Russians of military age as possible to Germany as prisoners before relinquishing territory. In early 1943, the Germans abandoned a large salient at Rzhev, taking with them livestock, grain, and any other useful material. They also sent adult Russian males to Germany to reduce the number of booty troops. However, after July 1943 the Germans seldom had the time to remove potential soldiers as the Red Army advanced quickly. Therefore the Soviet platoon had the opportunity to pick up the men in Mogilev.

In addition to the four older Belarusians, there were four other men over 35; three were Russians and one was an Uzbek. Two of the Russians, ages 49 and 50, had been drafted in 1942 as part of the mobilization of reserves. The third Russian, age 42, had lived in an occupied zone. He was drafted in 1943 and had previous combat experience. He was probably another booty soldier picked up by the platoon. The last man over age 35 was an Uzbek. Trained as a sniper, he had been in combat twice before. Along with the platoon sergeant, also from Uzbek, he was one of the best-trained soldiers in the platoon.

Younger men in the platoon generally had received better training. The 30-year-old was a Kazakh drafted in 1942 and, though twice in combat previously, had no listed military specialty. The 23-year-old, a Russian born in Sverdlovsk, was a machine pistol man. The 22-year-old was an Uzbek who had been drafted in 1942. The two 21-year-old men were a Russian born in Moscow, who carried a machine pistol, and a Chuvash who was trained as a mortar man. Without fail, the younger soldiers were better trained, and the older men and the booty solders were the riflemen with the least amount of weapons training. The sergeant was only 22; the artillery man 37; the mortar man 21; the sniper 40; and the two machine pistol men were 23 and 21, respectively. All of the riflemen were 42 or older. The platoon had extensive combat experience. Of the 15 men, 1 had four previous combat assignments; 2 had three; 5 had two; and 6 had combat experience at least once. Only one man had no previous combat experience, a Belarusian booty soldier. The year in which the men were drafted verified that older men were called up throughout the war. Of the six drafted in 1941, the age range was 21 (only 18 when drafted) to 51. The six drafted in 1942 ranged from 21 to 50; the three drafted in 1943 were in their forties. Two Russians had been drafted in each of the three years; four of the Belarusians had been drafted in 1941 and one in 1943. The men from central Asia were all 1942 draftees, indicating that the major expansion of the Red Army there in early 1942 drew on local manpower.

The civilian occupations of the men provided an insight into Soviet society before the war. The sergeant had been an office worker; two men from Mogilev had been workers, presumably in factories; and the others had been collective-farm workers. Skilled men were in great demand for the elite units and technical branches of service, resulting in a high percentage of the infantry being farmers. Even the office worker–sergeant was from Uzbek rather than Russia. Those men born near the large cities of Moscow, Ryazan, and Sverdlovsk listed their occupations as collective-farm workers.

The men of the platoon were not well educated. The sergeant had some technical school education, and one private had eight years of grammar school. Of the other 13, only 3 had five years of schooling, probably leaving school at the age of 11 or 12. Four had four years; 3 had three years; and 2 had only two years of schooling. The lack of education revealed that Soviet strides in improving education had not reached the age group in the army. Soviet statistics stated that 20 percent of the Red Army in 1939 had completed secondary school or beyond, and 60 percent had completed grammar school. The better-educated men apparently were not assigned to rifle companies.

In the platoon, most of the men had left school before the end of the Civil War. Improvement in education was possible only after the Civil War. Children who had dropped out of school would have felt uneasy returning when they were several years older than classmates at the same grade level. For example, during World War II, three of my classmates in the seventh grade of an elementary school in Detroit were three years older than the rest of the class. Their families had moved to Detroit from the South to work in defense plants. The children were unable to fit in with the other students, and none continued in school after age 14, when they could obtain a work permit. Russian children would have had even more difficulty returning to school in 1920. Furthermore, the new schools would have been unable to absorb a large backlog of older children.

The two Komsomols had four and five years of school, respectively. They were young, 20 and 23, and both came from central Asia, from Sverdlovsk and Chuvash. The majority of the men could scarcely read and write and spoke various languages, though probably all knew some Russian. Because of these differences, the platoon leader would have had difficulty training them and developing sophisticated tactics.

The median age in the platoon was 40 years. A rifle platoon with men as old as 49, 50, and 51 was inconceivable to Western armies. All of the Red Army men who were 42 and older were either not designated or were listed as riflemen. With one exception, all of the men under 42 had received special training. A 50-year-old rifleman with limited education could not be expected to carry out tactics relying on personal initiative as practiced by the Germans. Instead, the Red Army platoon leader had to rely on carefully rehearsed plans and maintain close contact with his men.

Three other documents provided useful comparisons, revealing the makeup of a mechanized brigade, a tank destroyer battalion, and an artillery battery in 1943. The first document described the 51st Mechanized Brigade on November 25, 1942. Although the table of organization called for 1,156 men, there were only 841 in the brigade. The brigade, formed on September 16, 1942, at Kosterovo, had no previous combat experience. In November it had been in the Caucasus as part of the 6th Mechanized Corps. The age breakdown was as follows:

19–21 years	171
23–25 years	323
26–30 years	223
31–35 years	84
36–40 years	37
Unknown	3
Total	841

The men were well trained; 646 had specialized training, including 198 who had attended regimental schools. Only 195 had no special training. The men were experienced; 222 had been assigned previously to combat organizations, but only 164 had real combat experience. The number of young men with limited combat experience was a consequence of the recent organization of the brigade. The brigade had an excellent cadre. The youth, experience, and training differed a great deal from the rifle platoon referred to above.

The second document described the 261st Tank Destroyer Battalion of the 340th Rifle Division. The 340th Division formed in September 1941 in Balachov in the Volga Military District. The only data in the document were the age groups of the 268 men in the battalion. Compared to the older men of the rifle platoon, most of the men in the battalion were under 35, as was the case in the mechanized brigade. Forty-five men were 20 years or younger; 40 were from 21 to 25; 139 were from 26 to 35; the remaining 44 were 36 and older.

The spread in ages was as expected. The casualty rate in a tank destroyer battalion was lower than in a rifle platoon, and many of the original men may still have been in the battalion in 1944. Divisions formed in September 1941 were made up of reservists, many of whom were in the 26-to-35 age group.

The third document described a battery of the 615th Howitzer Artillery Regiment. The regiment was the howitzer regiment of the 197th Rifle Division formed in April 1941 in Kiev. In July 1941, the regiment was withdrawn from the division and became the corps artillery regiment of the 29th Rifle Corps at Vilnyus. In December 1942, the regiment formed part of the 47th Howitzer Brigade of the 13th Artillery Division. As part of a prewar division, the battery had many younger men. Forty were age 21 or less; 52 were 21 to 35; and only 8 were over 35. Only 30 of the men were married; the other 41 were single. Although originally part of a division formed in Kiev in 1941, the unit had few Ukrainians. There were 51 Russians, 12 Ukrainians, 3 Belarusians, and 4 other nationalities. The report was dated January 8, 1944. Between the date of formation, April 1941, and January 1944, most of the Ukrainians may have transferred to other units. A regiment using 122 mm howitzers would have suffered few combat casualties.

The education level was quite high compared to that of the rifle platoon. Six had attended and nine had graduated from high school. Further, 21 had attended and 35 had graduated from elementary school. The rate of Communist Party affiliation was very high: 36 were party members, 18 were Young Communists, and only 16 were not party members. The party membership and education were tantamount to the artillery receiving better manpower.

All three documents confirmed that the younger and better-qualified men had been taken by the technical units and that the infantry received the others. The rifle platoons suffered the heaviest casualties during the grinding offensives that drove back the Germans.

The Germans extracted heavy casualties as they slowly gave ground after 1943, but the Russians were able to sustain the combat value of the rifle divisions with a steady stream of replacements. The number of men in rifle platoons decreased while the available men formed new supporting units. However, the combat value of divisions increased through more and better weapons. The Soviets continued to form additional support units of tanks and artillery throughout the war and constantly improved the armament. The Russians maintained about 6 million men at the front from January 1943 until the end, while the number of guns and mortars increased from 72,000 to 91,400. The number of tanks and self-propelled artillery pieces increased from 6,000 to 11,000. The Soviet Union had not exhausted its manpower in 1945; instead, more troops were used to operate heavy weapons while the number of riflemen declined.

Chapter 3

Mobilizing Arms Production

THE GERMAN PLAN for victory over the Soviet Union, Barbarossa, anticipated a series of quick victories, defeating the Russians before winter set in. With this plan in mind, the Germans believed that they could defeat the Soviet Union with their stock of weapons available in mid-1941. In the first half of 1941, the Germans had increased arms production sharply in anticipation of the invasion of Russia. The new weapons were improved models plus additional stocks to equip the many new formations created for the campaign.

At first, in the summer of 1941, all went according to plan. The Germans were so confident in the fall of 1941 that they reduced arms and ammunition production. However, events in the winter of 1941–42 changed plans drastically. The Soviet counteroffensive was unexpected and caused a major setback to the Germans. The Germans were forced to abandon thousands of weapons in their retreat from Moscow. By early 1942, the Germans realized that they had a serious war on their hands and that more of their industry would have to be turned to war production. Tank production is an example of the reaction to the realization that defeating the Russians would take an all-out effort. German tank production increased dramatically from 1941 to 1944.

The Soviets managed to hold on in 1941, trading space for time and profiting from Hitler's interference in operations. In the war of attrition that followed, the battle of production became decisive. Soviet production of artillery and armored vehicles increased steadily throughout the war, while production of artillery and rifles peaked in 1942 to meet the demands of new units and replacement of battlefield losses. In the final years of the war, the Soviets reduced artillery and small arms production. Armored vehicle production increased from 2,800 in 1940 to 29,000 in 1944; numbers of guns and mortars increased from 53,800 in 1940 to

129,500 in 1944; and production of rifles and carbines increased from 1,460,000 in 1940 to 4,050,000 in 1942 and then dropped back to 2,450,000 in 1944.

The Russians won the production contest because of the sacrifices made by the civilian sector and the basic strength of their economy, even though it was not equal to the total European economy. The European nations under German control produced 31.8 million tons of steel in 1940, compared to only 18.3 million tons produced by the Soviet Union in the same year. Regardless of this disparity, the Soviets were able to manufacture more weapons than the Germans. A large percentage of Russian industrial capacity was committed to war production, 45 percent in 1943, but not as great as that of the United States or Britain. In 1944, 66 percent of British manufacturing and 59 percent of American manufacturing were devoted to the war effort. The unique Soviet advantage was the concentration of its heavy industry on basic armaments to defeat Hitler rather than spreading its efforts over marginal military needs, for example battleships and heavy bombers, neither of which had an immediate impact on the war with Germany or were essential for defense.

The concept of concentration on primary goals was learned from the Americans. For more than a decade in the 1920s and 1930s, U.S. engineers had taught the Russians the techniques of low-cost mass production and planned obsolescence. U.S. manufacturers in the 1930s, in cutthroat competition to lower the cost of their products in a depressed American economy, had developed a philosophy of planned obsolescence. The objective was to limit the quality of a product to function efficiently for a predetermined life span, for example, increasing the tolerance level for machined parts. The end result was reducing the time to make the part and reducing the number of rejected parts. In the long term, the poorly matched parts would cause breakdowns, but this might be many times the expected lifetime of a transmission, for example. Determining the minimum requirement took skill. This philosophy reduced the cost of the original item. I had personal experience in this process in 1951 when a purchasing agent for the factory where I was working as a production scheduler accepted inferior parts for a lower price. I discovered the error and tried to prevent the use of the inferior parts but was overruled. The result was the breakdown of thousands of military trucks in Korea and a huge fine imposed on the company by the federal government.

Planned obsolescence by cutting tolerances, that is, increasing the margin of error, the acceptable variation from the ideal measurement, reduced the number of hours and the degree of skill required to complete a product but at the same time reduced the life span of the engine or weapon. However, the determining factor of the life expectancy of a weapon on the eastern front was not its degree of perfection but shells from German antitank guns. Even the best engine could not overcome the law of averages that led to destruction by enemy fire. Lend-lease English tank engines lasted much longer and therefore made them ideal training machines for Russian tank drivers, who needed many hours of experience. Soviet tank engines seldom lasted longer than a few hundred hours or about six months, the average life span of a tank on the eastern front.

Cost-effective, functional design simplified each part of a product. The raw materials, the method of fabrication (stamping steel parts for machine pistols versus machining the parts from a forging, for example), and the quality of the finish and appearance were determined by a pragmatic point of view. As one American veteran told me, the Russian tanks looked terrible. They were dirty and had a bad odor. Cost-effectiveness dictated a very rough finish on the T-34 tank. Aesthetic appearance was ignored on the battlefield.

The Soviets adopted the two ideas of cost-effective approach and planned obsolescence and applied them even more rigorously than had the U.S. originators. Weapons were produced with the minimum number of work hours and the smallest amount of material. American tanks were designed to last for 40 hours of combat and a year or more of service. The interior provided the crew comfort for long periods. In contrast, Soviet tanks were designed with an expectancy of 14 hours of combat and six months of service, with little concern for crew comfort. The turret of the T-34 had no floor, greatly simplifying production at the cost of crew comfort. The tank crew had to perch on seats hung from the turret ring. The floor of the main part of the tank, which did not rotate along with the turret, was stacked with shells for the 76 mm gun. In combat, the loader had to scramble around the floor of the tank for shells while the turret moved around him.

Throughout the war, efforts continued to reduce the cost of weapons. Between 1941 and 1943, the labor cost of producing the 76 mm regimental gun was reduced by 31 percent; the 152 mm howitzer, 41 percent; the T-34 tank, 51 percent; and divisional 76 mm guns, 73 percent. In 1942, 1,030 hours of machining produced a 76 mm divisional gun. By 1944, the same gun required only 475 hours of machining.

The Soviets adopted two other related techniques of American manufacture, mass production and long runs. Mass production divided a complex task, such as building an automobile, into many semiskilled or unskilled tasks. An individual could be trained in a few minutes to perform a single task very quickly. The worker would then do the task repeatedly, for example, placing pins to join the links of a tank track.

The Soviets went further than the Americans and abandoned any attempt at a refined appearance. Some activities required more training, such as welding together two pieces of armor plate. A skilled welder produced a fairly smooth bead where the two pieces joined. The welding on Soviet tanks was very crude. To enable unskilled workers to operate complex machine tools, skilled or semi-skilled workers set up the work and supervised the unskilled. Women and boys performed many tasks not requiring physical strength. During World War II, my father, a painter before the war, became a setup man supervising a group of 20 or so women machining parts for the M5 light tank being manufactured by the Cadillac Motor Car Division of General Motors. My father showed the women how to secure the part to the drill table and then drill holes at the marked places. He was there to help out if anyone had a problem and inspected the work when it was completed.

Long runs multiplied the savings in skilled labor. The Germans continually tinkered to improve the design of their tanks and other weapons, but regrettably at the cost of numbers produced. The Russians were loath to make changes that would delay production. Changes were made only when absolutely necessary, for example to provide a larger gun to counter heavier armor on German tanks. Designers could not modify weapons and interfere with production schedules unless the weapon promised substantial improvement. The Russians began and ended the war with the same small arms: machine pistols, rifles, pistols, light machine guns, heavy machine guns, and mortars. In contrast, the Germans introduced one or more radically new models of each weapon during the war. The improvements in Russian artillery were usually minor and made use of previous components. The new self-propelled guns used the chassis of earlier tanks and existing artillery pieces. The new Stalin tanks were improvements on the prewar KV, not an entirely new product such as the Tiger or the Panther, both of which incorporated many technological innovations.

Cost-effective design, planned obsolescence, mass production, and long runs enabled the Russians to produce weapons at far less cost in factory space, machinery, raw materials, and labor than the Germans. An essential factor was that the Soviet plants were planned for a smooth flow of production. Efficient large plants were necessary to build complex weapons. During the 1930s, American engineers designed and built all of the Soviet tank factories and many other factories for mass production. Many were improved copies of the most efficient American plants. The Germans could not adopt the American philosophy because their factories were smaller and not designed for mass production. Many Russian plants employed from 10,000 to 40,000 workers. This economy of scale made a major difference in the cost of the final product.

The quality of the weapons produced was also a significant factor. Faulty weapons could not win battles regardless of the number manufactured. The questions were whether the weapon would work and whether an increase in quality would justify the loss of quantity produced.

The Russian riflemen used bolt-action rifles throughout the war, as did the Germans. In 1941, the Russians had large stocks of foreign rifles. During World War I, Winchester in the United States sold Russia large numbers of Model 1895 bolt action rifles specially chambered for the Russian 7.62 Mosin cartridge. The Russians also had stocks of Canadian Ross .303 rifles, British Pattern 14 .303 rifles taken in Latvia, Czech 7.92 mm Mauser M1924s, and Polish Kar98s taken in September 1939. Some antiquated French M1886/93 Lebel rifles were issued to troops in Leningrad in 1941. Some weapons were taken from museum collections.

However, by 1942 Russian production ended the shortages. The standard rifle was the Mosin-Nagant 7.62 mm rifle, adopted by the Russians in 1891. In 1930 the Soviets shortened the rifle and simplified the sights, producing the M1891/30 carbine. In 1938 the sight of the carbine was improved along with other minor changes. In 1937 a sniper version of the rifle had a telescopic sight. In February 1944 a new carbine, the M1944 with an attached folding bayonet, was approved for the airborne troops. By 1944 the Soviets had large reserve stocks of carbines and production was curtailed.

The Russians used semiautomatic rifles for sniping because the sniper would not have to move to operate the bolt, whereas moving would reveal his position. In 1938, Tokarev designed the SVT38, which fired only semiautomatically. Although easily disassembled for cleaning, the rifle was fragile. In April 1940 the SVT40, a sturdier version, replaced the 1938 model. Only a few were produced with the full automatic option. In a curious reversal, the Americans issued bolt action rifles to snipers because they were more accurate and semiautomatic rifles to the other riflemen because they delivered a greater volume of fire to make up for the comparative lack of automatic weapons in the rifle company. There were no submachine guns or machine pistols in an American rifle platoon.

During the war, the Russians increased the proportion of machine pistols to rifles when they realized that a low-cost weapon was needed to produce a high rate of fire. The Russians did not use an automatic rifle. The difference between a machine pistol and an automatic rifle is that the former fires pistol-type ammunition and is less accurate. The automatic rifle fires more powerful rifle ammunition (requiring a substantial chamber and bolt) with much longer range. Automatic rifles were very difficult to control without a bipod and hinged butt plate because of the tendency of the barrel to rise. The machine pistol was much cheaper to manufacture because the low-powered ammunition did not apply as much stress on the weapon and stampings could be used instead of machined parts.

In 1940, George E. S. Shpagin designed the PPSH 1941, and mass production began. Stampings replaced machined parts, making the gun simple to manufacture. Also, the PPSH was easy to disassemble for cleaning and delivered a high rate of fire from a 71-round drum. The use of the machine pistols expanded dramatically during the war. In 1941, 99,000 were in use; in 1942, 1.5 million; and in 1944, 2 million. More than 5 million machine pistols were made by the end of the war, but demand exceeded supply as late as 1944. The PPS 1942 was made in Leningrad during the blockade, when the supply of machine pistols was running low and there was a shortage of metal and workers. The new machine pistol required only 6.2 kg of metal and 2.7 hours to manufacture, compared to 13.9 kg of metal and 7.3 hours to manufacture the PPSH. The weapon was very crude and only 50,000 were made in Leningrad.

In 1942 the PPSII-2 was issued with a curved 30-round magazine similar to an AK-47 instead of the drum. The machine pistols provided the Soviet infantry with heavy firepower to replace the reduced numbers in the rifle companies. While production of carbines decreased from more than 3 million in 1942 to 1.3 million in 1944, production of machine pistols increased from 1.5 million to nearly 2 million. Given the high attrition rate of small arms in combat, probably two-thirds of the men on the front lines carried machine pistols. The carbine continued as a personal weapon for the artillery and rear-echelon troops.

For sustained heavy fire, the Russians continued to use the Maxim machine gun copied from the British Maxim in 1905. Production increased from 53,700 in

1941 to 458,500 in 1944. The Soviets met the need for a light machine gun in 1928 when the Red Army accepted the DP27 light machine gun. The modified gun was very simple, reliable, and robust. It seldom jammed because of dirt. Its only disadvantage was that the standard rimmed cartridge was more prone to jam automatic weapons than the rimless cartridges used by the Germans and Americans. The gun used a 47-round drum that in some situations, such as firing from the hip on the move, was more desirable than the belt-fed machine guns of the Germans. Millions of automatic weapons were made throughout the war with few variations. In 1944 and 1945, the Russians manufactured 2.8 million machine guns and machine pistols.

The Russians, like the Germans and British, adopted an antitank rifle firing a round slightly more than .50 caliber. The PTRD41, designed by Degtyarev, was adopted in 1941. The weapon was heavy (17.4 kg), long (over 2 meters), and required a two-man crew. The muzzle velocity was 1,010 meters per second, enough to penetrate the armor on 1941 and 1942 tanks at moderate range, 25 mm at 500 meters. Another gun, the PTRS41, designed by Simonov, used the same 14.5 mm ammunition but was semiautomatic, used a five-round clip, and was 3.5 kg heavier. The Red Army used both rifles throughout the war, though both were ineffective against the later German tanks. In 1943 the antitank rifle company in the rifle battalion was reduced to a platoon. The Russians produced 471,500 antitank rifles during the war, losing 214,000, mostly from 1942 to 1945.

Losses in small arms were heavy in 1941, with 5,550,000 rifles and carbines and 189,000 machine guns lost as the Germans overran the Red Army. In 1942 losses were still high: 2,180,000 rifles and carbines and 101,000 machine guns, a result of the defeat in Ukraine in the summer. In 1943 losses of rifles and machine guns remained high at more than 1 million rifles and 100,000 machine guns. These losses were offset by the enormous production by the end of 1942. The stock of rifles in June 1941 was 7,740,000 plus 100,000 machine pistols. By January 1, 1943, production restored the huge losses of small arms. The stock was 5,620,000 rifles and carbines and 1,110,000 machine pistols, despite heavy losses in 1942. The Soviet Union cut production of personal weapons in 1944, indicating sufficient reserves for battlefield attrition. The Germans continued to increase production until the end to replace heavy battlefield losses.

In addition to equipping individuals with small arms, an army required a substantial artillery component. During the war, the Russians steadily increased the amount of artillery support for the infantry. The Red Army entered World War II with an excellent arsenal of artillery pieces that had been designed or improved in the 1930s, increasing the range, the rate of fire, the accuracy, and the destructive force of all of their artillery. During the war, the Red Army relied on artillery more than any of the other major armies in World War II. During the war, the Soviet Union produced more than 500,000 guns and mortars. The Russian arms industry produced more than enough artillery despite German occupation of the most industrialized part of its country.

The Soviets established requirements and then designed, selected, produced, and distributed artillery based on a few simple factors: the level of destructive power needed to be delivered by whom and at what distance from the weapon. In World War II there was need for a larger variety of weapons than in previous wars because the targets were far more diverse, including tanks and aircraft.

The Soviets referred to artillery in terms of the unit size to be supported: battalion guns (37 mm and 45 mm), regimental guns (76 mm), division guns (76 mm and 122 mm), and corps guns (107 mm to 152 mm). A rifle battalion required enough artillery support to break up attacks on their position within 100 meters of the defense line. When attacking, a rifle division needed enough artillery support to destroy trenches and strong points immediately ahead. The guns had to be light enough to manhandle and did not need long range. Corps guns, on the other hand, destroyed fortifications with heavy shells and enemy artillery at great distances.

The cannon companies in the rifle regiments had regimental guns; the divisional artillery regiment had light or field artillery; and corps and armies had medium and heavy artillery. Antitank guns defended against tank attacks and antiaircraft guns against air attacks. The field, medium, and heavy artillery included both guns and howitzers, all designated by the diameter of the bore. Each user had his special requirements—how much destruction had to be delivered at what distance.

A gun had a flat trajectory and long range stemming from its high muzzle velocity. The howitzer had a lower muzzle velocity, resulting from a smaller powder charge. A shorter barrel was adequate as the powder burned in less time. The advantage of the howitzer was that it could be fired with a high trajectory over hills and other obstacles. The plunging shell struck the target from a nearly vertical angle, an advantage when shelling troops in dugout shelters.

The destructive power of artillery dominated the battlefield. A 76 mm shell created a crater 1 meter in diameter and .5 meters deep; a 122 mm shell, a crater 3 meters in diameter and .7 meters deep; and a 152 mm shell made a crater 5 meters in diameter and 1.8 meters deep. Theoretically, seven shells from seventy-four 76 mm guns could destroy 1,000 square meters, allowing for more than 60 percent overlap of craters. Such a barrage would create a significant gap in a German defense line. During the war, the Russians concentrated on producing artillery designs in existence in 1941 with minor improvements.

Simplicity was the basic idea, as opposed to the German predilection for complexity. The Russians produced only a few types of guns with the simplest design possible in both operation and manufacture. Muzzle brakes reduced recoil and made lighter carriages practical. Many parts and ammunition were interchangeable and identical carriages were used on several types of guns.

The type of guns manufactured changed considerably during the war, as heavier weapons were made in the later years to be used in demolishing German fortifications. The production of mortars and 45 mm antitank guns was reduced toward the end of the war, while production of antiaircraft guns increased, especially the light guns, which made up nearly one-third of total production in 1944.

By 1940 production of artillery was at a high level, as new guns replaced older designs and the Red Army increased in size. Additional factories, including the Red Putilov Factory, were constructed in the late 1920s and early 1930s to manufacture artillery. By 1940 six major factories produced artillery: the Bolshevik and the Kirov factories (formerly the Putilov works) in Leningrad, the Stalin Machine Works in Kramatorskaya in Ukraine, the Kalinin Factory No. 8 near Moscow, the Molotov Factory at Perm, and the Ordzhonikidze Factory at Sverdlovsk. Eleven other factories, including one or more in Dnepropetrov, Mariupol, Nikolayev, Voroshilov, Gorki, Kolomna, Moscow, Stalingrad, Magnitogorsk, and Sverdlovsk also made guns, along with 22 smaller plants.

The arsenal in Kiev began with repairs and then made carriages of antiaircraft machine guns and 37 mm M1939 antiaircraft guns. In 1939 it began production of the Czech-designed 76 mm M1938 mountain gun. In 1941 the Kiev Arsenal was the major source of antiaircraft mount production. It was evacuated beginning in June 1941 and absorbed by the Votkinsk No. 235 plant.

The Bolshevik Plant in Leningrad made naval guns and 76 mm guns (M1902/30) in the 1930s. The factory repaired damaged guns after the city was surrounded, while continuing to make 76 mm regimental guns. There was no further need for naval guns on the Baltic Sea.

The Kirov Plant in Leningrad made 76 mm tank guns, 76 mm regimental guns, and 76 mm M1936 F-22 guns, 76 mm M1938 mountain guns, and 45 mm tank guns as well as 50 mm, 82 mm, and 120 mm mortars. The factory also made KV tanks. Frunze No. 7 in Leningrad turned to repair work after the city was surrounded.

Kalinin Plant No. 8 at Kaliningrad made antiaircraft guns, 45 mm antitank guns, and tank guns. Some of its machinery was evacuated to the Molotov Factory at Perm when the Germans drew near Kalinin in September 1941. The number of shifts was reduced from three to two, and the number of workers declined from over 12,000 to 10,600 as workers were transferred to Sverdlovsk. Nevertheless, the plant continued in production and the Germans were driven back during the winter. Most of the personnel had returned from Sverdlovsk by April 1942, as the factory was producing daily forty 85 mm antiaircraft guns, sixteen naval 76 mm antiaircraft guns, fifteen army 76 mm antiaircraft guns, forty-three automatic 45 mm antiaircraft guns, and seventy 45 mm antitank guns. More than 180 guns were being assembled every day, or over 5,000 per month.

The Stalin Plant No. 9 at Sverdlovsk was built in 1937 as part of the URALMASH complex. It began producing 122 mm M1910/30 howitzers and in 1940 shifted to the M1938 M-30 model. During the war the plant had 25,000 workers, mostly women and youths. Part of Plant No. 8 from Kaliningrad was evacuated to Sverdlovsk and added to the Stalin factory. In September 1943 the daily production included twenty 45 mm antiaircraft guns, thirty 76 mm antiaircraft guns, forty-five 76 mm tank guns, fifteen 122 mm howitzers, four 85 mm tank guns, four 152 mm howitzers, and two 203 mm heavy howitzers. Later the Stalin Factory produced the 100 mm and 122 mm SUs (the Russian abbreviation for self-propelled artillery). The Kalinin and Sverdlovsk plants worked together throughout the war.

The Kirov Plant No. 13 in Bryansk was evacuated to Ust-Katav in the Urals and made 82 mm mortars and mounts for 85 mm antiaircraft guns. Later the plant made rockets, 76 mm tank guns, and in 1944 it made 85 mm tank guns. The Stalin Plant No. 92 at Gorki, built under the first Five-Year Plan from 1931 to 1934, began production in 1934. The factory had a new design bureau and specialized in field artillery and tank guns. During World War II, it was the leading producer of artillery. It employed 30,000 workers, of which 30 percent were women, 30 percent youths, 45 percent men unfit for the army, and 5 percent wounded men released from the army.

The daily production of one building alone was nine 122 mm howitzers, six 152 mm howitzers, and parts for fifteen more. Other buildings made the ZIS-3 76 mm gun, the 76 mm F-34 tank gun, and the ZIS-5 76 mm tank gun. In March 1943, Building 1 was making more than 120 76 mm guns per day. Buildings 13 and 27 assembled 140 guns of various calibers each day. Later the plant made 57 mm antitank guns and 85 mm tank guns and played a major role in artillery production.

Molotov Plant No. 172 was the former Perm Factory with its long history of artillery production. In September 1941, the plant was expanded by the addition of parts of Kalinin Plant No. 8 evacuated from the Moscow area. In April 1943, the factory employed 40,000 workers, 60 percent women and 10 percent youths, working two 12-hour shifts. The plant made thirty 45 mm antitank guns, thirty 76 mm field guns, twelve 152 mm howitzers, and five 45 mm antiaircraft guns each day in April 1943. The plant also made 122 mm howitzers, 122 mm guns, 152 mm guns, M1838 76 mm regimental guns, 25 mm M1940 automatic anti-aircraft guns, and 152 mm gun-howitzers also used on the SU-152 and JSU-152. During the war, the factory provided artillery for 116 artillery regiments. The complex included more than 16 buildings, with individual buildings producing carriages, barrels, and other parts, while several buildings were assembly lines.

The Barrikady Plant at Stalingrad had been built to make copies of the Czech Skoda super-heavy artillery pieces under contract before the Germans took Prague. In 1936, production of the 122 mm M1931 corps guns, the 203 mm M1931 B-4 howitzer, the 152 mm M1935 BR-2 gun, and the 280 mm M1939 BR-5 mortar began. In 1939, the plant began the manufacture of 76 mm M1939 USV division guns. During the war the factory also made 120 mm mortars. When the Germans reached Stalingrad in August 1942, some workers and machinery had gone to Votkinsk, but the plant continued to make guns until captured by German troops. The factory was the scene of a prolonged bloody battle, a part of the struggle for Stalingrad.

Plant No. 235 in Votkinsk was developed in 1938 by converting a factory that had built narrow-gauge railroad locomotives. In 1941 it had acquired German machinery to manufacture the 107 mm M1940 M60 corps gun. In the fall of 1941, it absorbed the arsenal evacuated from Kiev and Machine Works No. 14 from

Galevo on the Kama River. Some equipment also came from the Budennyi Plant No. 352 at Novocherkassk. In August 1942, additional workers and machines came from Stalingrad. In September 1942, the plant had 12,000 workers. Early in the war, the main products were 152 mm M1938 M10 howitzers. Later the plant made 45 mm antitank guns, 76 mm divisional guns, 57 mm antitank guns, and 76 mm tank guns. In June 1942 the factory was making over 1,500 guns per month, and in February 1943 the daily production of the factory included fifty-six 45 mm antitank guns and thirty 76 mm field guns. The factory became the second largest artillery producer in the Soviet Union during the war.

The Budennyi Plant No. 352 at Novocherkassk began production of the 107 mm M1940 M60 gun and the 122 mm M1931/37 A-19 corps gun in 1941. The factory was evacuated to Votkinsk in the fall of 1941 and was absorbed by Plant No. 235.

Voroshilov Plant No. 586 at Kolomna began as a repair facility but in 1939 was converted to the manufacture of the new automatic 37 mm M1939 antiaircraft gun. In the fall of 1941, it was evacuated to Krasnoiarsk along with a factory from Kaluga to form Plant No. 4 making 37 mm antiaircraft guns, 120 mm mortars, and depth charges.

The Kunzevo Plant No. 46, located near Moscow, was built in 1932 and expanded in 1941. In December 1943 the factory employed 15,000 workers making fifty 45 mm and 57 mm guns and thirty 76 mm field guns daily. Factory No. 183 at Nishnij-Tagil made 250 to 300 76 mm guns per month in 1944.

After the Stalingrad plant was destroyed, of the 13 plants in production in June 1941, only 8 factories remained, excluding the plants in Leningrad that were in limited production. The three in Leningrad, the Kiev plant, and Stalingrad were no longer providing weapons to the main front. Of the eight remaining, five were in the Urals near the tank factories (Gorki, Molotov, Sverdlovsk, Votkinsk, and Novocherkassk); two were near Moscow (Kaliningrad and Kolomna); and one was near the front at Bryansk. Three of the plants in the Urals had been built in the 1930s as part of the Five-Year Plans, and all were among the major producers of artillery. After Stalingrad was retaken, the plant was restored, and production of 122 mm tank guns began late in the war. When the siege of Leningrad was lifted, its three plants were restored and in 1944 made the 100 mm M1944 BS-3 field gun, among other weapons.

The total number of guns and mortars produced during the war was 526,200. Of these, 100,000 were used on tanks and SUs. The heavy losses of the first few months of the war heavily strained stocks, when the many new formations needed artillery. In June 1941 the Soviet Union had 112,800 guns and mortars and in the next five months made 58,400. However, in that same period the Russians lost 101,100, leaving only 70,100 guns and mortars (including 21,500 50 mm mortars) in December 1941. The number of guns and mortars over 50 mm decreased from 76,500 to 48,600. Russian production dropped drastically from 1940 to 1941. The loss of the western zone where most of the artillery had been made was devastating, and evacuated industries did not resume production until 1942.

Total losses in guns and mortars exceeded 100,000 in both 1941 and 1942. Most of the pieces lost were mortars (60,500 in 1941, 82,200 in 1942), 45 mm antitank guns, and 76 mm field guns. Production of the 76 mm guns was more than adequate to replace the losses in 1942. The stock of 76 mm guns was 15,300 at the beginning of the war and dropped to 9,500 in January 1942. By January 1943 the stock was at 23,000 and by January 1945 it had increased to 68,800. In June 1941 the Red Army had 32,000 and despite losses had 89,600 at the end of the war. After early 1942, there was never a shortage of artillery to replace losses and equip new divisions.

German intelligence in their reports tended to inflate Soviet artillery production by about 20 percent. There is seldom a reference to a Soviet artillery unit being short of guns. Actually, supply was more than adequate for the needs of the Russian artillery divisions, brigades, and regiments by the end of 1942, and the numbers of these units increased steadily throughout the war.

A third major category of weapons was armored vehicles. Russia's top priority in late 1941 was to replace the thousands of tanks lost in the first months of the war. Many Soviet tank factories were captured or evacuated. To provide the most tanks in the shortest time, the Russians concentrated on building four existing types: the medium T-34, the heavy KV, and the light T-60 and T-70. The designs were simplified and any unnecessary variations or improvements were prohibited. Changes were made only to reduce the cost of manufacture, either in work hours or in material, or to make major essential improvements in the gun, armor, or engine. Soviet tanks appeared rough and poorly made, but a higher standard was used to finish important parts. The ideal design was one just good enough; anything better was wasted effort. The outstanding characteristic of Soviet tanks was simplicity, making them easy to manufacture, operate, and maintain.

The Red Army began the war with 22,600 tanks, almost all of them varieties of light tanks. The Russians lost 20,500 tanks in 1941 and manufactured only 5,000. In 1942 losses decreased to 15,000 while production increased to 27,900. By June 1943, the Red Army had 20,600 tanks on hand. For the remainder of the war, production slightly more than compensated for losses. However, the proportion of light tanks dropped as production concentrated on heavy and medium tanks. The result was a much more powerful tank force than had existed in 1941.

Production of SU guns increased after 1942. By 1944, the total of tanks and SUs produced reached 34,700, nearly 3,000 per month. German intelligence estimated the distribution of Soviet tanks on October 31, 1944, as 3,160 at the front; 2,060 in reserve behind the front; 2,880 in the rear area; 4,370 in armored units, the location of which Germans were unaware; 930 in the Caucasus, the Far East, and Iran; and 4,800 in replacement units, repair depots, and in transit. The German estimated a total of 18,200 tanks, but the actual total was 20,600.

The Germans estimated Soviet tank factory production based on captured documents and prisoner of war statements. A production worker would not know annual production, although he might have known the daily rate at his factory.

In developing their estimates, the Germans considerably reduced the numbers given by prisoners, placing the Sverdlovsk production at 200 monthly instead of 1,200, Chelyabinsk at 100 to 200 instead of 540, and Omsk at 200 instead of 600.

The Soviet totals on hand were higher than the German estimates. The German estimate of a stock of 6,835 was well below the actual number of 20,600 available to the Soviets on January 1, 1943. In June 1943, the Germans estimated a possible 12,500 including 7,050 in known units, 4,000 in unlocated units, and about 1,500 not in units, far below the actual number of more than 22,000. The Germans estimated the Soviet stock at 13,581 versus the actual number of 25,400 in January 1945. Thus the Germans seriously underestimated both Soviet production and losses in the last two years of the war.

Although the total number of tanks on hand at the beginning of the war and at the end were similar (25,200 in 1941 and 25,200 at the end), the relative proportion of light, medium, and heavy shifted toward the heavier tanks. In June 1941, there were 21,200 light tanks and only 1,400 medium and heavy tanks. In May 1945, there were 16,300 medium and heavy tanks and only 8,800 light tanks. The totals produced by type according to Soviet figures are shown in table 3.1.

The self-propelled SU served as an infantry support weapon like the tank, or as an antitank weapon. Although a powerful asset to the defense, the towed antitank gun was clumsy to handle on offense. Hooking the gun to its towing vehicle, moving it forward over rough terrain, unhooking it, and bringing the gun into position made it less than ideal during offensive operations. German tank-supported counterattacks were a constant menace, requiring heavy investment by the Soviets in both towed and self-propelled tank destroyers. The most effective form of tank destroyer was the self-propelled gun. The Russians formed nearly equal numbers of regiments of towed and self-propelled guns. Both types of regiments had multiple roles, fighting tanks and supporting the infantry with either direct or indirect fire. The term *mechanized artillery* is a closer translation of the Russian than most terms used to describe artillery pieces mounted on vehicles. The terms *mechanized artillery, SU,* and *self-propelled artillery* are used interchangeably. The Red Army formed more self-propelled artillery units than any other army in World War II.

Table 3.1   Total Soviet Tank Production

Light and Medium Tanks		*SUs*	
Light tanks	14,508	SU-76	12,671
T-34	35,119	SU-85	2,050
T-34/85	29,430	SU-100	1,675
KV and KV-85	4,581	SU-122	1,148
JS	3,854	SU-152	4,779
Total tanks	87,492	Total SUs	22,323
Total SUs and tanks	109,815		

None of the Russian SUs had turrets. The Russian SU-76 was open topped, lightly armored, and based on a light tank chassis. Other Russian types had heavy armor and closed tops. All functioned as assault guns, mobile antitank guns, and substitute tanks. The Russians halted production of the original SU-122 with the howitzer in November 1943. Production of the SU-85 stopped in June 1944 because by then the same gun was available on the fully armored T-34/85. The increasing number of German Panthers and Tigers in 1944 led to the development of more powerful guns. The new SUs were designed primarily as antitank weapons, the other roles being left to the SU-76s that continued to come off the assembly lines in increasing numbers.

Tanks were manufactured in more than a dozen factories from Leningrad to Stalingrad. In Gorki, the Molotov GAZ No.1 plant made light tanks and self-propelled guns. This huge factory, designed, built, and initially operated by the Ford Motor Company under an agreement made in 1927, originally produced copies of the Ford Model A automobile. The plant was modeled on the Ford River Rouge plant near Detroit. The River Rouge plant concentrated in one complex all of the facilities to build an automobile, beginning with raw materials. The Gorki plant began production on January 1, 1931, with American machinery. Designed to build 140,000 autos per year, the plant was enlarged in 1936 and 1937. In 1938 the plant had 45,000 workers and produced 84,288 GAZ AA light trucks, 23,256 GAZ M autos, 6,314 GAZ AAA two-ton trucks, and a few BT tanks.

After June 22, 1941, the Molotov plant continued making 1.5-ton GAZ trucks and T-60 light tanks. Later the factory made the T-70 until October 1943, when production switched to the SU-76 using the same chassis. By 1944 the plant had 60,000 workers, 45 percent women, 10 percent boys ages 16 and 17, 5 percent invalid soldiers, and 40 percent older men. There were two 12-hour shifts for some workers and three 8-hour shifts for others. In 1944 the Molotov plant reduced truck production because of the large number of American imports, and production concentrated on the SU-76. By September 1944, production of the SU-76 reached 380 per month.

The Krasnoye Sormovo No. 112 plant, also in Gorki, had a long history of tank manufacture, having produced the first Soviet-made tank in 1920. Before the war, the plant had 27,000 workers making the T-32 medium tank. In July 1941, production of T-34s began. In September 1941, when the evacuation of industry started, the only plants making the T-34 were the Stalingrad tractor plant and the Krasnoye Sormovo. The Sormovo plant had the facilities to manufacture a cast turret for the T-34 that was superior to the welded turrets made in Stalingrad. The first T-34/85s with a new enlarged cast turret were produced in December 1943 at Krasnoye Sormovo. In September 1944, that plant's production was 300 T-34s per month. The tractor factory at Stalingrad was the first tractor plant to be designed and equipped by Americans. The Soviets selected the site in 1926 and began work, but little was accomplished until 1929, when American technical assistance arrived. The plant was designed by Albert Kahn and built under the supervision of a Detroit architect, John Calder, who became a troubleshooter at other plants. American companies provided the equipment, including Rockwell, Niagara, Bliss, Seper, Westinghouse, and Chain Belt. The plant made copies of the International Harvester 15/30 tractor. Construction of the plant began in June 1929, and by June 1930 the buildings were up and with most of the machinery from the United States and Germany in place. The plant, the largest in Europe, was designed to build 50,000 tractors per year.

Before the war, the Stalingrad tractor factory employed 20,000 workers making agricultural tractors and light tanks. During 1941 and 1942, Stalingrad was the major producer of T-34s, while the other plants were being evacuated. Production continued until the Germans stormed the factory itself in late 1942. After the city was retaken in 1943, the factory was rebuilt, and by 1944 it employed 40,000 workers. The restored factory became the primary tank repair center, refurbishing up to 600 per month and building 150 new T-34s monthly.

The Putilov Factory (Kirov) in Leningrad made the KV heavy tank before the war. The oldest engineering plant in Russia, the Putilov Factory was rebuilt and expanded in 1929 with the help of the Ford Motor Company. Part of the plant was evacuated to Chelyabinsk in September 1941 along with the Izhorskiy factory, which made armor plate at Kolpino just south of Leningrad. Only 525 machine tools and 2,500 workers from the Kirov plant were able to leave Leningrad before the blockade halted evacuation. A few skilled workmen later were sent out of the city by air.

The four largest tank producers during the war were the Ordzhonikidze factory at Sverdlovsk, the Chelyabinsk tractor factory, the Ural Tank Works (Stalin) No. 183 at Nishnij-Tagil, and Lenin Plant No. 174 at Omsk. During the war, part of the Kirov factory in Leningrad was evacuated and added to the Chelyabinsk factory, but the Germans blockaded Leningrad before the evacuation could be completed. Factory No. 75, which made tank engines in Kharkov, was also added to the Chelyabinsk tractor works, along with part of the Stalin heavy machine factory from Kramatorsk, part of the pump and compressor factory from Melitopol, machine tools from the metal works in Mariupol, and the Red Proletariat machine works from Moscow. The new combined factory, which included almost all of the facilities to manufacture a tank, was named Kirovskiy Works No. 100, better known as Tankograd.

The Chelyabinsk factory employed 60,000 employees in 1944. The workers were 50 percent women, 15 percent boys of 16 and 17, 5 percent invalid soldiers, and only 30 percent able-bodied men. The factory operated seven days per week, in two shifts of 12 hours each with one hour off at midshift. Workers had only two free days each month.

The first KV tank was completed at Chelyabinsk in October 1941. In 1943, the KV-85 replaced the KV and in November 1943 the JS (Joseph Stalin) replaced the KV-85. Chelyabinsk also produced heavy SUs based on the KV and JS chassis. In April 1942, production of T-34s began, up to 15 per day. By January 1944, the SU-85 and the T-34/85 replaced the T-34. Average daily production in 1943 was 17 or 18 T-34s, 5 or 6 KV-85s, and 6 KV-14 SUs. In May 1944, production was 6 KV-14s and 12 JS-13s daily. According to Soviet sources, the level of production at Chelyabinsk was about 180 heavy tanks and SUs monthly in 1943 and 540 heavy tanks plus 100 T-34s per month in 1944.

Chelyabinsk was an excellent example of the strengths and weaknesses of the Soviet production system. Manufacturing heavy tanks required powerful cranes to move the components (turrets and hulls) to assemble the tanks. Chelyabinsk was one of the few factories with this equipment. The design of the factory followed Henry Ford's idea of assembly-line production and the vertical concentration of production. In contrast, the horizontal technique concentrated the production of a common component, such as engines, in a few plants and transported the components to various plants for assembly in a variety of finished products. For example, the Germans built the Mann tank engine in one plant and sent the engines to various other plants for use in a variety of tanks. The vertical method concentrated production of all components for a single finished product in one location, limiting the incoming shipments to raw materials. Chelyabinsk was planned to make tractors with the vertical method and converted to heavy tank production by the addition of evacuated factories with their workers in 1941. Because of the increased complexity of producing tanks compared to tractors, fewer units were made at far greater labor cost. The workforce at Chelyabinsk increased from 25,000 to make tractors to 60,000 in 1944 to make tanks.

The advantage of the vertical system was that it created no added burden on the limited rail network to move heavy components from distant locations. The advantage of the horizontal system was that the various plants profited from large-scale production and could be located near the source of raw materials. However, using the vertical system, making 20 engines per day fell short of the economy of large-scale production. Concentrating the production of heavy tanks in Chelyabinsk was possible because its remote location protected against air attack, and the threat of sabotage was neglible. The Germans could not risk such a concentration because any interruption would halt the production of all heavy tanks.

The Chelyabinsk factory worked on a cycle. From the sketch of the assembly plant included in one German report, the tanks were assembled on a line nearly half a mile long. Soviet photographs reveal the building method. The road wheels were attached to the hull on an auxiliary line. The 20 ton chassis was then picked up by two cranes and hoisted to the beginning of two parallel assembly lines in the center of the building. The motor was dropped in, and then the turret and gun were added, both major components coming from auxiliary lines probably located in separate buildings. The tanks could be pulled forward on the road wheels as work progressed. One of the final steps was the addition of the tracks. The completed tank could then be driven off the end of the line.

An alternate technique used by the Germans in their smaller plants did not require the tank chassis to move. Batches of tanks could have been assembled at various points in the building, starting with the chassis and adding the hull, the engine, and finally the turret. When a batch was finished, all of the tanks would be rolled out of the building at once and a new batch started. The difficulty of moving the heavy chassis once assembly had begun, and the probable scarcity of assembly space equipped with overhead cranes, precluded large, open aisles to facilitate moving the finished tanks. Soviet photographs show very crowded work space in the tank factories.

The second largest tank factory was the Ural Tank Works (Stalin) No. 183 at Nishnij-Tagil. In September 1941, the Locomotive and Tank Factory No. 183 at Kharkov was moved to Nishnij-Tagil, added to the existing factory, and renamed the Ural Tank Works. The Kharkov plant, which employed 14,000 workers before the war, sent hydraulic presses and heavy machine tools. Other machines came from Mariupol, Leningrad, and Moscow.

The first Nishnij-Tagil T-34s were completed on December 25, 1941. Daily production increased from 5 to 15 by December 1942, to 22 in January 1943, and to 30 in July 1943. The monthly production of T-34s in 1943 was 850. In March 1944, production began on the T-34/85. The factory also made 250 to 300 long-barreled 76 mm antitank guns monthly. The factory employed 40,000 workers, including women (50%), boys of 16 and 17 (10%), and invalid soldiers (5%) who worked either 8-hour or 12-hour shifts. The work was hard and food was short. Bread was rationed according to the work assignment, from 400 grams (a 1-pound loaf) to 800 grams per day.

Another T-34 plant was located at Omsk-Lenin Plant No. 174. Before the war, the Lenin plant in Omsk had employed 5,000 workers making tractors. In 1941, additional machines and men came from Plant No. 174 in Leningrad. Work conditions were similar to those in Nishnij-Tagil. The plant first made T-60 light tanks but soon switched to producing T-34s. By 1944, 15,000 workers were producing up to 20 T-34s per day and 200 per month.

The Ural Heavy Machine Tool Factory (URALMASH) at Sverdlovsk also made T-34s and other military equipment. The large complex began with raw materials, made its own steel, and produced finished heavy equipment. Most of the original machinery was German. Construction was supervised by 150 foreign engineers and employed 12,000 workers. One building was one-fourth of a mile long. The complex included foundries, hammer and press shops, forge shops, heat treating, mechanical departments, machine fabrication, and assembly. On July 15, 1933, the factory began production of mining and metal industry equipment along with military equipment.

Before the war, the plant at Sverdlovsk had employed 27,000 workers making tractors and some medium and heavy tanks. The factory began making parts for the T-34 in 1942 and by the end of the year was assembling complete tanks. By May 1944, the factory was turning out 200 T-34s per month. In September 1943, the plant began production of SU-85s using the T-34 chassis, and by May 1944 was producing 15 SU-122s per day.

The Kuibyshev Factory No. 38, located in Kirov, northeast of Moscow, was the second major light tank factory. The prewar Kolomensky Locomotive Works No. 38 at Kolomna, south of Moscow, began making T-60s in July 1941 and continued until it was evacuated to Kirov in the fall of 1941. More men and machines came from Plant No. 37, and they combined to form the new Kuibyshev Factory No. 38. Plant No. 37 had developed light tanks before the war and continued to make T-60s until September 1941, when it was evacuated. When No. 38 resumed production of the T-60 at Kirov, it became one of the two major sources of the T-60, along with the Gorki GAZ factory.

Research and development on light tanks continued at Factory No. 38, resulting in an improved T-60. In 1942, production of light tanks increased to 30 per day. The T-70 went into production in September 1942. In October 1943, light tank production ceased and the factory concentrated on SU-76s. Production of the SU-76s had begun in December 1942, but the faulty design limited output. In the spring of 1943, full-scale production of the SU-76 began at both the GAZ plant and at No. 38. In addition, more than 1,200 German Mark III panzers and Sturmgeschutz IIIs were converted into SU-76s at No. 38 in the fall of 1943. By June 1944, monthly production at Kirov included 550 SU-76s, 2,700 GAZ trucks, 350 armored cars, and the assembly of American trucks shipped in crates. In September 1944, the plant had 8,000 to 10,000 workers.

Tank production took place in other factories in the east. The Kaganovitch factory in Charabarovsk employed 4,000 workers before the war. During the war, the plant repaired tanks for the Far East and assembled some T-70s and T-34s.

In summary, before the war many Russian factories made components and assembled tanks. With the advance of the Germans, the Soviet high command decided to maintain the plants at Stalingrad and Gorki and to create five major centers at Kirov, Nishnij-Tagil, Chelyabinsk, Omsk, and Sverdlovsk, enlarging existing factories with men and machines from factories in Leningrad, Kharkov, Moscow, and other cities. Although production fell to 500 tanks per month in October 1941, by March 1942 it reached 1,000 and by the end of 1942 more than 1,500, as the new plants came into full-scale production. Heavy tanks came from Chelyabinsk; medium tanks from Nishnij Tagil, Gorki, Sverdlovsk, Omsk, and Chelyabinsk; and light tanks from Gorki and Kirov, providing the Red Army with enough to both replace losses and create new units. At the end of 1942, the number of Soviet tanks on hand exceeded 20,000, and it continued to increase until the end of the war, when 35,000 were on hand. From mid-1942 the Russians had an ample supply of tanks to maintain the strength of their units. In January 1945, the German Army had about 12,000 tanks and assault guns on all three fronts and in noncombat formations. Probably fewer than 10,000 were on the eastern front. German losses in January 1945 were 1,375 tanks and assault guns, more than 10 percent of the total. With overwhelming numbers of tanks and SUs, Soviet forces were able to break through the strongest defenses. The Red Army no longer feared the German tank-supported counterattacks that had turned victory into defeat in 1942 and early 1943. The results were far-reaching advances and rapid conquest of enemy-held territory by the Red Army.

The turning point in weapons production came at the end of 1942. Before that time, there were shortages. Sending weapons to the troops in Ukraine in the

Table 3.2   Weapons Inventories in 1941 and 1942

Weapons	December 1941	November 1942
Guns and mortars	22,000	77,851
Tanks	1,954	7,350
Combat aircraft	2,238	4,544

summer of 1942 was hampered because of limited rail capacity. When the Nazis drove into the Caucasus, sweeping aside the Russian defenders, the Soviets had to deploy the reserve armies before they were ready and arm them with whatever weapons were at hand. On August 27, 1942, the Stavka sent the 1st Guard and the 24th and 66th Armies to defend Stalingrad. The armies were poorly equipped, manned by old reservists, and short of fuel and ammunition. In the 9th Army defending the Caucasus in August 1942, the recently formed 417th Rifle Division had only 500 rifles. The 151st Rifle Division of the same army equipped half of its men with foreign rifles. Only 30 percent of the men of one infantry brigade were armed with foreign rifles, and there were no machine guns or artillery.

By the end of 1942, the supply of weapons for the Red Army had improved. The inventory of heavy weapons on hand had increased dramatically compared to the year before (table 3.2). The November 1942 totals exceeded the number of weapons in the hands of the Germans and their satellite forces on the eastern front. The Soviet rifle division in December 1942 had a table of organization of 9,435 men, 727 machine pistols, 605 machine guns, and 212 antitank rifles. With only about two-thirds of the men, the division had more machine guns than the prewar division. The rifle company had 12 machine pistols and 12 light machine guns, double the number in December 1941. The supply of antitank rifles was ample. The Russians were winning the production battle by the end of 1942 (table 3.3).

At the end of the war, the Soviet Union had 11 million men in the armed forces, including 6 million in the army. There were about 6.5 million men on the eastern front. The Red Army had 91,400 guns and mortars, 2,933 rocket launchers, 11,000 tanks and SUs, and 14,500 military aircraft. The Poles, Czechs, and other allies had 326,500 men, 5,200 guns, and 200 tanks on the eastern front. In

Table 3.3   Total Weapons Produced from 1941 to 1945 (in Thousands)

Weapons	Soviet Union	Germany
Mortars	347.9	68.0
Guns	188.1	102.1
Tanks and SUs	95.1	53.8
Military aircraft	108.0	78.9
Motor vehicles	205.0	375.0

comparison, the Germans on the eastern front had only 3.1 million men, 28,500 guns and mortars, 4,000 tanks and self-propelled guns, and 2,000 aircraft. Only in production of motor vehicles did the Germans exceed Soviet levels. The import of American vehicles substituted for Russian production.

In summary, at the beginning of the war, the Red Army had a vast arsenal of weapons, although some were obsolete. In the first three or four months of the war, the Soviets lost or consumed most of their prewar stocks of weapons and munitions. Simultaneously, production was severely disrupted by German occupation of the western territory, where much of the Russian military productive capacity had been located. Weapons production became the first priority in late 1941 and continued to be first through 1943. Losses continued at a heavy rate, but by early 1942 production exceeded losses in all categories, and quantities available increased steadily, with the exception of six months of heavy losses in armored vehicles in the second half of 1943. By early 1943, the Red Army had a clear superiority in weapons that increased as the war progressed. The Soviet Union, with an economy severely disrupted by occupation of its most productive land, analogous to occupation of the United States east of the Mississippi, was able to outproduce Germany. This productive capacity was a major cause of Germany's defeat.

Chapter 4

Maintaining the Divisions

IN THE SUMMER of 1941, the Red Army suffered catastrophic losses, forcing the Soviet Union to introduce drastic changes to replace the destroyed divisions and to maintain them during the bloody battles that followed. Calling up reserves and drafting men at a younger age provided the manpower to recreate the divisions.

As the war progressed, there was a steady drain of killed, wounded, and missing. Both the Germans and Soviets had to find millions of replacements every year. The Russians developed a sophisticated system that churned out millions of soldiers by lowering the draft age, reducing the number of men in a division, and shortening the training cycle for new recruits. Although the Red Army experienced heavier losses than the Germans, the Russians developed a more efficient replacement system.

While the Russians were able to maintain about 6 million soldiers on the front with Germany and an additional 5 million on other fronts and behind the lines, the Germans reached a peak of 12 million men in 1944. However, the Germans had only 3.1 million on the eastern front in July 1943, and by February 1944 the total had dropped to 2.4 million as the demands of other fronts drew strength away from the east.

The Russian routine of inducting and training new men each year had a major impact on the timing of Soviet offensives, even though the condition of the roads dictated where and when operations occurred. In the spring and fall of 1944 about half of the annual class, young men who had reached the age of 18, were inducted and trained in schools in the various military districts. Riflemen received up to four months of training, while tank crew members were trained for as long as a year. Beginning in January and again in June of each year, up to 1 million new replacements were available to the Red Army to fill divisions depleted in the prior six months. Of course there was a flow of replacements during the intervening months too, primarily from men returning from hospitals, but the biggest bumps in manpower came around January and June.

Maintaining the numerical strength and, more important, effectiveness of a military unit once it entered combat was crucial in World War II. Although short campaigns similar to previous German experiences in Poland, Norway, France, and the Balkans produced little concern for rotation or replacements, the long struggle on the eastern front demanded a well-organized system for replacing losses and relieving the survivors. A human being could withstand a limited amount of combat stress, beyond which he would no longer react positively and became more concerned with survival than achieving goals. Stress was cumulative, each individual having an "account," so to speak, from which energy withdrawals were made each time danger was faced. The size of individual accounts and the dangers perceived by each person varied widely. Few could endure the stress of continuous frontline combat for more than a year. Commanders had to be concerned with the emotional and physical condition of the individual combatant. Exhaustion from prolonged combat reduced the chances of survival as well as the ability to carry out assignments. Exposure to disease, injury, or death had to be reduced to the lowest possible level, and an atmosphere was needed that encouraged the hope of survival. Few Soviet soldiers or individuals from any other nation could endure a year of continuous intense combat, even if they were able to survive enemy action.

To relieve the stress in all wars, an informal truce often developed in the quiet sectors: "We won't shoot if you don't shoot." This arrangement allowed units to hold quiet sectors for many months. The pattern of offensive operations on the eastern front was a few weeks of intense combat to break through the opponent's defense line followed by a period of exploitation at a lower risk level. Soon another stalemate set in as the attacker outran his supply lines. Human exhaustion and wear and tear on vehicles also contributed to the slowdown of an operation. The loss of men in the rifle companies from death, wounds, or sickness weakened their ability to sustain an offensive.

There were several approaches to maintaining the combat effectiveness and integrity of a unit. The preferred method was to rotate a complete unit to the rear after an operation, refit it with newly trained men and returning wounded, and give the survivors a respite. Replacements had to learn their roles before combat, and that was best accomplished by withdrawing the division from the front line. At the same time the more aggressive veterans, who tended to have higher casualties after prolonged service on the front, received a needed break from frontline duty. Unless rested, the unit faced a steady deterioration of quality.

The alternative of adding replacements to a division at the front exposed inexperienced men and denied the veterans relief. Adding replacements while a division was in combat led to excessive losses among the new men. In World War II, if a replacement survived four days, his chances of surviving the war increased considerably.

The third alternative was to disband a worn-out unit. The disadvantage was the loss of the accumulated experience of the officers and noncommissioned officers (NCOs), who maintained the unit's tradition and integrity. Most of the disbanded Soviet divisions were probably beyond redemption because they had been encircled and the men had been killed or captured, leaving only a few stragglers who escaped. After the bitter battles in Ukraine in 1942, only one Soviet division was disbanded until the end of the war.

The Soviets frequently rotated units from the line, depending on the situation. While the division was behind the line, replacements arrived and were trained. Stalin's order of March 16, 1942, required that divisions receive replacements while in reserve behind the lines and that a division could not receive replacements during combat. Stalin repeated his admonition in an order on May 1, 1942. A refreshed division returned to the line to replace another spent division that went through the same process. This replacement method required extra units or a commander with the courage to reduce his frontline strength. The advantages of rotation were manifold: New men had time to assimilate into their platoon; veterans had welcome relief from combat; and the army commander had a reserve in the event of an unexpected severe crisis.

Rotation required the formation of extra divisions. The disadvantage of forming too many divisions was an increased need for equipment and support units that seldom experienced losses. During a period of few losses, the temptation was to create more units with the excess of replacements, which the British did in 1941 and 1942. When the fighting intensified, a nation might be at a loss to provide the necessary replacements, and divisions had to be broken up. The Russians did not do this, although the remnant of a division was occasionally added to another division.

Most replacements came from two sources: returning wounded and newly trained men. Returning the wounded man to his own unit occasionally created a problem when too many wounded returned directly to their own units regardless of need. A unit that had suffered many casualties and replaced them with new men would be over strength once its wounded were returned, leaving other units short of men. This occurred in the German Army in early 1944. The Russians tried to return men to their previous units if at all possible, but there were a few instances when a division was over strength.

A division would profit when the newly trained men came from the division's original geographical area. The new men fit in quickly, as there were no language barriers. The alternate approach drew men from the nation at large for both the original unit and for replacements. Given the diverse makeup of the Soviet Union and its many languages, the problem of intermingling was especially severe. If the regional basis were retained, how restricted should that basis be—by state or province, region, county, or even town? Regionally oriented units had better cohesion because the men shared the same language and customs. Obtaining the right proportion of replacements from each region was difficult because of the uneven casualty rates. In the end, the Soviets abandoned the practice of regional replacements and used any available replacements to fill the gaps in the rifle companies.

In the final years of the war, men who had been in the area occupied by the Germans in 1941 were drafted into service and termed booty troops, as they were the result of the recapture of territory. There were two types of booty troops. The most numerous were older men who had trained before World War II, as the Soviet Union had compulsory military training since its Civil War. They were immediately inducted into units. The other group were the young men who needed training. A boy age 14 in 1941 when the Germans took his village was 18 in 1945 when the Red Army retook his village. Every year, 500,000 boys reached the age of 18 in the occupied territory, so that in 1943 a million additional young men were available, plus another half million in 1944 and 1945. Toward the end of the war, the supply of new men exceeded losses and allowed the return of technicians to civilian life to begin rebuilding the Soviet economy.

Combat effectiveness demanded that men, weapons, and supplies be maintained at a workable level, not necessarily according to the official table of organization. The workable number, although possibly below the authorized strength, was at a level considered combat effective, for example, rifle companies with about 100 men. Eventually, after 1942, the Russian authorized tables were changed to reflect a more efficient or more attainable situation.

The Soviet mobilization system excelled in the task of creating new units. The methods of providing replacements, returning wounded to combat, and reconstructing worn-out divisions were all related to the mobilization process. The Russians increased the number of rifle divisions rapidly during the late 1930s as well as in 1940 and 1941. The territorial divisions, composed mostly of part-time soldiers, had drawn their men from a restricted geographical area. However, the territorial divisions were eliminated in the late 1930s, technically ending the relationship of divisions to regions. The new philosophy created an "all-Union" army, drawing men from all areas of the Soviet Union.

Regional affiliation was an especially thorny problem for the Soviets because the Red Army had over 100 nationalities, each with significant numbers. The largest were the Russians, Ukrainians, Belarusians, Tartars, Jews, Kazakhs, Armenians, Georgians, Uzbeks, Mordvinians, Chuvashes, Azerbaijanians, Bashkirs, and Ossetians. The Red Army required that nationality units be trained in two languages, because the manuals were in Russian. The insurmountable problem was training a platoon of men who did not understand Russian and did not even have a common second language.

The real issue was not only language but also questionable loyalty to the Soviet Union. Because of questionable loyalty, the czarist regime had exempted some Caucasian nationalities from military service. Even the Communists considered some nationalities untrustworthy or otherwise unsuitable for military service. Before the Soviet Law of Universal Military Training in 1938, some nationalities had been exempt from military service: the Lapps from the north, some Caucasian nationalities, and others from less developed regions. The Soviets, even late in the war, distrusted certain nationalities. In November 1944, the 2nd Guard Army ordered all Kalmyks, Chechens, Ossetians, and Crimean Tartars, along with the nationals of enemy countries, to be relieved from duty and sent to the rear.

The distrust seems to have been justified. The Germans were able to recruit thousands of prisoners from Azerbaijan, Georgia, and Turkestan to fight for Germany in the Ost battalions. These groups hated Stalin and readily joined the Germans. The Germans reformed the 162nd Infantry Division on May 21, 1943, from Ost battalions and the staff of the former German division.

Added to these difficulties were cultural and religious differences as well as historical racial conflicts. Because of these differences and because the Soviet Union had a limited transportation system, in practice, divisions formed before the war drew their men from a single district for compatibility. Even after the war had begun, new divisions drew their men from a single compatible district. In the fall of 1942 the Panfilov Division, named for a Kazakh hero, was formed from men from the Kazakh Republic.

Later in the war, most units had a mixture of Russians, Ukrainians, and Belarusians, with a few other nationalities. An artillery battery of the 233rd Rifle Division in December 1944 was 45 percent Russian, 45 percent Ukrainian, and 10 percent other nationalities. The enlisted men of the 101st Rifle Brigade in 1943 were from Kazakhstan, but the officers were Russians. Although the official policy after 1938 rejected regionally oriented units in favor of an all-Union army, necessity produced not only divisions but entire armies that drew their men from a single military district or from two adjoining districts. However, realistically the Soviets could not maintain the nationality orientation of units through selective replacements. Replacements came from any available source, and therefore the problems of language and assimilation continued throughout the war.

To maintain a ground army of over 6 million men on the eastern front, the Red Army needed masses of replacements. The Red Army outnumbered the Germans about two-to-one and suffered casualties at the same rate. In the late fall of 1942, the available men were needed for new artillery and armored units, reducing the number of infantry replacements. The average rifle company included only 145 men and a rifle battalion 609. In 1943, the rifle company was down to 120 and the battalion 513. In 1944 the rifle company was at 90 men, with the battalion at 405.

Although Soviet tactics improved as the war progressed, reducing losses, breaking through well-prepared German defenses was still costly in men. In March 1943, the Soviets launched ten attacks of more than a thousand men and six minor attacks on the German 260th Division. The Germans counted over 1,500 dead, compared to their own losses of only 150 killed, 27 missing, and 539 wounded.

Another Red Army rifle regiment suffered 1,638 casualties in 12 weeks from December 1, 1943, to February 24, 1944, an average of 20 per day, including 227 killed, 373 missing, 967 wounded, and 71 sick. On April 2, 1944, the regiment had only 600 men. During the winter months, other armies had far higher rates of sickness, suggesting that the Soviet regiment had evacuated only the most seriously ill. The missing 373 were apparently prisoners. Although some wounded returned, permanent losses (killed and missing) of 600 men in three months was serious. An efficient replacement system was required.

Because of the threat of war in 1939, the training period for recruits was cut and the draft age lowered. The army absorbed many more recruits and training became a serious undertaking. In September 1939, the draft age was lowered from 21 to 19, so that by June 1941 four classes were in the army instead of two, as draftees normally served two years. Each class included about 1.5 million men, so that there were 6 million new men in the army in June 1941. In addition, reservists from 14 classes were called up during the remainder of 1941 to replace the heavy losses of the summer. Absorbing the men and creating new units created a monstrous administrative problem. The men had received military training in sports organizations, where they had learned marksmanship and individual combat skills.

The reserves reported to a reception center that conducted medical examinations and assigned men to companies. Each company received an allotment of military specialties. Men received uniforms and equipment and shipped personal property home. These companies were then assigned to the new divisions formed in the fall of 1941.

After the first wave of divisions had left for the front, the reception centers transferred their duties to replacement regiments that each division left behind in its home station after the division went to the front. In 1942 new recruits were sent to replacement regiments. Most new men had received military training either at school, in the Komsomol, or in the Ossoawiachim, a paramilitary organization. The replacement regiments trained recruits, formed them into companies, and sent them to replacement regiments attached to armies at the front that allocated the replacements to divisions as needed. The better educated recruits went to the technical arms and services. Because the Revolution of 1917 had eliminated the upper class and reduced the middle class, few well-educated men were available for the army in 1941. Less than 12 percent of the Soviet soldiers had a high school or higher education, and more than 60 percent had completed only elementary school.

The infantry training depended on the situation at the front. Normally training lasted two to four months or more and varied with the arm of service; for example, infantry training was shorter than tank or artillery training. Tank crews trained from 8 to 12 months. Stalin's order of March 16, 1942, had stressed improved training for the recruits. Training was vigorous and emphasized endurance, close combat, night fighting, combat in forests and marshes, camouflage, deception, field fortifications, and discipline.

Future NCOs trained in army and front replacement regiments or in the school battalions of the rifle divisions from three to four months. Some NCOs trained in the rear at special schools. The 2nd Guard Cavalry Corps received a large contingent of young, tough, well-trained NCOs to replace heavy losses in December 1941. Good NCOs were usually not plentiful. In November 1942, the 51st Mechanized Brigade had only 841 NCOs instead of the authorized 1,156. Most were graduates of an NCO course and under 25 years of age, but 195 had received no special training; only 222 had prior command experience; and only 164 had prior combat experience.

Russian replacements normally flowed in companies or battalions from training units to field replacement regiments assigned to each front and field army. These regiments also served as processing centers for returning wounded, conscripted civilians (booty troops), and stragglers. The number of men processed by a field replacement regiment in a month was often more than a thousand. The replacement regiments transferred men after a short period to the divisional replacement battalions. If the situation permitted, the training took place in the divisional replacement battalions immediately behind the front in the techniques of sniping, reconnaissance, and working in a unit.

Each rifle division incorporated a replacement battalion, also called a school battalion, for training newly arrived replacements and to hold recuperating sick and wounded. The division cautiously made every effort to ease the entry of the new men. The new troops received additional training in group, platoon, company, and battalion tactics, as well as individual training. Only rarely did the situation at the front and the lack of training cadres shorten the training period.

The 271st Rifle Division had a school battalion with three rifle companies and a machine gun company with up to 130 men in each company. The 30th Rifle Division had a similar battalion. New recruits received six to eight weeks' training in the school battalion before joining a rifle company. The school battalion also held slightly wounded men, sick, and stragglers, in addition to training new replacement platoon leaders.

By February 1944, the Germans had identified over 300 replacement regiments. Another 500 had been identified in the past but were either abolished or redesignated. Several training camps were huge. The camp near Kostroma had five regiments, each with four battalions. Each replacement regiment normally had 3,000 men in training, although prisoners reported as many as 4,000 to 6,000 in some regiments, and one regiment held 10,000 men. In September 1942, a training brigade at Kostroma had received 11,000 men of the class of 1924, who were trained for more than six months until March and April 1943. Various regiments specialized in training heavy machine gunners, riflemen, snipers, submachine gunners, and antitank riflemen. Each regiment normally had three battalions with 150 to 250 cadres each. At the end of training in March, the replacements formed into companies and battalions and went to the front. By mid-May, only the cadres remained.

The army field replacement regiment also administered the returning wounded, limited-service men, and men being transferred from service organizations. When territory was liberated, all military-age combat-fit men were immediately drafted and assigned to units, except the youngest men who had received no prewar training. In October 1943, untrained men inducted in newly acquired territory were sent to army field replacement regiments for instruction before assignment to rifle divisions.

The divisions also had training battalions for recruits sent from the replacement system. The training battalion of the 95th Guard Rifle Division, located near Staszow, consisted of two rifle companies, a heavy machine gun company, a light machine gun company, and a rocket launcher company. Training in this battalion lasted only three weeks and was probably advanced training for men who had received prior training in other units.

In May 1944, the reserve and training units formed eight training divisions. During 1944 and 1945, 1,020,000 officers and men were trained in the Moscow Military District in 60 replacement units.

The replacement process is illustrated by the experience of two prisoners captured by the Germans. Lt. Sobolev, captured in October 1944, gave minute details of his military service. He was inducted on November 9, 1942, at the age of 19 and sent to an antiaircraft replacement brigade at Tiflis in the Caucasus. After one month of training, he was sent to the 20th Antiaircraft Division near Tuapse. In January 1944, he was reassigned to the infantry and, after 20 days of infantry training in the 180th Replacement Regiment, was sent to officer training school for three months. In May 1944, he was assigned to the 318th Rifle Division.

Another example is Pvt. Baranov, who was born in 1925 and drafted on August 30, 1943, from the newly liberated area around Orel. He was trained in the 72nd Replacement Regiment and on December 24, 1943, was assigned to the machine pistol company of the 508th Rifle Regiment of the 174th Rifle Division. The machine pistol companies usually had the best soldiers in a regiment.

In my personal experience in 1946, eight weeks of basic training was not enough for most of the recruits to learn essential skills. Having had three years' training in the Junior ROTC, I was familiar with most of the subjects being taught and had considerable experience firing the M1 rifle. During the eight weeks of basic training, I was taught how to fire the Browning automatic rifle, the 60 mm mortar, and the .45 caliber pistol. Two hours of marching and physical training daily added more than 20 pounds of muscle. However, other recruits learned very little in the two months, while sleeping through instruction sessions and malingering at every opportunity. Many, if not most, of the Russian recruits would have received military training before being inducted and discipline would have been more rigid, plus the important fact that they would have been highly motivated, in contrast to American draftees in 1946.

Fremde Heer Ost compared the information on the Russian system to the German Replacement Army in 1943 and again in 1944. In 1943, the Soviet replacement organization was half again as large. The Germans had 1,021 battalions with 206,900 cadres while the Soviet system had 1,866 battalions (622 regiments) with 280,000 cadres. In 1944, even though there were nearly a million men in the German Replacement Army, the German system had shrunk to only 560 battalions with 133,200 cadres, while the Soviet replacement system in 1944 increased, with about 10 percent more battalions and nearly a third more cadres; 1,815 battalions (605 regiments) plus 336 school battalions (84 regiments) for NCOs, a total of 2,151 battalions with 407,000 cadres. The Russians were providing improved training to new recruits while the Germans were reducing their training.

Men were drafted according to their date of birth, and those sharing a common birth date formed a class. The class of 1923 consisted of men born in 1923 drafted in the winter of 1941–42 as 18-year-olds. The drafting of the class began in May 1942, when only half the men were 18. In August 1942, the Russians called up 1.4 million 17-year-olds from the class of 1925. The Red Army called up the 17-year-olds early to allow more time for their training and withheld them from combat until they reached 18. The younger men often went to new units, where they received additional training as the unit organized. The men of the class of 1925 were not sent to divisions as replacements until August, September, and November 1943, when most of them were 18, more than a year after they had been drafted.

The Russians began to call up the class of 1926 (17-year-olds) in January 1943, six months earlier than the previous class. The class of 1926 was much larger than those of previous years because of the higher birthrate in 1926. Living conditions had improved in 1926, and the birthrate rose to 43.6 per thousand or 6,409,000 births based on a total of 147 million, the estimated population of the Soviet Union in 1926. The division between male and female births was approximately equal, amounting to a total of 3,200,000 males in the class of 1926. Some children would have died before their 17th birthday. The Civil War had ended by 1926 and, though there were shortages of food and many children died of starvation in the 1920s, there were far more survivors than the Germans had estimated. Rather than adding only 1.5 million recruits to the Red Army in 1943 as in previous years, the total was over 3 million, including men picked up in liberated areas and women enlisted in the armed forces.

Combined with the men from the class of 1925 and other sources, the Germans assumed that in 1943 the Russians would have enough men to replace their losses plus an additional million to form new units. In a study prepared in 1943, the Germans estimated that 2.6 million Russians would be drafted in 1943; 1.3 million would be used to replace losses; 400,000 would reinforce worn-down units; and 900,000 would go to new units.

Members of the class of 1927, drafted in 1944, were not used in combat until 1945. In February 1945, the Germans estimated that only 400,000 of the class of 1927 were in units and that 1.3 million were still training. All of these studies mesh with Russian documents and contradict the assumption that the Soviets sent young men into battle without training. After 1942, the recruits received extensive training and only the booty troops, many of whom had previous training and even combat experience, were sent directly to units.

The Soviet replacement system trained and sent to the field army a prodigious number of replacements in 1941 and 1942, but in the beginning quality suffered.

Replacements for the rifle companies were especially poor in the early years of the war. In March 1942, the replacements sent to the front were either young recruits with a minimum of training or were over age. Some were less than 18 years old and others were over 40. The 1st Shock Army received men 46 and 47 years old. In June 1942, Timoshenko rightly complained that the replacements scarcely knew the rudiments. They were peasants, office workers, shopkeepers, and schoolboys who could not fire an antitank rifle or a 50 mm mortar.

However, the situation improved in late 1942. During the buildup at Stalingrad for the winter offensive of 1942–43, commissars met new soldiers coming to the 65th Army at the rail unloading point and sent them to a rifle division or other unit. There the commander and the unit commissar indoctrinated the new recruits on unit traditions and spoke with each man. The men received their weapons, and an experienced soldier was made responsible for each new man. The army made a special effort to provide commissars who spoke additional languages, as one-third of the men on the Stalingrad Front did not speak Russian.

The issue of quality extended to new units sent into combat before they were ready in 1942. Yeremenko, a front commander at Stalingrad, complained in August 1942 that the new reserve armies lacked equipment and included poorly trained old reservists hastily formed into divisions. As the struggle in Stalingrad dragged on and the number of casualties soared, the Russians continually fed thousands of replacements to the divisions in combat. Faced with that crisis, the quality of replacements deteriorated. Some of the replacements were criminals who had volunteered to fight in return for their freedom. Released prisoners formed entire battalions. On September 21, 1942, 8,000 replacements were sent across the Volga in one night and distributed to various divisions. Two days later, 2,000 men were sent to the 13th Guard Division, including some boys from Stalingrad ages 17 to 19, presumably with very little training.

In 1943, the 226th Rifle Division commander had complained that replacements arrived badly trained and some with no uniforms, probably booty troops. The new men acquired in the liberated territory were not comparable to the regular replacements. However, conditions had improved by 1943. As the Soviets prepared for the Battle of Kursk in 1943, the Red Army needed a huge intake of fresh manpower. Exhausted divisions from the Stalingrad Front needed refitting and new units were needed to provide for the defense of Kursk. In the first half of 1943 the Red Army lost 781,000 men and women, and 1.9 million were hospitalized, a total of nearly 2.7 million troops. Returning wounded probably exceeded the number hospitalized in that period, providing 2 million experienced soldiers. The 1.5 million new recruits increased the total to 3.5 million, for a calculated net gain of 800,000. In fact, the total manpower of the Red Army on the eastern front increased from 5.3 million on January 1, 1943, to 6.46 million on June 30, 1943. The Red Army gained over a million men in the first six months of 1943. The additional half million resulted from more hospital returnees, recruits taken in the first six months, and a combing of service units. There are repeated references in prisoner of war interrogations at Kursk of men being drafted in the newly liberated areas, which would have boosted the number of recruits in the first six months of 1943. Regardless of the source, the Soviets had an enormous pool of over 3.5 million men to restore battered divisions, to increase the table of organization of existing units, and to create new units.

In all of 1943, the Red Army lost 1,977,000 troops (male and female) and 5,506,000 were hospitalized, most of the losses occurring in the first half of the year. The Red Army lost 656,000 men in the first quarter of 1943 and 1.4 million were hospitalized (a total of 2 million losses). The loss rate dropped precipitously in the second quarter, with only 125,000 killed and missing and 471,000 hospitalized (a total of fewer than 700,000). In early 1943 the Voronezh and Southwestern fronts suffered 45,219 losses and 41,250 hospitalized from March 4 to March 25, 1943, a total of nearly 90,000 in three weeks. Despite the losses in early 1943, the total strength of the field forces of the Red Army grew from 5.3 million on January 1, 1943, to 6.4 million on January 1, 1944, a gain of 1.1 million men. Of the 5.5 million hospitalized, 73 percent returned to duty in 60 days and more came later, leading to a net loss from wounds and sickness of fewer than 800,000. Many of the invalids were assigned as instructors in the replacement regiments, releasing able-bodied men for combat. One can only conclude that given the loss of nearly 2 million killed and 800,000 invalids, plus a net gain of 1 million in the field army, the number of recruits added to the Red Army during 1943 apparently was about 3.5 million men and women! This total supports the estimate based on the birthrate.

The Soviets called up about half of the annual class of recruits in the spring and the other half in the fall of each year. Roughly 1.5 million men were added in the spring of 1943 to complete their training by the end of June. German interrogation of prisoners taken at Kursk revealed that many replacements did arrive in June 1943. At the same time, more than a million wounded men returned to their units. The total number available in the replacement streams was about 2.5 million. Replacement regiments sent 2,857,000 troops to the front line from January 1 to July 15, 1943. This number probably includes returning wounded and men gleaned from the service units and retrained as riflemen. Over 1.3 million men were gleaned from service units between May and December 1943. In the six months ending in December 1943, the Germans estimated that the Red Army had received 3.4 million replacements, including 896,000 from the replacement training regiments, plus returning wounded and booty troops. Individual divisions had received from 300 to 1,000 replacements each month. Some divisions had received many more, such as the 71st Guard Rifle Division, which received 3,500 in November 1943.

A German analysis of a sample of data on 513,000 replacements received by the Red Army in 1943 indicated that 92.3 percent were new recruits from training centers, 6.5 percent were returning wounded, and 1.2 percent were men gleaned from the rear and service units. The percentage of returning wounded was very low, reflecting the inability of the prisoners who provided the information to distinguish the source of the replacements. The breakdown on training is very surprising: untrained, 40.9 percent; short training period (less than one month), 26.7 percent; 1 to 12 months' training, 32.4 percent. The breakdown by age reinforces the thesis that many of the men may have been picked up in the Rzhev salient when the Germans withdrew. The untrained men were booty troops: under 18 years of age, 13.3 percent; 18–25 years of age, 32.3 percent; 25–35 years of age, 21.9 percent; 35–40 years of age, 22.5 percent; over 40 years of age, 10.0 percent. The high percentage of untrained men and men with scant training and the age groups reflects the inclusion of booty troops as replacements. These men were better trained than the intelligence report suggested, as most had prior military service either before the war or among the partisans. Young men drafted in the recaptured area returned to the training regiments. The 54.4 percent over age 25 represented most of the 70.6 percent of untrained and briefly trained men. The 32.4 percent that had 1 to 12 months' training correlated with the 45.6 percent under age 25.

Russians made up 75 percent of the half-million replacements, and all other nationalities the remaining 25 percent. From July to October 1943, replacements included in the various reports had totaled 1,173,283. Covering only four months, this information was the basis for the estimate of 3.4 million provided in 1943. Most of the replacements were from the class of 1925 (18-year-olds) or civilians from the liberated territories. A study of the reports of eight Soviet armies in the center showed that 28 percent of the replacements had been from the class of 1925. Still in training in the rear were recruits from the classes of 1926 and 1927.

To provide officers for these huge numbers of troops, the entire system of training officers was revamped. Officers came from two sources: battlefield commissions and officer training schools. Military schools were established offering two- and three-year programs. In 1939 there were 14 military academies and 109 military schools. With the outbreak of war, new measures provided thousands of officers for the new divisions. In 1941 the Red Army had increased the number of academies to 19 and maintained 203 military schools training 240,000 students. By 1943 there were 310 officer training schools with courses that lasted from three to seven months. Infantry schools trained machine gun and mortar officers, and artillery schools trained artillery and heavy mortar officers. In selecting candidates, men with secondary school education were given preference.

Front and army replacement regiments also conducted officer classes from two to six months with emphasis on frontline experience. By October 1941, each field army had formed a school for potential junior officers with special three-month courses. Similar schools were created in the military districts and on the fronts. For example, in November 1942, Lt. Sobolev was drafted at age 19. He attended an NCO school for one month and, after some combat, attended an officer training school for three months beginning in February 1944. Frontline training was part of the curriculum of all officer schools.

The Red Army had begun the war woefully short of senior-grade officers because of the purge of the late 1930s, when Stalin removed practically all of the senior commanders of the army because of a suspected plot to overthrow him.

This vicious move left him short-handed for senior officers when war broke out. Stalin apparently considered Hitler less of a threat than his own generals. Commissars who were equal to the commanding officer were added to all Red Army units to ensure that the army could not be used against Stalin. The realization that he lacked experienced commanders probably influenced Stalin to agree to the nonaggression pact with Hitler.

The Voroshilov Academy trained commanders of divisions and larger units, chiefs of staff, and chiefs of operation sections. The course lasted four to six months. The general staff officers trained at the Frunze Academy. Regimental commanders and staff officers also trained at front and army schools. Lack of academy training was not a block to higher ranks. By 1945, 120 former enlisted men were commanding regiments, and others who had obtained higher ranks served on staffs. Battlefield commissions went to those who displayed heroism and to NCOs who had demonstrated exceptional ability. The dearth of professionally trained officers was shown by the 51st Mechanized Brigade, which formed in October 1942 and by November had 358 officers, of which only one had academy training. Of the others, 257 had been to officer training school and 80 had attended short courses. They were young: 150 were under 25, and 148 were between 25 and 35. Only 148 had been in combat before, suggesting that more than 200 were either recent graduates of schools or had transferred from rear area units to form the new unit. By late 1942, because the supply of officers was greater than needed, the length of courses increased to nearly a year for infantry officers and up to 18 months for other branches, providing better training in the schools and academies. In late 1943, some surplus officers, especially engineers, were returned to civilian positions to begin planning for reconstruction.

When an officer had completed his training or left a hospital, he went to an officer replacement regiment, of which 42 had been identified by the Germans in 1944. Each front had at least one regiment; most fronts had two; and one had three. The strength varied from 200 to 4,000 officer replacements, and in one instance 7,000. The reserves of officers were highest in 1943 when the demand was high and declined in 1944 as officer losses tapered off. In 1944, each replacement regiment had from 500 to 1,000 officers. Returning wounded officers rejoined their previous regiments. In 1943, 250,000 wounded officers had returned to duty. Because the shortage ended, training schools lengthened their courses, and the academy training increased from one to two years. The abolition of the position of deputy commander for political affairs (commissar) in May 1943 had made 122,000 more officers available. The commissars were eliminated first in the rifle companies and then in the staffs of the corps, division, brigade, fortified sector, and other units.

July 1943 may have marked the high point in the rifle strength of the Red Army. The Red Army conscripted men with prior military service in newly retaken territory and thrust them directly into rifle companies. In October 1943, young men drafted in the liberated territory returned to the replacement training regiments.

The service units and hospitals surrendered combat-fit men to reinforce the rifle divisions. In September 1943, gun crews had been reduced from nine men to six, and the surplus men went to the rifle companies. Even with these emergency measures, a rifle division averaged between 5,000 and 6,000 men with only a few guard divisions at 7,000. The strength of the rifle divisions continued to decline to provide men for new tank and artillery units. The army also needed more service units, as it moved away from the production areas and depots near Moscow.

In October 1944, the replacements received by 10 Soviet divisions and four other units were mostly Ukrainians and were in the older age groups, probably booty troops. Other nationalities included Azerbaijanians, Uzbeks, Tartars, Poles, and Belarusians. The booty soldiers were often in the 40- to 50-year-old bracket. Returning wounded constituted a small percentage of the replacements received by the divisions.

Throughout the war, the civilian population had been a ready source of replacements. When Belov with the 2nd Guard Cavalry Corps was surrounded near Viasma in February 1942, he inducted former Red Army men from partisan units and other civilians to the age of 45. In one month, he recruited 2,436 men for his corps. At Stalingrad, Eremenko had mobilized every man in the city between 18 and 50. Initially, they formed in detachments with work clothes and later received uniforms and some training. These ragtag men had provided the Soviet divisions with tens of thousands of replacements.

As the Red Army liberated Soviet territory, more men became available from civilian sources, as well as partisans and soldiers who had remained behind in 1941. In March and April 1944, the 6th Army had mobilized every man in the reoccupied area with the objective of raising the strength of its rifle divisions to 6,000 men. From March to May 1944, the 2nd Ukrainian Front took in 265,000 men from the formerly occupied territory. In the same period, the 3rd Ukrainian Front took in 79,000 men. In some units, more than half the men were booty troops. The newly acquired soldiers received 10 days' training before assignment to units. Two weeks after an area was retaken, the Russians drafted all men between 16 and 50, leaving the women to do the farm work.

Two other sources of manpower in the reconquered territory were the partisans, used immediately as replacements, and liberated Ost workers (men forced to work for the Germans), who after a short training course went to the front. In February 1945, six divisions had received nearly 5,000 replacements, 60 percent of whom were former Ost workers.

Women also replaced men in the rifle divisions and in the supporting units. As in no other army in World War II, the Soviets made extensive use of women in both combat and noncombat roles. Women fought as pilots and snipers but more frequently acted as military police and communications personnel. More than 2 million women served in the Soviet armed forces during the Great Patriotic War.

In early 1943, with a pause in operations, the Soviets had turned their attention from forming new armies to rebuilding reduced formations. After Stalingrad, when the Russians no longer lost entire armies to German encirclements, attention turned to replacing the heavy losses. Individual battlefield competence improved as thousands of men went to schools and received additional training. These men returned to their units and reinforced the strong divisions that defeated the Germans at Kursk.

Beginning in 1943, there was a sharp drop in the number of killed and wound in major operations. At Stalingrad 324,000 were killed and more than 319,000 were wounded or became sick. At Kursk only 70,000 were killed while 108,000 were sick or wounded. The change in the structure and functioning of the Red Army is illustrated by an examination of some sample strategic operations. The ratio of rifle divisions and tank corps demonstrates the growing power of the Soviet armored forces. The decline in the average loss per day during the offensives indicates a reduction of the level of dependence on infantry attacks.

The ratio of killed and missing to sick and wounded changed considerably (table 4.1). At Moscow the ratio was 2:3 and at Izyum 2 killed or missing for each sick or wounded soldier. At Stalingrad the totals were nearly equal and at Kursk 1:1.5. After Kursk the ratio hovered between 1:3 and 1:4 for the rest of the war. Most of the sick and wounded returned to duty within six months. After Kursk, most rifle divisions and tank corps taking part in these sample operations would have required a 200-man replacement company made up mostly of returning wounded every two to four days to maintain their level of strength.

In the Belarus operation, the trend continued. At Berlin the ratio was less than one permanent loss to three temporary losses. At the same time, the daily rate of losses declined sharply after the Orel operation from 126 per division and tank corps to only 61 in Belarus. The low rate continued to the end of the war, an obvious indication that weapons, not masses of men, were winning the battles.

After a lull in early 1943, operations resumed in July, losses escalated, and the quality of the rifle replacements declined as the best personnel were sent to new armored and artillery regiments and brigades. In November 1943, the 226th Rifle Division received 200 badly trained replacements with no uniforms. Even then the demand was not met. Service units were combed for combat-fit men. In December 1943, the 336th Rifle Division had reduced its service units by 40 percent to provide riflemen, while additional combat-fit men were replaced by limited-service men. The service personnel trained as riflemen in a special school unit. The target was to increase the rifle companies to 100 men. In June 1944, the 2nd Guards Army ordered a scouring of its service units for men under 40, or if good soldiers, under 45. Each division had to produce at least 400 men from its service units to replace men over 45 in the rifle companies.

Returning wounded provided high-quality replacements. After recovery, the wounded wanted to return to their original units. Official policy did not automatically allow this, but in practice, the wounded went to the replacement regiment of the army from which they had come to complete their convalescence. In 1941 Belov, in command of the 2nd Guards Cavalry Corps, complained that wounded men had not been allowed to return to their original units. Because wounded soldiers deserted to get back to the 2nd Guards Cavalry Corps, Belov

Table 4.1 Numbers of Killed and Missing Compared to Numbers of Wounded and Sick

Operation	Dates	Days	Divisions	Tank Corps	Men	Killed/ Missing	Wounded/ Sick	Total	Average Loss Per Day	
									Total	Per Unit
Moscow	12/5/41–1/7/42	50	105	0	1,022,000	140,000	231,000	371,000	7,400	70
Izyum	6/28/42–7/24/42	26	74	6	1,310,000	370,000	198,000	568,000	21,846	273
Stalingrad	7/17/42–11/18/42	123	70	3	1,000,000	324,000	319,000	643,000	5,228	51
Kursk	7/5/43–7/23/43	19	77	8	1,273,000	70,000	108,000	178,000	9,900	116
Orel	7/12/43–8/18/43	38	82	8	1,288,000	113,000	317,000	430,000	11,315	126
Belarus	6/23/44–8/29/44	68	172	12	2,412,000	180,000	591,000	771,000	11,338	61
Lvov-Sandomir	7/13/44–8/29/44	48	72	7	1,002,000	65,000	224,000	289,000	6,020	76
Jassy	8/20/44–8/29/44	10	91	6	1,314,000	13,000	54,000	67,000	6,700	69
Baltic	9/14/44–11/24/44	72	135	7	1,546,000	61,000	219,000	280,000	3,900	27
Budapest	10/29/44–2/13/45	76	52	7	720,000	80,000	240,000	320,000	4,210	71
Oder River	1/12/45–2/3/45	23	138	16	2,203,000	43,000	150,000	193,000	8,390	54
Berlin	4/16/45–5/8/45	23	161	20	2,062,000	81,000	280,000	361,000	15,700	86

established a reserve regiment stationed at the rear of his corps to accept the wounded. The returning wounded were a significant factor because for the most part they had been well trained. In February 1944, the 176th Guard Rifle Regiment of the 59th Guard Rifle Division reconstituted its third battalion, which had been abolished in November 1943 because of a temporary manpower shortage. Most of the men were returning wounded, along with some booty troops.

At the end of 1944, the quality of the replacements was better than in 1942. One Russian unit had received replacements in October 1944 to increase the strength of the rifle companies from 50 men to 110. Most of the replacements were 18- and 19-year-olds, with a few 17-year-olds, from central Russia and the Urals. A few were from Belarus and some were older men. The recruits had received six months' training in the replacement regiments.

The most effective element of the Soviet process of maintaining combat strength was its rotation of divisions. Having created over 500 rifle divisions, the Red Army was able to take worn-out units behind the lines for refitting to a far greater extent than any other major power. Divisions were sent to the rear for rebuilding rather than having losses replaced at the front. In the first 12 months of the war, divisions were formed with new conscripts and sent to the front, although the men were not completely trained or equipped. On March 16, 1942, Stalin's order no. 1457 prohibited the addition of replacements to divisions in combat. New replacements were to be added only to divisions behind the lines for rehabilitation. Therefore the commander from time to time was forced to withdraw divisions from the front line.

Some units were repeatedly refitted. In August 1941, the 3rd Airborne Corps had escaped from the Kiev pocket with severe losses. It was refilled with replacements and reappeared as the 87th Rifle Division in December 1941, taking part in the winter offensive. Again depleted, it was pulled out, rebuilt, and took part in the Kharkov offensive as the 13th Guards Division. By July 1942 it was down to 666 men, who swam across the Don River after acting as a rear guard. In September 1942 it was rebuilt again and entered the battle for Stalingrad at full strength.

Later in the war, units that had sustained losses were withdrawn to the rear, rebuilt with replacements, and held as part of the Stavka Reserve. This process provided the Soviet high command with a strategic reserve that could be employed decisively. In the winter of 1942–43, 108 rifle divisions were sent to the front from the Stavka Reserve, along with many other units. In the summer and fall of 1943, more than 200 rifle divisions were provided from the reserve. The classic example is the creation of the Steppe Front behind Kursk in the summer of 1943. When the Germans finally penetrated the Russian defenses in July, armies from the Steppe Front were sent forward to drive back the advancing Germans and initiate a counteroffensive.

As the number of units increased, the limited number of replacements had to be shared with new artillery and armored units. Divisions began receiving replacements while still on the front line. As a result, the rebuilding behind the lines was not as thorough. In October 1943, the 71st Rifle Division was withdrawn from the line and received 100 officers, 450 NCOs, and 3,950 men in two weeks. The division also received 1,800 rifles, 120 light machine guns, 47 heavy machine guns, and 430 machine pistols. Even with these additions, the division had only 7,200 men and was short of weapons.

In view of the losses in the rifle divisions and the increase in armored and artillery units, the Russians did not maintain the rifle companies at the same strength. The authorized strength of the rifle division had dropped from 10,566 in July 1942 to 8,000 in the summer of 1943, and then to 6,800 in October 1943. In 1943 and during the first half of 1944, the bulk of the divisions were seldom involved simultaneously in active operations. The replacement system was able to maintain the rifle companies at about 100 men. However, in 1944 practically all of the armies were engaged and the bonus of the booty troops had been exhausted. The artillery and armored units had first call on the available recruits both as replacements and to create additional units. The inevitable result was the shrinkage of the rifle units. In March 1944, the rifle division was down to 5,400 men with only 2,200 riflemen. Actual strength was even lower. The 212th Rifle Division had only 5,200 men in December 1944. In September 1944, the 242nd Rifle Division was placed in reserve to absorb replacements. The 2nd Battalion of the 897th Rifle Regiment received 90 men, consisting of 13 new Ukrainian recruits and 77 returning wounded. The service units were combed out and the men sent to the rifle companies. As a result, rifle company strength rose to 70 or 80 men.

In the last six months of the war, the Soviets reduced the size of the divisions to create new armored and artillery units. In February 1945, there were three authorized levels of rifle divisions: 4,500 men, 4,000 men, and 3,600 men. The last level had only 12 rifle companies with 76 men and 9 light machine guns each. That same month, the 950th Rifle Regiment of the 262nd Rifle Division had reduced its 3rd Battalion to a cadre of six officers. The remaining two battalions, antitank company, 76 mm gun battery, and 120 mm mortar company had only 109 officers, 141 NCOs, and 381 men, for a total of 631 men. On February 15, 1945, the regiment received 15 officers and 137 men from the 231st Replacement Regiment, increasing the strength of the regiment to 783. With only three rifle companies in each of two battalions, the rifle company strength was about 100.

By April 1945, the Red Army was heavily armed and capable of defeating the remaining German forces. However, a last-ditch defense of Berlin led to street-by-street fighting that took a heavy toll. One of the bloodiest battles of all was a political rather than a strategic operation. The war was over and a simple blockade would have forced a German surrender in a matter of days. If the Russians could wait for weeks at the gates of Warsaw for the political problem to be resolved, they should have been able to wait at Berlin, but Stalin insisted that the Red Army take Berlin even if it cost thousands of Russian lives.

At the end of the war, the average rifle division had only 4,000 men. Divisions became the equivalent of regiments in their rifle strength but were heavily armed with automatic weapons and had the healthy support of a divisional artillery regiment, not a bad situation. The Soviets strove to give the riflemen maximum support. When a division withdrew to refit, the artillery regiment remained at the front to provide extra support to other divisions. The Russians did not maintain large rifle companies in 1945 but instead relied heavily on artillery and tanks for firepower. The rifle units were given lavish numbers of submachine guns and light machine guns, and as long as there were enough men to fire the automatic weapons, the combat value of the company was not depleted seriously.

The use of bold tactics costing heavily in Russian lives needed a system that provided large numbers of replacements and organizations that could continue to function with a low level of manpower. Considering the material available and the task of defeating the German Army in the field, this system was probably the only one that would work.

Chapter 5

Frustrating the Germans: Moscow, 1941

ON JUNE 22, 1941, the Germans launched Operation Barbarous with three drives directed at Leningrad, Moscow, and Rostov. Not expecting the attack and in the midst of a massive reorganization, Stalin refused to believe warnings, including one on March 5, 1941, from Richard Sorge, a Soviet spy in Tokyo with access to the German embassy. Stalin suspected that reports of a pending German invasion were a trick by the British to involve him in a war against Hitler to divert Germany from attacking Britain.

The first four months of combat reduced the Red Army drastically from 4.4 million men to 2.3 million. On June 22, 1941, the Red Army had 198 rifle divisions and 31 motorized divisions. Of these 229 divisions, 117 were deployed on the eastern front, 47 in the Stavka Reserve, and the remaining 65 were scattered in the military districts and the Far East. Of these divisions, 47 were formed in June 1941. In reality, the Russians had about 180 rifle and motorized divisions available for combat on June 22. By the end of December 1941, the Red Army order of battle no longer listed 155 of the divisions, indicating that the prewar army had been destroyed.

However, in July 1941 the Russians formed another 109 new divisions, restoring the number of Red Army divisions to the level of June 1. The new divisions formed in June and July (156) were assigned to combat formations in August and September. The new divisions slowed the German advance, replacing the 97 divisions lost between July and September. The Red Army actually had more active divisions on October 1, 1941, than they had on June 1. The fierce battles of October and November cost the Russians an additional 50 divisions, but they did slow the German advance. Meanwhile, a second wave of 148 new divisions and 88 new rifle brigades were created by the Russians between August and November and were sent to the front in November and December. In December, with the new divisions in place, the Russians launched their counteroffensive, losing only seven divisions in the month. The Russian offensive ground to a halt in January as the Germans reinforced their front with divisions from France and elsewhere.

Close examination of the records raises a few questions, the most significant being why did Stalin, if he was assured that the Germans would not attack as stated in most sources, form 47 new rifle divisions in June 1941, increasing the total number of rifle divisions by a third in a single month before the invasion? The second question is why were the Russians able to stop the Germans in front of Moscow despite the heavy losses sustained in the summer? The weather was not the complete answer, because cold weather affects both sides. The mud in September hindered the Germans more than the snow in December, but they still managed to surround and kill or capture more than 800,000 Russians. The heavy snow in December favored the Germans as it blocked the advance of Red Army units.

The carnage began on the first day of the war and, by the end of July, 17 divisions were no longer in the order of battle, although only 10 divisions were officially abolished during the month (table 5.1). The lost divisions included 12 by the Western Front that took the heaviest blows from the Germans, and 5 from other fronts. Some divisions lost in July were not formally abolished until the following months.

Table 5.1 Rifle Divisions Lost in July 1941

Division	Front/Army	Date Abolished
27A	West 3	September
85A	West 3	September
86A	West 3	September
204mtr	West 3	July
205mtr	West 3	July
49A	West 4	July
205mtr	West 4	September
4mtr	West 10	July
29mtr	West 10	July
113A	West 10	September
208mtr	West 10	August
109mtr	West 20	July
172A	Center 13	September
210mtr	Center 13	July
69mtr	Reserve 24	July
184A	NW 11	September
221mtr	Transcaucasus District	July

In the tables in this chapter, the assignment is the last indicated for the lost division. Capital A following the division number indicates that it was the first formation of that number. Subsequent formations are indicated by B, C, and D. Numbers including slash marks show the various numbers used by the same formation, for example, Poliarnaia/28A. This indicates that the Poliarnaia Division was later given the number 28.

August was even more devastating. Some 28 divisions were lost: 7 by the Western Front, 12 by the Southern Front, and 9 by other fronts. However, only five were formally abolished in August (table 5.2).

During September, the Red Army lost an additional 53 divisions (table 5.3). In the pocket east of Kiev, the Southwestern Front lost 27 divisions in September. The Western Front holding the road to Moscow lost 9 more divisions; the Leningrad and Northwestern Fronts lost a total of 7; and the Bryansk Front lost 6. The Reserve Front and the Southern Front lost 4 more. On September 19, 1941, 51 divisions were officially abolished, including some that had disappeared from the order of battle in August (table 5.4).

Heavy rain fell during September, and the Russians began to counterattack supported by increasing numbers of T-34 tanks and artillery. By October 7, 1941, the Germans overran this first wave of new divisions and killed or captured more than 800,000 men in the Viasma pocket west of Moscow.

Despite the heavy losses, a second wave of divisions faced the Germans in mid-October. The Western Front defending Moscow was reformed by Marshal Z. K. Zhukov and a new Kalinin Front was created on October 17, 1941. By October 31, the advance of the Germans on Moscow was halted by the new Russian

Table 5.2 Divisions Lost in August 1941

Division	Front/Army	Division	Front/Army
61A	Center 21	139A	South 6
110A	Bryansk 13	141A	South 6
167A	Bryansk 21	190A	South 6
208mtr	West 10	197A	South 6
37A	West 13	60mtn	South 12
158A	West 16	72mtn	South 12
233A	West 20	189A	South 12
145A	West 28	192mtn	South 12
140A	West 28	216mtr	South 12
102A	Reserve 24	173A	SW 26
209mtr	West	213mtr	SW 5
44mtn	South 6	67A	Leningrad 8
80A	South 6	185mtr	NW 27
58A	South 6	223A	NW 27

Table 5.3   Rifle Divisions Lost in September 1941

Front	Army	Division
SW	5th	62A, 124A, 131A, 193A, 195A, 200A, 215A, 228A
	21st	55A, 117A, 187A, 219A, 232A, 266A, 277A
	26th	41A, 97A, 116A, 159A, 196A, 264A, 289A, 301A
	37th	28mtn, 87A, 146A, 295A
South	18th	130A
Reserve	24th	24A, 102A, 151A
Bryansk	21st	75A
	37th	147A, 165A, 175A, 206A, 284A
West	10th	2A, 8A, 13A, 17A
	20th	229A
	22nd	98A
	28th	46A, 56A
	29th	253A
NW	11th	18A, 118A
Leningrad	8th	16A, 28A
	23rd	198mtr
	55th	237A
	Reserve	235A

armies and the knee-deep mud. Russian losses were heavy as the hastily assembled armies fought the weary but skillful Germans.

In October another 34 divisions were lost: 17 by the Western Front, 6 by the Kalinin Front, 4 by the Bryansk Front, and 7 by other fronts (table 5.5). However, only 11 were officially abolished. The 7mdno was the 7th Volunteer Division formed in Moscow. There were two divisions using the number 51 at the same time. The 8mdno/51A(2) was the second division with the number.

By the end of October 1941, 131 divisions had been lost and had disappeared from the order of battle, although only 77 had been officially abolished. By that time the German advance on Moscow was stopped. Losses began to dwindle in November as the Soviets stabilized the front with the arrival of new troops. In November, 16 divisions were lost, although only 11 were abolished (tables 5.6, 5.7). Again, two divisions were using the same number, 106, at the same time. Both were abolished in November.

In December, only 7 divisions were actually lost, although 65 divisions were formally abolished to clear the books (tables 5.8, 5.9). Most of the abolished divisions had disappeared from the order of battle in September and October.

The total for the six months was a staggering 155 divisions of a total of 229 available at the outbreak of the war, nearly equal to the 159 divisions on the eastern front and in the Stavka Reserve at the beginning of the war. The tank corps were annihilated in the same period. The only remaining tank corps was in the east. The Soviets had indeed lost their prewar army.

Table 5.4 Divisions Abolished in September 1941

Front/Army	Division	Month Lost
South 6	44mtn, 58Amtn, 80A, 139A, 141A, 197A	August
South 12	60mtn, 72mtn, 189A, 190A, 192mtn, 216mtr	August
SW 5	62A, 215mtr	September
SW 26	173A	August
	264A, 289A	September
SW 37	28mtn	August
	87A, 295A	September
Reserve 24	102A	August
	151A	September
West 3	27A, 85A, 86A	July
West 10	113A	July
	2A, 8A, 13A, 17A	September
West 13	37A	August
West 20	233A	August
West 22	98A	September
West 28	46A, 140A	August
	56A	September
West 29	253A	September
West	209mtr	August
Center 21	61A, 167A	August
Center 13	172A, 110A	August
Bryansk 37	284A	September
Leningrad 8	67A	August
	Poliarnaia/28A	September
Leningrad 23	198mtr	September
Leningrad 55	237A	September
NW 11	184A	July
	118A	September
NW 27	223A	August
	18A	September

Nations that had suffered less had given up and made peace with the Germans, such as the French. The difference was that space gave the Russians more time to create new armies. However, the French and British had ample time to create additional armies between September 1939 and May 1940 but chose not to do so. Given the resources available to both countries in their colonies and in the British Commonwealth, the response to the invasion of Poland was feeble. Neither wished to repeat the bloodbath of World War I. The French surrendered and the British withdrew behind the English Channel and hoped for a miracle.

Stalin, on the other hand, had steadily enlarged the Red Army since 1939. Even after the disaster in the summer of 1941, which was a far greater calamity than the losses in France in May 1940, he scurried to assemble divisions to slow the

Table 5.5 Rifle Divisions Lost in October 1941

Front	*Army*	*Division*
Northwestern	27th	181latvian
	34th	257A
Western	5th	312A
	16th	152A
	19th	91A, 166A, 189A
	20th	73A
	24th	7mdno/29A, 103mtrA, 106mtrA, 9mdno/139B, 309A
	29th	171A
	43rd	149A, 211A, 303A
	49th	248A
	Reserve	164A
	Stavka 28th	140B
Kalinin	22nd	112A, 170A, 214A
	30th	162A
	31st	244A, 247A
Bryansk	3rd	287A
	13th	134A, 298A
	50th	278A
Southern	9th	8mdno/51A
	12th	274A
	Crimea 51st	321A
	Stavka Reserve	410

Table 5.6 Rifle Divisions Lost in November 1941

Front	*Division*	*Army*
Northwestern	292A	Volkhov 4
Western	129A	West 5
	38A	West 16
	242A	West 30
	260A	West 50
	8mdno/8B	West
Bryansk	279A	Bryansk 50
Southwestern	42A	SW 3
	280A	SW 3
	282A	SW 3
	212mtr/A	SW 26
	135A	SW 40
Other	273A	South 12
	184B	Crimea 51
	421	Crimea Coastal
	407	Stavka Caucasus

Table 5.7   Rifle Divisions Abolished in November

Front/Army	Division
Bryansk 50	6estonianrb/279A
West 5	129A
West 24	106A (1)
West 50	260A
West	8mdno/8B
SW 21	187A, 277A
South 12	273A
Crimea 51	106A (2)
Crimea Coastal	Odessa/421
Caucasus	407

German advance and then began to rebuild the Red Army into the powerful machine that defeated Hitler.

To replace those losses and create an army to defeat the Germans, Stalin planned in June 1941 to mobilize 350 divisions. With the classes of 1919 to 1922 already in service, the Russian war mobilization plan detailed the formation of new divisions using recalled reservists and 1.5 million young soldiers of the class of 1923 who were completing their training. By June 30, 1941, the Russians had mobilized about 5.3 million reserves from 14 classes, 1905 to 1918 (men aged 23 to 36 years), who had previous military training. In addition to the reservists, new inductees were used to create new units. The army had received an astonishing additional 3,544,000 men between July 1 and December 1, 1941.

Professor James Goff estimated that 229 rifle and motorized divisions were available on June 22, 1941, and 483 new divisions were formed during the war, for a total of 712. Col. David Glantz estimated that the total reached 707. Both estimates were based on totals published in Soviet sources. Poirier, in his excellent work on the Soviet order of battle, gave 724 as the total number of formations. The steady stream of new divisions enabled the Soviet Union to

Table 5.8   Rifle Divisions Lost in December 1941

Front	Division	Front/Army
Western	7mtr/A	West 16
	126A	West 16
	106mtr	West 24
	299A	West 50
Other	2mdno/2B	Crimea Coastal
	275A	Caucasus 37
	Voroshilov	East 25

Table 5.9 Rifle Divisions Abolished in December 1941

Front	Army	Division
Leningrad	8th	16A, 28A
	Reserve	235A
Volkhov	4th	292A
Kalinin	22nd	214A
	30th	162A
	31st	244A
West	5th	312A
	16th	7mtr/7A, 38A, 126A, 152A
	19th	89A, 91A, 166A
	20th	73A, 229A
	24th	103mtr/103A, 106mtr, 9mdno/139B, 309A
	29th	171A
	30th	242A
	43rd	149A, 211A, 303A
	49th	248A
	50th	299A
	West Reserve	164A
Reserve	24th	24A
Bryansk	3rd	287A, 134A, 298A
	21st	75A, 167A
	37th	147A, 165A, 175A, 206A
	50th	278A
Southwest	3rd	42A, 280A, 282A,
	5th	124A, 131A, 193A, 295A, 200A, 228A
	21st	55A, 117A, 219mtr/219A, 232A, 266A
	26th	41A, 97A, 116A, 159A, 196A, 301A
	37th	146A
	40th	135A
Crimea	51st	4nkvd/184B
	Coastal	2mdno/2B
Stavka	28th	13mdno/140B

remain in the war. Many details of the mobilization plan can be assumed by an analysis of the division histories. The Red Army doubled from 117 divisions to 232 from 1940 to June 1941. In the second half of 1941, 258 new divisions were formed. The new divisions received the numbers of the destroyed divisions. These numbers compare closely with the totals presented in Soviet published sources: 229 divisions active on June 22 and 237 raised in the next six months. The difference resulted from the definition of *new division* as opposed to refitting a depleted division.

Many divisions raised in the second half of 1941 had a distinctive regimental numbering scheme, suggesting that they were part of a definite plan. There were

80 sets of numbers, each with two to four divisions having related regimental numbers. Each set of numbers followed a pattern related to the military districts. Consecutive artillery regiment numbers showed the relationship between some divisions. Other divisions had random groups of regimental numbers within a limited range. Most sets came from one military district. A few sets had one division from the North Caucasus and the other from the Volga District, or one from the Ural and one from the Siberia District.

The Red Army was expanding rapidly even before the Germans attacked. In June 1941, 47 divisions were added to the order of battle, although they were retained by the military districts (table 5.10). In the next few months, they were transferred to the field armies.

A few rifle brigades were formed in June as well. In the Leningrad District, these included the 1mtnrb/13rb/201B (first formed as the 1st Mountain Rifle Brigade, redesignated as the 13th Rifle Brigade, and finally upgraded as the second formation of the 201st Rifle Division) and the 8Arb/136B/63Gd. The 1st Mountain Brigade was assigned to the 11th Army in the Northwestern Front and the 8th Brigade to the reserve of the Northern Front. In the Volga District, the 53rd Rifle Brigade was formed and in December was sent to the 2nd Shock Army of the Volkhov Front. In the east the 1st (16th Army) Brigade was formed and assigned to the 1st Army in the Far East. These were minor events but a clear indication that the Red Army had little interest in rifle brigades at the beginning of the war.

No new tank brigades were formed in June 1941. Any available tanks were sent to the tank divisions in existence at the beginning of the war that were not fully equipped or had suffered losses.

The existing prewar mobilization plan was shattered by the ferocity of the German invasion that destroyed 155 divisions in six months. No one could have foreseen such a calamity. Rather than a planned expansion of the Red Army in the summer of 1941, Stalin hastily scraped together divisions as quickly as possible with whatever was at hand.

Table 5.10 Divisions Formed in June 1941

Military District	Division
Archangel	58mtn, 111
Central Asia	68, 83mtn, 194mtn, 238
Kharkov	214
Moscow	118, 235
North Caucasus	28mtn, 157, 165, 175
Odessa	47mtn, 106, 116, 156, 196, 206
Orel	89, 120, 145, 149, 217, 219, 220, 222
Transcaucasus	4, 9mtn, 20mtn, 31, 63mtn, 76mtn, 77mtn, 136, 138, 221, 224, 236
Transbaikal	36, 57, 65, 82, 93, 94, 114, "M"

New divisions were created in the military districts, which were administrative organizations charged with inducting and training men, forming new units, and other duties, similar to the German Wehrkreis and the American Corps Area in 1940. In the 18 months before the war, most districts had created a number of divisions equal to those existing before 1940. By June 1941, the military districts of Archangel, Far East, Kharkov, Orel, Odessa, North Caucasus, Siberia, Transcaucasus, Volga, and Ural produced the same number of divisions as they had before. The Baltic District produced six divisions based on the existing units of the three former independent nations. In a similar fashion, the Germans had incorporated units of the Austrian Army into the German Army in 1938.

After June 1941, the districts occupied by the Germans produced very few divisions. Before the war these heavily populated districts had a consistent pattern of forming large numbers of divisions, but they played little if any role in later mobilization plans. For the 109 divisions created in July 1941, the western districts played a minor part. The Western Special District formed 24 divisions before the war and only 3 after it began. Kiev Special District formed 34 before the war began, 4 after. In contrast, Leningrad produced 17 divisions during the second half of 1941, including 10 Leningrad Opolchenye (volunteer) divisions. The Moscow District formed 31 before the war and 67 divisions after—far more than usual. The Moscow District may have formed divisions from recruits and reservists evacuated from the districts overrun by the Germans.

The sparsely populated districts of Central Asia and Transbaikal made a small contribution before the war but sharply increased their activity after the war began. Central Asia formed 4 divisions before the war began and 11 after. The Volga District raised 10 before and 16 after. The Transcaucasus Military District formed 13 before June 1941 and 21 divisions between July and December 1941.

An example of the mobilization process was the formation of 19 rifle divisions and 5 cavalry divisions in the Kharkov and Odessa military districts at the end of July 1941. Despite the urgency, more than a month elapsed before the divisions were formally organized, owing to a lack of part of their artillery, small arms, signal equipment, engineer equipment, and even uniforms, although the military district headquarters obtained some material locally. When the divisions were ready, eight rifle divisions and two cavalry divisions went to the Southwestern Front. Nine rifle and three cavalry divisions went to the Southern Front, and two rifle divisions and two tank brigades to the Stavka Reserve. Between July 22 and December 1, 1941, 227 rifle divisions were created to replace lost formations, including 84 reformed rifle divisions and 143 new rifle divisions. The reformed rifle divisions were in fact new divisions that were given the numbers of divisions that had been destroyed. German intelligence identified only 74, indicating the success of the Soviet system in deceiving the Germans.

The GUF, the Reserve Armies Administration, created in July 1941, supervised the formation of strategic reserves. In July a major effort began to expand the Red Army. The GUF created new divisions and entire armies to replace those destroyed. By July 15, 1941, the Reserve Front had six armies with 31 divisions, and additional armies were forming in the east. The divisional designations in tables 5.11 through 5.16 reflect their lineage; for example, the 1st Leningrad Volunteer Division was renamed the 1st Leningrad Volunteer Guard Division, and finally became the second formation of the 80th Rifle Division. The assigned date refers to the month in which the division was assigned to a command involved in combat. The Front/Army column lists the front or military district and the army number.

A total of 109 divisions were formed in July 1941, primarily by calling up reservists. Most of the divisions were in combat by September 1941. The Leningrad Volunteer Divisions were organized by the local Communist Party leader and performed well. Stalin copied this concept in name by designating some of the new divisions formed in the Moscow District as volunteer divisions. They also performed above average and many later became guard divisions.

The Leningrad divisions were used to defend Leningrad. Most of the Moscow divisions were assigned to the armies on the Reserve Front, the Western Front, and the Bryansk Front, which formed a second line of defense in front of Moscow in September. The 10 Odessa divisions went to the Southern Front in August, and 8 were lost in the early months in Ukraine. The 12 Orel divisions were sent to the Bryansk Front and the Reserve Front in August. Nine were lost in the following months in the defense of Moscow. One was sent to Leningrad. Three of the four Central Asia divisions went to the Stavka 52nd Army to defend Moscow. The four Archangel divisions remained in the north. The five Kharkov divisions went to the Southwestern Front along with seven other divisions formed in the Southwestern area. Seven were lost in the next few months. The three Ural divisions were scattered, and the four from the Far East remained there with the 1st Army.

Only a few new rifle brigades were formed in July, again illustrating a lack of interest in the formation. In Leningrad, four naval rifle brigades were formed, and

Table 5.11   New Volunteer Divisions Formed in Leningrad in July 1941

Division	Date Assigned	Front/Army
1ldno/1ldno Gd/80B	9/41	Leningrad 8
2ldno GdA	9/41	Leningrad 42
2ldno GdB	8/41	North
3ldno GdA/44B	9/41	Leningrad 42
3ldno GdB	9/41	Leningrad 54
4ldno G/4 Res/5 ldno/13B	9/41	Leningrad 42
2ldno/85B	9/41	Leningrad 8
3ldno/67B	9/41	Stavka 7
4ldno/86B	9/41	Leningrad 55
6ldno/189B	9/41	Leningrad 42
7ldno/56B	9/41	Leningrad 42

Table 5.12 Moscow Volunteer Divisions

Division	Date Assigned	Front/Army
1/60	9/41	Reserve 33
2/2B	9/41	Reserve 32
2/129B	7/41	West 16
4/110B/84G	9/41	Reserve 31
4/155B	1/42	Moscow Zone
5/113B	7/41	Moscow Zone
5/158B	1/42	Moscow Zone
6/160 (west)	11/41	West 33
7/29A	9/41	Reserve 32
8/8B	9/41	Reserve 32
9/139B	9/41	Reserve 24
13/140B	9/41	Reserve 32
17/17B	9/41	Reserve 33
18/18B/11G	9/41	Reserve 33
21/173B/77G	9/41	Reserve 33

all were assigned to armies defending Leningrad. The 1st Mountain Brigade (later the 1st Rifle Brigade and then the 113th Rifle Brigade) was also formed in July, but its assignment is unknown. The 1st Marine Brigade (later the 48th Marine Brigade) was formed in July but not listed in the order of battle until August 1942 as the 48th Marine Brigade in the Leningrad Coastal Operating Group. The 3rd Marine Brigade was also formed in July and appeared in the order of battle in September 1941 in the Leningrad Reserve. The 4th Marine Brigade was also formed but never appeared in the order of battle. Again, no new tank brigades were formed in July. Any available tanks were used to replace losses in the tank divisions. The emphasis was on new rifle divisions.

Clearly the new divisions, many of which were assigned to combat formations as early as August and most by September, were short on training, although the recalled reservists did not need much. The divisions were urgently needed to protect the vital areas of Leningrad, Moscow, and Ukraine. The focus of the assignments was on defense. There was no indication of gathering an offensive force in September.

The second wave of new units began with 78 divisions formed in August, an amazing number compared to the 90 divisions formed by the United States in the entire war (table 5.17). There was a startling change in the relative number raised west of the Ural Mountains, an indication that this was a new program that would use new inductees from other districts in addition to reservists and would provide more training time. Few divisions were formed in the districts attacked by the Germans, including Moscow and Leningrad, although many divisions had been formed in those districts the month before. Four volunteer divisions were formed in the Crimea to reinforce the defense there and were later given regular numbers.

Table 5.13 Rifle Divisions Formed in July 1941 in the
Moscow Military District

Division	Date Assigned	Front/Army
211A	8/41	Reserve 43
242A	7/41	West 30
243	7/41	West 29
244A	7/41	Reserve 31
245	7/41	Reserve 34
246	7/41	Reserve 31
247	7/41	Reserve 31
248A	7/41	Reserve 24
249A/16G	7/41	Reserve 31
250	7/41	West 30
251	7/41	West 30
252	7/41	West 29
254	7/41	NW 11
256	7/41	West 22
257	7/41	Moscow 34
259	7/41	Moscow 34
260A	8/41	Bryansk 50
262	7/41	Moscow 34
265	7/41	North
266A	8/41	Bryansk 21
268	8/41	Leningrad 8
269	8/41	Bryansk 31
272	8/41	Karelian 7
279A	8/41	Bryansk 50
280A	8/41	Bryansk 3
282A	8/41	Bryansk 3
285	8/41	Stavka 52
288	8/41	Stavka 52
290	8/41	Bryansk 50
291	8/41	Leningrad 23
298A	8/41	Bryansk
305A	8/41	NW
307	8/41	Bryansk 13
322	11/41	West 10

The major blocks of new divisions were created in the Caucasus, the Ural District, the Volga District, and the Siberian District, presumably with new recruits as there were few reservists in those districts. Most of these divisions trained for four months and were assigned in December to the armies that counterattacked the Germans at the gates of Moscow. The new divisions in the south were committed in September and October to stop the German advances there. Another exceptional difference was that very few of the divisions formed in August were

Table 5.14   New Rifle Divisions Formed in the Odessa Military District

Division	Date Assigned	Front/Army
226A/95G	8/41	South 6
230A	8/41	South 6
253A	8/41	South
255A	8/41	South 6
261	8/41	South 12
270A	8/41	South 12
273A	8/41	South 6
274A	8/41	South 12
275A	8/41	South 12
296A	8/41	South 9

lost in later battles. They remained in service until the end of the war. Of the 15 lost, 5 were lost in the Crimea.

A significant number of divisions were sent to the Volkhov, Kalinin, and Northwestern Fronts north of Moscow and the Bryansk Front south of Moscow, arriving in December. These fronts were not directly in the path of the German attack, but rather were the areas from which the counteroffensive would be launched in December 1941. The divisions formed in the south, where the Germans were advancing rapidly, were sent into battle in September and October. The divisions around Moscow were assigned in November and December after four or five months' training. Stalin deliberately withheld these divisions to prepare for a crushing blow rather than feeding them immediately into battle in September and October.

Table 5.15   New Rifle Divisions Formed in the Orel Military District (12)

Division	Date Assigned	Front/Army
258A/12G	8/41	Bryansk 50
267A	8/41	Stavka 52
271	8/41	Stavka 51
276A	8/41	Stavka 51
277A	8/41	Bryansk 21
278A	8/41	Bryansk 50
283	9/41	Bryansk 13
287A	9/41	Bryansk
294	9/41	Leningrad 54
299A	8/41	Bryansk 50
303A	8/41	Reserve 24
309A	8/41	Reserve 24

Table 5.16 New Rifle Divisions Formed in Other Military Districts

	Division	Date Assigned	Front/Army
Central Asia Military District	310	8/41	NW
	312A	8/41	Stavka 52
	314	8/41	Stavka 52
	316A/8G	8/41	Stavka 52
Archangel Military District	Febolic/27B	8/41	Karelian
	263	11/41	Karelian
	281	7/41	North
	286	9/41	Leningrad 54
Kharkov Military District	284A	8/41	SW 37
	293A/66G	8/41	SW 40
	295A	8/41	SW 40
	297A	8/41	SW 38
	300A/87G	8/41	SW 38
Southwest Area, District Unknown	223A	7/41	South, North Caucasus District?
	264A	7/41	SW 26, North Caucasus District?
	289A	8/41	SW 26
	301A	8/41	SW 26
	304A/67G	7/41	SW
	317	10/41	Transcaucasus 56
	415	11/41	West 49, Far East District?
Ural Military District	273B	5/42	Stalingrad
	311	8/41	Leningrad 48
	311	9/41	Stavka 7
Far East	21	7/41	East 1
	22	7/41	East 1
	26	7/41	East 1
	239	7/41	East 1

Ten rifle brigades were formed in August 1941, mostly in the north (table 5.18). Most of the rifle brigades in August were formed from navy personnel as the navy lacked the ability to create the service units for divisions. Two brigades were formed in the east to replace some of the divisions sent to the eastern front. The remaining four brigades were eventually upgraded to rifle divisions.

Large-scale formation of tank brigades began in August 1941 to replace the shattered tank divisions, an indication that Soviet tank production was increasing rapidly (table 5.19). The brigades were created in the Moscow Military District and in the fronts. In some instances, the remnants of a tank division were used to form a brigade. Soviet industry produced more than 6,500 tanks in the second half of 1941, and these new tanks were used to equip the new brigades.

Table 5.17 Rifle Divisions Formed in August 1941

	Division	Date Assigned	Front/Army
Moscow Military District	292A	8/41	Stavka 52
	324	12/41	West 10
	326	12/41	West 10
	328/31G	12/41	West 10
	330	12/41	West 10
	332	12/41	West 10
Orel Military District	323	12/41	West 10
	325A/90G	12/41	West 10
	327A/64G	12/41	Volkhov 2sh
	329A	12/41	West 5
	331	12/41	West 20
Crimea Volunteer Divisions	1cdno/320A	9/41	Stavka 51
	2cdno/321A	9/41	Stavka 51
	3cdno/172B	9/41	Stavka 51
	4cdno/184	9/41	Stavka 51
Kharkov Military District	393A	10/41	SW 6
	395	10/41	South 18
	383	10/41	South 18
	411	10/41	?
Odessa Military District	421	9/41	Stavka Coastal
Transcaucasus Military District	386A	11/41	Transcaucasus 46
	388A	11/41	North Caucasus Coastal
	390A	11/41	Crimea 51
	392	12/41	Caucasus 46
	394	12/41	Caucasus 46
	396A	11/41	Crimea 51
	398	11/41	Crimea 51
	400	11/41	Crimea 51
	402	10/42	Transcaucasus
	404	12/41	Caucasus 44
	406	1/42	Transcaucasus 46
	408	9/42	Transcaucasus Tuapse
	409	2/42	Transcaucasus 45
	224A	11/41	Crimea 51
Ural Military District	355A	12/41	Kalinin 39
	357	12/41	Kalinin 22
	359	12/41	Kalinin 31
	361A/21G	12/41	Kalinin 39
	363A/22G	12/41	Kalinin 30
	365A	11/41	West 30
	367	12/41	Karelian
	369	12/41	Kalinin 39
	371	10/41	West 30

(*continued*)

Table 5.17   continued

	Division	Date Assigned	Front/Army
	373	12/41	Kalinin 39
	375	12/41	Kalinin 29
	377	12/41	Volkhov 4
	379	12/41	Kalinin 30
	381	12/41	Kalinin 39
Volga Military District	334	12/41	NW 4sh
	336	12/41	West 5
	338A	12/41	West 33
	340	12/41	West 50
	342A/121G	12/41	Bryansk 61
	344	12/41	West 50
	346	12/41	Bryansk 61
	348	12/41	Kalinin 30
	350	12/41	Bryansk 61
	352	12/41	West 20
	354	11/41	West 16
	356	12/41	Bryansk 61
	358	12/41	NW 4sh
	360	12/41	NW 4sh
North Caucasus Military District	337A	12/41	Stavka 57
	339	10/41	South 9
	343A/97G	10/41	Caucasus 56
	353	10/41	Caucasus 56
Siberian Military District	362	2/42	Kalinin 22
	364	3/42	NW 1sh
	366A	12/41	Volkhov 59
	368	3/42	Stavka 7
	370	2/42	NW 34
	372	12/41	Volkhov 59
	374	12/41	Volkhov 59
	376	12/41	Volkhov 59
	378	12/41	Volkhov 59
	380	2/42	Kalinin 22
	382	12/41	Volkhov 59
	384A	2/42	NW 11

Most of the 20 new brigades were formed immediately behind the front line by reorganizing a battered tank division. All but two were assigned before October, indicating they consisted of experienced men. Most were assigned to fronts in the center and the south in purely defensive roles.

The divisions and brigades created in August formed the armies that launched the Moscow offensive in December. They had four months of unit training and

Table 5.18 New Rifle Brigades Formed in August 1941

District	Brigade	Date Assigned	Front/Army
Leningrad	5navalb/71B	8/41	Leningrad
Murmansk	5Arb/289B	8/41	Murmansk
Archangel	12navalb	11/41	Karelian 14
Archangel	32rb/319C	2/42	Leningrad
Black Sea	7navalb (Black Sea)	8/41	?
Black Sea	8Anavalb	8/41	?
Volga	31rb/1B	12/41	NW 3sh
Siberia	41Arb/180B	12/41	West 1sh
East	2eastrb	8/41	East 25
East	6eastrb	8/41	East 1

were well equipped compared to the divisions formed in June and July that were sent into battle as soon as they were formed.

Comparatively few rifle divisions were created in the next three months as the emphasis changed from immediate commitment to battle to building and training those that had been formed in previous months. However, the Central Asia

Table 5.19 New Tank Brigades, August 1941

	Cadre	Brigade	Date Assigned	Front/Army
Moscow Military District	34th Tk Div	1	9/41	SW 21
		2	9/41	South
	1st Tk Div	5	9/41	SW 40
		6	10/41	Caucasus 56
		7	9/41	SW 38
	32nd Tk Div	8B	9/41	NW 11
		9	9/41	Stavka 4
		142	9/41	SW
Reserve Front		143	9/41	West
Bryansk Front		121	8/41	Bryansk
	110th Tk Div	141	9/41	SW 13
	50th Tk Div	150	9/41	SW 21
Western Front	17th Tk Div	126	8/41	West
	18th Tk Div	127	9/41	West 16
	57th Tk Div	128	9/41	West
Southwestern Front	12th Tk Div	129	9/41	SW 21
Southern Front	11th Tk Div	132	8/41	South
Kharkov District	37th Tk Div	3	9/41	SW
		4	10/41	West 16
		12	9/41	SW 6

District emerged as a major source (table 5.20). Most of the 31 divisions were assigned to the south after three months' training.

Twenty other divisions were formed in September 1941 in various locations (table 5.21). Very few data have been found on the last seven divisions formed in September. These divisions were never assigned to a frontline unit. They may have been used on the Turkish border, in Iran, or in the Far East.

An additional three divisions arrived from the Far East in September, two more in October, and another in November 1941 (table 5.22). These divisions had little impact on the battles, in contrast to popular belief. All but one were assigned to the center defending Moscow.

Fifteen more rifle brigades were formed in September 1941, far fewer than implied in earlier literature (table 5.23). Seven were in Leningrad and the northern sector and were sent immediately into combat. The remainder were held back until November or December and took part in the Moscow offensive in December.

Table 5.23 demonstrates that the brigade organization was used sparingly in the north to add formations to the defense of Leningrad and to add more riflemen to the planned Moscow offensive in December, even though there were insufficient service units to form divisions.

The phenomenal development in September 1941 was the formation of 34 new tank brigades (table 5.24). New tanks were rolling out of the factories and being formed into brigades that were sent to the field army in the following month in preparation for the counterattack. Twelve brigades were formed from remnants of tank divisions.

Practically all of the new tank brigades were hastily assembled and sent back to the front. Only the four brigades formed near Stalingrad with the new tanks produced there were held back for an appreciable time.

In October 1941, only 18 new rifle divisions were created because of the lack of support troops, especially artillery (table 5.25). Five new rifle divisions were

Table 5.20 Divisions Formed in the Central Asia District, September 1941

Division	Date Assigned	Front/Army
333	12/41	Stavka 57
335A	12/41	Stavka 57
341A	1/42	South 57
345A	12/41	Caucasus Coastal
347	10/41	Caucasus 56
349	1/42	South 57
351A	12/41	Stavka 57
385	12/41	Moscow District 24
387	12/41	Bryansk 61
391	12/41	Moscow District

Table 5.21   Other Divisions Formed in September 1941 (20)

Division	District	Date Assigned	Front/Army
Mechno	?	9/41	SW 40
Voroshilov	Far East	9/41	East 25
37B	?	9/41	Karelian
28A	?	9/41	Leningrad 8
61B	Transcaucasus	9/41	Transcaucasus
106A	Odessa	11/41	South 56
186B/205B	Archangel	9/41	Karelian 14
204A/78G	Far East	7/42	Stalingrad 64
295B	?	9/41	SW 21
306A	Moscow	None	
410	Moscow	None	
416A	Volga	None	
397A	?	None	
389	?	None	
399A	?	None	
401	?	None	

assembled in the south and immediately assigned to the front. Five more divisions were formed, two of which were abolished early in 1942.

Eight other rifle divisions were formed in October: three in the Caucasus, one in Central Asia, and four in unknown districts (table 5.26). Six were immediately sent into combat, one was held in Central Asia until March 1943, and the last never saw action.

By October 1, 1941, the Red Army had received substantial reinforcements. The Red Army then included 213 rifle divisions, 30 cavalry divisions, 5 tank divisions, and 7 airborne brigades. The rifle divisions averaged only 7,500 men, and the ground forces opposing the Germans had 3,245,000 men, 2,715 tanks, and 20,580 guns and mortars. However, many units were held back to receive more unit training.

Table 5.22   Far East Transfers, 1941

Division	Date of Arrival	Front/Army
21	9/41	Stavka 7
26	9/41	NW 11
32A	9/41	Stavka 4
78A	10/41	West
413	10/41	Bryansk 50
239	11/41	West 50

Table 5.23 New Rifle Brigades Formed in September 1941

District	Brigade	Date Assigned	Front
North	11/120Crd	9/41	North
Karelia	61/83rd	12/41	Karelian
Leningrad	6Naval/183Brd	9/41	Leningrad
Leningrad	7Naval/72Brd	9/41	Leningrad
Leningrad	9A	9/41	Leningrad
Leningrad	10	9/41	Leningrad
Leningrad	11	9/41	Leningrad
North Caucasus	39A	12/41	Kalinin 4sh
Volga	51A/119Brd	12/41	NW 3sh
Volga	52A/207Brd	12/41	Moscow District
Volga	59	12/41	Volkhov 2sh
Siberia	43A/258Brd	11/41	West 5
Siberia	44/62Crd	11/41	West 1sh
Ural	49/208Brd	12/41	West 16
Ural	61/83rd	12/41	Karelian

The renewed German attack on Moscow in September cost the Russian forces heavy casualties. A few divisions came from the Far East, but most of the new divisions came from the Siberia, Ural, and Central Asia districts. During the war, the Far East sent many replacements to Europe, but there was no large movement of entire divisions. Most new divisions formed in the Far East remained there.

A flood of rifle brigades was formed in October 1941 as the Russians strove to ready as many units as possible for the December attack. The 55 brigades formed represent about 220,000 men, but they had little artillery or automatic weapons (table 5.27).

Much of the second wave of rifle divisions and rifle and tank brigades was completed in September, and the new divisions formed in October and November were odds and ends rather than part of a massive mobilization effort. The numerous rifle brigades formed in October were mostly naval personnel without service units and only one battalion of artillery. The 55 brigades were formed for the most part in the Volga, Ural, Siberia, and North Caucasus districts from naval men that were brought in from Leningrad, the White Sea ports, and the Black Sea ports. Most of these brigades were upgraded to divisions later in the war. They were a temporary measure to make use of sailors who were cut off from their ships and home ports by the German advance. After creating the many divisions in August and September, the Russians were short of artillery and support units to additional divisions and resorted to the brigade organization. These brigades were trained for three months before taking part in the Moscow offensive. The brigades relied on the field army headquarters to provide them with artillery and logistical support when they entered combat.

Table 5.24 New Tank Brigades Formed in September 1941

	Brigade	*Date Assigned*	*Front/Army*
Moscow District	48td/17	10/41	West 43
	18	10/41	West 5
	19	10/41	West 5
	20	10/41	West 5
	22	10/41	West 5
	23	10/41	West
	24	10/41	West 43
	25	10/41	West 5
	26	10/41	West
	27	10/41	West 16
	147	10/41	West 16
	102td/144A	9/41	Moscow
	145	9/41	Moscow
	105td/146A	9/41	Moscow
	109td/148	9/41	Moscow
	21	10/41	Kalinin 30
	34td/16	9/41	Leningrad 54
North Caucasus District	45	1/42	Stalingrad
	47B	4/42	Bryansk
	48	4/42	SW 6
	49	4/42	Bryansk
Stavka	11	10/41	Bryansk 50
	16td/46	9/41	Stavka 7
Bryansk Front	42td/42	9/41	Bryansk
	108td/108	12/41	West 10
Leningrad Front	122	9/41	Leningrad 54
Northwestern Front	125A	10/41	NW
Southwestern Front	43td/10	9/41	SW 38
	14	9/41	SW 38
	10td/133	9/41	SW
	13	9/41	SW 6
Southern Front	15	9/41	South
	8td/130A	9/41	South
	10td/131	9/41	South

In November, 11 rifle divisions were formed and immediately assigned (table 5.28). Six of the divisions were second formations of divisions lost in the previous months. Apparently they were not part of the mobilization plan but merely took advantage of available remnants of divisions and odd regiments. All of the divisions were immediately assigned rather than being held back for more training, as was the case with divisions formed in August and September. Two of the divisions were formed in the Far East and remained there.

Table 5.25 New Rifle Divisions Formed in October 1941

	Division	Date Assigned	Front	Notes
Transcaucasus	20Bmtn	10/41	Transcaucasus 46	
	213	10/41	Central Asia	
	151B	10/41	Caucasus 56	
	253B	10/41	South 37	
	216A	10/41	SW 38	
East	205A	10/41	East	In 7/42 to Stalingrad 4t
	208A	10/41	East 25	In 7/42 to Stalingrad 64
	Spassk	10/41	East 1	Abolished 1/42
	Poltava	10/41	East 25	Abolished 3/42
	Grodek/187	10/41	East 1	

Also in November, 18 rifle brigades were formed, most of which were sent into combat in December (table 5.29). The rifle brigades had only a single artillery battalion and few service troops. Instead they received their artillery support and logistical support from the army to which they were assigned. The rifle brigades tended to be grouped within selected armies, which would then be given additional service troops to support the brigades. Most of the brigades were from the Ural, Siberian, and Volga districts. Most were assigned to the Western, Northwestern, and Volkhov fronts and took part in the battles around Moscow. Fourteen were later upgraded to divisions in 1942 and 1943, clearly indicating they were merely a temporary expedient to add units to the central fronts for the offensive. Two brigades (29A and 38A) later became guard rifle brigades.

Of the few tank brigades formed in November 1941, six were created in the Far East (table 5.30). The source of the tanks for the new brigades in the east is unclear. Perhaps they were redistributed from existing units. New tank production was used in Europe to fill the tank brigades formed in the previous months and to replace losses. The 143B brigade was formed from remaining elements of

Table 5.26 Other Rifle Divisions Formed in October 1941

Division	District	Date Assigned	Front/Army
20mtn/20	Caucasus	11/41	Transcaucasus 46
107A	?	10/41	Kalinin 30
151B	Caucasus	10/41	Caucasus 56
298B	?	10/41	Karelian
213	Central Asia	3/43	Voronezh 64
216A	?	10/41	SW 38
253B	?	10/41	South 37
407	Caucasus	None	

Table 5.27 Rifle Brigades Formed in October 1941

	Brigade	Date Assigned	Front/ Army	Date Abolished
Orel District	18A/338B	12/41	West 5	
	19/227B	12/41	West 49	
	20/159C	12/41	NW 3sh	
	21/47	12/41	NW 4sh	
Moscow District	26	12/41	West 41	5/43
	27A/316B	12/41	NW 3sh	11/42
	28/174C	11/41	West 20	
	30A/274B	12/41	West 49	
	74A/292B	6/42	NW 11	
	130naval/ 6Brb/174B/46G	4/42	South	
Kharkov District	10A	10/41	None	10/41
	23/325B	12/41	Volkhov 2sh	
	25A	12/41	Volkhov 2sh	7/42
Far East	2east (2nd Army)	10/41	East 2	
	5B	10/41	East 25	
Volga District	54/325B	12/41	NW 3sh	
	55A/260B	11/41	West 1sh	
	57/316C	12/41	Volkhov 2sh	
	58	12/41	Volkhov 2sh	2/44
	60/257C	12/41	West 5	
	66marine/ 11Gdmarineb	12/41	Karelian	
	67marine/45B	1/42	Karelian Kemp Group	
	84/84marine/ 227B	11/41	West 1sh	
	85/85marine/83	1/42	Karelian Mas Group	
Ural District	46/319C	12/41	NW 34	
	47/70B	11/41	West 1sh	
	48/215B	12/41	NW 3sh	
	50A/3Gdrb	11/41	West 1sh	
	63marine	?	Archangel	6/42
	64/64marine/ 82	11/41	West 20	
	65/65marine/ 176B	12/41	Karelian	
	130/154B	10/41	South 12	

(*continued*)

Table 5.27   continued

	Brigade	Date Assigned	Front/ Army	Date Abolished
Siberian	69marine/69mtnb	10/42	Stavka 7	
District	70marine/70mtnb	12/41	Stavka	
	71Amarine/2Gdrb	12/41	West 1sh	
	72/72marine/72mtnb	12/41	Karelian 14	
	73/73marineb	1/42	Stavka 7	8/43
North Caucasus	11 (South)/107B	11/41	South 56	
District	12A	11/41	Crimea 51	8/42
	13 (South)/161B	11/41	South 56	
	14/321C	12/41	Moscow	
	37/204B	11/41	West 16	
	68marine/29C	3/42	SW	
	74A/74marineb/292B	12/41	Moscow	
	75A/75marineb/ 3Gdrb	12/41	Moscow	
	76marine/23B	1/42	SW	
	77/77marineb/341B	1/42	Karelian 14	
	78A/78marineb/ 318mtn	11/41	South 56	
	79A/79marineb	12/41	Caucasus Coastal	7/42
	80/80marineb/176B	12/41	Stavka	
	81/81marineb/117Gd	2/42	SW	
	82/154B	12/41	Leningrad 26	
	83/83Amarineb	12/41	Caucasus 51	
Unknown	27 (Iran)	10/41	Iran Transcaucasus 45	
District	130marine/6Brb/ 174B	10/41	South 12	10/42

the 142nd and 143rd Tank Brigades, an indication that there was a shortage of tanks to fill out all the other brigades that had been formed.

The first wave of divisions had delayed the German offensive in September. The second wave was completed by November 1941. In October 1941, many of the divisions of the second wave were formed into nine reserve armies. One of the reserve armies, the 10th, was formed with experienced regular army cadres that made up 15 percent of the army. Most of the men were reserves with prior military experience. The army was 90 percent Russian, 4 percent Ukrainians, and various other nationalities, including 3,245 Mordvinians in the 326th Division. Some 5 percent were Communists and 3 percent were Komsomols (Young Communists). In November, the 10th Army commander requested additional

Table 5.28 Rifle Divisions Formed in November 1941

Division	District	Front	Notes
2cav/109		Crimea Coastal	
223B	Transcaucasus	Transcaucasus	Formed from a rifle regiment
234	Moscow	Moscow Zone	
62B	Moscow	SW 40	Abolished 11/42
87B	Moscow	SW 40	Formed from paratroop units
46B	North	Volkhov 52	
241	North	NW 27	Formed from the 28th Tank Division
257B/91G	North	NW	
287B	Southwest	Bryansk	
209	East	East 36	
210	East	East 36	

Communists to stiffen the army. More than 700 arrived, mostly wounded men with combat experience discharged from hospitals.

One-third of the officers were regular army, the others reserves. The division commanders had training and experience. The staff officers and regimental commanders were regulars, many of whom had been promoted recently. Only a few of the officers were graduates of a military academy, but most had attended

Table 5.29 Rifle Brigades Formed in November 1941

District	Brigade	Date Assigned	Front/Army	Date Abolished
Moscow	29A/1Gdrb	11/41	West 1sh	
Orel	17A/264Brd	12/41	West 20	
Orel	34B/301Crd	8/42	?	
Kharkov	22	1/42	Volkhov 2sh	3/44
Kharkov	24	12/41	Volkhov 2sh	3/44
North Caucasus	15/51Brd	12/41	Moscow Zone	
North Caucasus	16/30Brd	11/41	South 56	
Ural	N86/63Brd	2/42	NW 34	
Ural	62/257Crd	12/41	West 1sh	
Central Asia	34A/233Brd	12/41	West 49	
Central Asia	35/208Brd	11/41	West 20	
Central Asia	36	12/41	West 16	5/44
Central Asia	38A/4Gdrb	12/41	Moscow Zone	
Central Asia	40/207Crd	12/41	West 16	
Siberia	42/226Brd	12/41	NW 3sh	
Siberia	45/63Brd	12/41	NW 3sh	
Volga	56A/133Brd	11/41	West 1sh	
Volga	58	12/41	Volkhov 2sh	

Table 5.30 New Tank Brigades Formed in November 1941

District	Brigade	Date Assigned	Front/Army
West	146B/29Gtb	11/41	West 16
Moscow	143B/66Gtb	3/42	Kalinin 30
Kharkov	35	12/41	West 30
East	72	11/41	East 25
East	73	11/41	East 2
East	74	11/41	East 2
East	75	11/41	East 1
East	76	11/41	East 25
East	77	11/41	East 1

advanced training schools. The rifle and artillery battalions were commanded by reserve officers, few of whom had combat experience.

The nine rifle divisions of the 10th Army came from the Moscow and Orel military districts. Table 5.31 shows the military districts and formation dates.

The 57th Cavalry Division came from Central Asia and the 75th Cavalry Division came from Siberia. The divisions were comparatively well armed for training units. There were more than 65,000 rifles for 100,000 men, 1,209 machine pistols, and 2,000 heavy and 41 light machine guns. The 10th Army divisions each had about 100 machine pistols and 200 machine guns. The army had 249 regimental and divisional artillery pieces, about half the authorized number but adequate for training. The army had few mortars, antiaircraft guns, or antitank guns, items that were scarce in Russia at the time, but sufficient in number for training. The most serious lack was signal equipment. The army had only one signal company, an impediment to training, as messages had to be delivered by couriers on horseback.

The divisions had trained before assignment to the 10th Army. One of the better divisions, the 328th, had six weeks' prior training. However, only 60

Table 5.31 District and Formation Date of 10th Army Rifle Divisions

Division	Military District	Formation Date
322nd	Moscow	7/41
323rd	Moscow	8/41
324th	Moscow	10/41
325th	Orel	10/41
326th	Moscow	8/41
328th	Moscow	9/41
329th	Orel	9/41
330th	Moscow	8/41
332nd	Moscow	7/41

percent of the men had completed their rifle marksmanship training, and only 25 percent had learned to throw grenades. After three weeks in the 10th Army, the 328th Division was still providing individual training to men, NCOs, and junior officers. Artillery and heavy weapons crews lacked experience.

Other divisions in the 10th Army, the 324th and 325th divisions, had more problems with their level of individual training. Regardless of shortcomings, in November the army practiced unit maneuvers and antitank defense techniques as well as participating in long marches to toughen up the troops. On November 24, 1941, some of the divisions left for the front. One division that went to the front had four months' training, but two divisions had less than two months. Three divisions, the 322nd, the 323rd, and 330th, were given priority training in preparation for combat. The 322nd went to the 50th Army at Kaluga. The 329th went to the 26th Army at Volkhov. The other divisions remained with the 10th Army, except the 330th, which later served with the 49th Army. In late November, the 10th Army received tanks, motor vehicles, and artillery and boarded trains for the front. On November 28, 1941, German air reconnaissance spotted trains at Ryazan that were carrying units of the 10th Army.

In addition to creating entirely new armies, the Soviets rebuilt armies weakened in combat. The 50th Army was rebuilt at Tula in mid-October. Three extremely depleted rifle divisions (293rd, 413th, and 239th) arrived from the front, each with from 500 to 1,000 men. The men were exhausted, their uniforms were in tatters, and they had very little equipment. Within two months, the three divisions of the 50th Army had been refitted and reinforced to authorized strength. In December, more divisions were added to the 50th Army: four rifle divisions, three cavalry divisions, a depleted tank division, and independent tank regiments. The rapid reconstruction of the 50th Army was probably typical of many armies in the fall of 1941.

Stalin methodically built up a reserve for the coming counterattack; 4 divisions were in reserve in October, 22 in November, and 44 in December. Despite the severe dislocation and the devastating losses inflicted by the Germans in the first six months, the Soviets created a second new Red Army. In November, the Red Army stood at 3.4 million men and 1,954 tanks at the front.

The winter offensive was conducted primarily with infantry, which produced heavy losses. The Germans were driven back from Moscow and held in the north and the south. The Russian attack was not a blitzkrieg surrounding German units and capturing thousands, but rather a frontal assault that drove the Germans back on a broad front.

One reason for the brutal tactics was that weapons were in short supply in 1941. Even before the Germans attacked in June 1941, Russian arms production, though substantial, had not been adequate to equip all of the new units formed in 1940 and 1941. The needs of the new divisions mobilized in the fall of 1941 placed an incredible strain on the existing stocks of weapons.

In June 1941, the Red Army had less than 30 percent of the automatic weapons called for in the tables of organization. Western Front troops had only 60 percent of the authorized number of rifles. The 34th Cavalry Division had no weapons at all in July 1941, and later did not have enough rifles to equip all of the men.

In the south in June 1941, the rifle divisions of the 5th, 6th, 26th, and 12th armies had enough weapons for the available men. The 17 divisions in those four armies had from 8,400 to 10,200 men with one exception; the 173rd Rifle Division had only 7,177 men. Only two of the divisions had more than 10,000 men. The table of organization called for 14,483 men, so all of the divisions were under strength. The divisions had from 7,300 to 11,000 rifles but machine pistols were short, only 300 to 400 in most divisions compared to the authorized 1,200. Machine guns were in good supply, with 450 to 700 per division compared to the authorized 558. The most serious issue was the many obsolete types of small arms dating back to World War I still being used by the troops. An example was the machine gun inventory that included the Degtyarev, the Maxim-Tokarev, the Lewis, the 1910 Maxim, and the Colt. The last three dated to World War I.

The defeats of the summer of 1941 led to reductions of the table of organization of the rifle divisions, especially in automatic weapons. The number of machine pistols in the rifle division was reduced from 1,200 to 171, machine guns from 558 to 270. The number of men authorized was reduced to 10,859. The rifle company had only six machine pistols and six light machine guns. The howitzer regiment was removed from the rifle division to provide army artillery.

The extreme losses suffered in the first months of the war and the evacuation of the arms industry to the east placed a severe strain on weapons and munitions production, which declined 50 percent in 1941. Tank production was less than 20 percent of prewar figures. The most critical short-term loss from the German advances and relocation of factories was ammunition production. By November 1941, Russia had lost more than 300 munitions plants, which had produced 8.5 million artillery shell cases, 3 million mines, and 2 million bombs per month. Steel production dropped from 11.4 million tons in the first half of 1941 to 3.9 million tons in the second half. Chemical plants producing explosives were overrun by the Germans. By August 1941, artillery ammunition production began to decline from 5 million rounds in August 1941 to 3 million rounds in December. The total production from July to December was only 26 million rounds, while more than 50 million were expended as prewar stocks were exhausted.

Much of the equipment lost was obsolete or obsolescent, so the remaining stock in December 1941 was of better quality, for example, T-34 and KV tanks instead of BT light tanks. Russia entered the war with a large stock of obsolescent tanks. One published breakdown in types listed 500 heavy tanks (KVs), 900 medium tanks (T-34s), and 21,200 light tanks, which included 11,000 BTs and 6,000 T-26s. Another Soviet source gave the total of modern heavy and medium tanks as 1,861, including T-34s and KVs, both of which were better than any German tank. The 11,000 BTs and T-26s were better than the German Mark II, but the remaining 5,000 were of little value. The Germans destroyed or captured more than 20,000 Russian tanks in 1941.

Tank production in the second half of 1941 was only 6,542 tanks, but many had been produced in the early months. Production dropped sharply as the Germans advanced. Another source listed tank production from June 22 to December 31, 1941, as only 5,600, half of which were light tanks. The supply conference held in September 1941 had established a requirement of 1,100 tanks per month. Of that total, the Russians expected to receive 500 per month from the British and Americans, and expected to produce only 600 per month themselves.

Soviet heavy and medium tank production after early 1941 concentrated on the T-34 and the KV to the exclusion of other types. New production of light tanks concentrated on the T-60 and the T-70. Production of the T-60 light tank began in July 1941. The disruption by the German advance reduced the monthly output of T-34s from Stalingrad and T-60s from Gorki and Kirov from 2,000 in June 1941 to 1,400 in September.

By the winter of 1941–42, the logistical support of the army had faltered. Ammunition was severely rationed. The new armies forming were not completely equipped. Strategic reserves of metal were nearly exhausted, and the supply of raw material to the arms industry was unstable. Desperate tank producers were breaking into warehouses and rail cars to steal material. Movement of freight was slowing and total production was dropping. In December 1941 production began to turn around but had not reached the point where all losses could be replaced.

Tank production was a high priority for the coming year. Automobile plants were converted to light tank and self-propelled artillery production during the war, but they had already started some tank production before the war. The two light tanks manufactured in 1941 and 1942 were the T-60 and T-70. The T-60 weighed 6.4 tons, had a crew of two, carried a 20 mm gun and 15 to 35 mm of armor, and had a speed of 45 km per hour. The T-70 was an improved T-60 with a 45 mm gun and armor of 15 to 45 mm and weighing 9.8 tons. The Soviets stopped production of light tanks in 1943 and turned the manufacturing facilities to the production of SU-76s.

Tractor plants made some medium and heavy tanks before the war and were converted to full-time tank production once the war began. The Soviet replicas of American factories were often larger than their models. The Chelyabinsk plant had three times the capacity of its model, the Caterpillar plant at Peoria, Illinois. The Stalingrad and Kharkov tractor plants had twice the capacity of their model, the Milwaukee plant of the International Harvester Corporation.

In 1941, most Soviet tanks were produced in a few plants located in European Russia, Ukraine, and the Urals. In the face of the advancing Germans, the Russians moved the machinery from tank factories in Kharkov and other threatened locations to the east to expand existing factories. Thus, factories in the east, built from 1930 to 1932, produced the tanks that defeated the Germans in later years before lend-lease goods flowed in any great quantity.

The Russians used the T-34 medium tank with improvements throughout the war. It weighed 30.9 tons, carried a 76 mm gun, had a crew of four, speed of 55 km per hour, and armor from 45 to 52 mm. The M1939 76 mm gun was a high-velocity piece, with a 30.5-caliber barrel, compared to the short 24-caliber 75 mm gun on the German Panzer IV in 1941. The early T-34 with its two-man turret required the tank commander to be the gunner. The turret provided little vision for the commander. The tank was exceedingly uncomfortable for the crew, with the gun loader seat attached to the turret, as the bottom of the compartment was filled with ammunition. In a drawn-out engagement, the loader would have to scramble around on top of the piles of shells. There were problems also with the transmission, and the tracks had a brief life expectancy.

The heavy tank in July 1941 was the KV-1 weighing 47.5 tons, with a crew of five, an M1940 41.5-caliber 76 mm gun, 75 to 100 mm of armor, and a speed of 35 km per hour. The KV-2 had a 152 mm howitzer for destroying bunkers. The Russians made only a few of the KV-2s because the tank was difficult to manufacture and there was a limited need for the heavy projectile.

Soviet artillery varied widely in quality and quantity. In 1941, three artillery programs developed the standard weapons of the Red Army, but these weapons were not available in June. The enormous losses of artillery in the first six months of the war forced the Russians to search their depots for every serviceable weapon. Among the many older guns used were the following. French guns included the 75 mm M1897, the 120 mm M1878, the 155 mm M1877, and the 280 mm Schneider mortar. British types included guns of 4.5 inches, 6 inches, 8 inches, and 9.2 inches, and the 12-inch howitzer. Pre–World War I Russian types were the 76 mm M1913 short gun, 107 mm M1910 gun, and the 105 mm M1915 Obukhov howitzer. Other types included the Austrian 47 mm Bohler antitank gun and the Lithuanian 105 mm M1935 Skoda gun.

Soviet production of small arms, tanks, and artillery suffered greatly from the advance of the German Army in 1941. Though many factories were evacuated, months passed before they were in full production. The result was that the new divisions formed in the fall of 1941 were short of small arms and artillery. Little effort was made to create new tank brigades until late in the year because all available tanks were needed to replace losses in the tanks units that survived the onslaught in the summer.

In summary, the last half of 1941 was a disaster for the Soviet Union. One-third of the population lived in occupied areas in December. The Red Army had been emasculated once in the summer and replaced with the first wave of new divisions. The Red Army lost 155 divisions from July to December but created 157 new divisions in June and July. Those division slowed the Germans, but many were destroyed in September. The second wave of 148 new divisions and 88 brigades was formed beginning in August, was able to stop the Germans, and counterattacked in December, inflicting the first major defeat experienced by the German Army in World War II.

The Russians accomplished this feat with their own resources. British and American lend-lease did not have a significant impact until 1942. The Japanese attack on Pearl Harbor did not reduce the Soviet fear of attack by Japan in

Manchuria. The Russians sent only seven divisions from the east in the first year of the war and continued to increase the size of the Far Eastern fronts.

Few nations could have survived such an onslaught. In World War I, Russia had succumbed under much less pressure. Somehow Stalin had convinced the many Soviet nationalities to fight for their country, which the czar had failed to do in 1917.

Chapter 6

From Disaster to Victory: Stalingrad, 1942

THE GERMANS managed to salvage their position in January 1942 and gathered a huge force to launch the summer 1942 campaign. To fill the ranks, the Germans called on the Romanians, Hungarians, and Italians to provide entire armies to guard the flanks of their spearheads as they crushed the Soviet forces, first at Izyum and then in the running battles in Ukraine and the Caucasus. Once again the Soviets were faced with chaos and responded with two powerful counteroffensives, one in front of Moscow, which did not succeed, and a second at Stalingrad, which inflicted the greatest defeat on the Germans to that point in World War II.

Despite the heavy losses inflicted by the Germans in the second half of 1941, the Soviets were able to mobilize divisions to replace those lost in two waves or mobilization groups by the end of November. The first wave stopped the Germans in front of Moscow and the second wave drove them back in December. A third wave was created beginning in December 1941. For the remainder of the war, only a few new divisions were formed. Conversion of airborne troops to ground warfare added about 30 divisions by the end of the war. Instead of being worn down by the Germans, the Red Army grew stronger as the war progressed. Despite the incursion of the Germans, which seriously disrupted the prewar mobilization plan, the Russians were able to form 260 divisions in 1941 and 158 in 1942.

The first five months of 1942 were comparatively quiet, and the Russians lost few divisions (table 6.1). In March the Stavka reviewed the strength of the Red Army, its equipment, and its supply situation. Because the army lacked trained and experienced reserves, a decision was made to remain on the defensive in the summer, prepare defenses, and concentrate on the Moscow area. In May, Marshal

Table 6.1　Divisions Lost January–May 1942

Month	Front/Army	Division
January	Kalinin 30	107A
March	Kalinin 30	365A
May	West 33	338A
May	SW 57	317A
May	Crimea 44	276A
May	Crimea 44	1cdno/320A
May	Crimea 44	63mtn/63
May	Crimea 51	398A
May	Central Asia District	405

S. K. Timoshenko, in command of the southern armies, presented a new plan for a major offensive in the south to retake Kiev, but the Stavka objected. Timoshenko then presented a plan to envelop Kharkov with two drives, one from Izyum and the other farther north at Volchansk. Stalin approved the latter plan. Due to the lack of experienced commanders and trained divisions, disaster followed at Izyum.

As a result of the purge of the Red Army leadership before the war, in April 1942 there was a shortage of experienced commanders for the new divisions and brigades. The rifle corps organization was eliminated and the size of the army reduced to about seven divisions to compensate for the lack of higher-grade officers. This weakness would plague the Red Army in the spring and summer battles in the south.

Losses escalated in June from the disastrous attempt to preempt the German attack in the south in the spring of 1942. Although the Soviets penetrated the German lines, the salient was cut off at Izyum and many divisions were destroyed in June. The Germans also destroyed the divisions in the Crimea when Manstein led the 11th Army in a well-executed campaign in June, clearing the peninsula. After destroying the Izyum pocket, the Germans swept through Ukraine, destroying many Soviet divisions in its path.

In the summer of 1942, the Red Army was in serious difficulty. The Germans were driving eastward through Ukraine, and the additional forces placed in their way by Stalin were unable to stop them. Fresh satellite armies from Romania, Hungary, and Italy followed in the wake of the advancing Germans, shoring up the northern flank of the offensive. The only bright spot was the tenacious defense on the north shoulder of the German attack.

As the Germans pressed forward, they destroyed divisions almost on the scale of the summer of 1941. Popular opinion in the West was that the Germans controlled the summers, reinforcing the idea that it was the cold weather rather than fresh Soviet divisions that prevented Hitler from taking Moscow in December 1941.

Table 6.2 Divisions Lost in June 1942

Front/Army	*Division*
Crimea 44	396A
Crimea 47	224A
Crimea 51	390A, 400, 404
Crimea Coastal	3cdno/172B
SW 57	150A
SW 57	351A
SW Reserve	463/103B
Bryansk 6	41B, 47mtn, 466/248B, 253B, 467/266B, 270A, 337A, 393A, 411

In June, the Russians lost 18 divisions as the Germans drove through Ukraine (table 6.2). In July, the number of divisions lost remained high as losses continued in the south and additional defeats were suffered by the Volkhov Front in the north (table 6.3).

Some 25 divisions were lost in the defeats at Izyum, in the Crimea, and in Ukraine in May and June and another 17 in July. Despite the loss of 44 divisions in the first seven months, the Soviets were able to launch a massive counterattack in November that trapped the German 6th Army in Stalingrad. This performance surpassed the remarkable performance in the December 1941 offensive. An entire German army was surrounded and captured at Stalingrad and three satellite armies were severely mauled.

The Soviet response to the crushing blows in 1941 seems unbelievable. Little wonder the Germans took a number of risks in 1942 and were surprised at the magnitude of the Soviet counteroffensive.

The truly remarkable story behind the Soviet victory is the massive mobilization of the third wave of new units. Two groups were raised beginning in December 1941. The first group was used in the spring attack in the south at Izyum and more were thrown into the effort to protect Ukraine in the summer of 1942. However, the most significant use was the transfer of the second group,

Table 6.3 Divisions Lost in July 1942

Front/Army	*Division*
Kalinin 22	355A
Volkhov 2sh	46B, 92A, 267A
Volkhov 52	305A
Bryansk 48	451/228B
Stalingrad 21	227A, 297A, 447/301B
SW 38	434/162B, 199A
Crimea Coastal	25A, 95A, 109A, 345A, 386A, 388A

consisting of entire armies, to the Stalingrad Front and using them to surround and destroy the German 6th Army.

The rapid expansion beginning in December 1941 was made possible by the influx of 1 million new recruits and the call-up of additional reservists. By January 1942, the young men drafted in the summer of 1941 had completed their basic training and were organized into 74 new divisions and 69 new rifle brigades, with older reservists serving as cadres. The new rifle divisions had an authorized strength of 10,000 and the brigades about 5,000, making a total of roughly a million men.

Most of the divisions were formed in central Asia and the Caucasus, although the men came from other districts as well. The 400 number divisions do not appear in the published Soviet order of battle but were listed under the numbers of destroyed divisions, which they later received (table 6.4). Professor James Goff has identified these divisions and the numbers they were subsequently given. In April 1942, the renumbered divisions appear with the notation that they were forming in various districts under their new numbers, which had been recycled from divisions destroyed in 1941. However, by the time the divisions appeared in the order of battle, they had been in existence for as long as three months. The reason for this anomaly was apparently to deceive the Germans, although they eventually learned of the existence of some, but not all, of the 400 divisions from prisoner interrogations.

In addition to the group of divisions shown in table 6.4, the Soviets formed 20 more divisions in December 1941 (table 6.5). Ten more divisions were formed in January 1942 (table 6.6). Five were formed in the Moscow District and remained there during the summer. Three divisions were added to the central fronts from the Archangel and Ural districts. One division came from the far east and was sent to the Southwestern Front, and the last division was formed in the Crimea.

Another major effort in December 1941 was the formation of 70 rifle brigades (table 6.7). With a simple structure of four rifle battalions, an artillery battalion, and a limited number of service troops, the brigades could be quickly assembled with the newly trained recruits, using reservists as cadres. A large percentage of these brigades were later upgraded to divisions when more artillery and service units became available. Others were used as temporary expedients to hold the newly trained men. The 22 brigades from the Volga and Central Asia districts were never given combat assignments. These brigades disappeared from the order of battle after December 1941 as the new recruits were sent to the front as individual replacements. Only a few brigades were sent into combat assignments immediately. The majority had four or more months of training before being assigned to a combat unit.

In sharp contrast to the number of rifle divisions and brigades formed in December and the large number of tank brigades formed in November, only eight tank brigades were formed in December 1941 (table 6.8). Most available tanks had been absorbed by the November brigades and there may have been few left over for new brigades in December.

Table 6.4 Divisions Formed in December 1941 and January 1942, the 400 Series

Division	Date Formed	District	Date Renumbered	Date Assigned	Front/Army
422A/397B	12/41	Volga	1/42	3/42	Kalinin 3sh
423/195B	10/41	South Ural	3/42	7/42	Voronezh 60
424/196B	12/41	South Ural	1/42	7/42	Stalingrad 62
425/200B	12/41	South Ural	2/42	4/42	Stavka, 5/42, NW 11
426/147B	12/41	Moscow	4/42	5/42	Stavka 7R
427/149B	1/42	Moscow	1/42	2/42	West 61
428/206B	12/41	South Ural	1/42	7/42	Voronezh 40
429/211B	12/41	South Ural	1/42	5/42	Bryansk 48
430/152B	12/41	South Ural	1/42	3/42	Stavka 58
431/58B	12/41	Volga	12/41	4/42	West 50
432/159B/61G	1/42	South Ural	3/42	7/42	Voronezh 60
433/214B	12/41	South Ural	7/42	7/42	Stalingrad 64
434/162B	12/41	South Ural	1/42	4/42	SW 28
435/164B	12/41	South Ural	1/42	7/42	West 31
436/165B	12/41	South Ural	12/41	5/42	Volkhov 59
437/166B	11/41	South Ural	1/42	5/42	NW 53
438/167B	12/41	South Ural	1/42	7/42	Bryansk
439/170B	1/42	South Ural	2/42	4/42	NW 34
440/171B	12/41	South Ural	12/41	4/42	NW 34
441/219B	12/41	South Ural	5/42	7/42	Voronezh 6
442/282B	12/41	Siberia	2/42	4/42	NW 11
443/284B/79G	12/41	Siberia	1/42	4/42	Bryansk
444/175B/13G	12/41	Siberia	3/42	4/42	SW 28
445/112B	1/42	Siberia	1/42	7/42	Stalingrad 64
446/298B/80G	12/41	Siberia	1/42	3/42	West
447/301B	12/41	Siberia	3/42	3/42	Stavka 28

(continued)

Table 6.4 continued

Division	Date Formed	District	Date Renumbered	Date Assigned	Front/Army
448/303B	1/42	Siberia	3/42	7/42	Voronezh 60
449/309B	12/41	Siberia	1/42	7/42	Voronezh 6
450/312B	12/41	Siberia	1/42	7/42	West 20
451/228B	11/41	Siberia	11/41	4/42	South
452/229B	12/41	Siberia	12/41	7/42	Stalingrad 64
453/232B	12/41	Siberia	1/42	7/42	Voronezh 60
454/235B	12/41	Siberia	3/42	4/42	NW 53
455/237B	12/41	Siberia	2/42	7/42	Bryansk
456/97B/83G	12/41	Transbaikal	1/42	2/42	West 16
457/116B	12/41	Transbaikal	12/41	3/42	West 50
458/8C	11/41	Central Asia	12/41	4/42	Bryansk 3
459/29B/72G	12/41	Central Asia	12/41	7/42	Stalingrad 64
460/38B/73G	12/41	Central Asia	1/42	4/42	SW 28
461/69	12/41	Central Asia	12/41	4/42	West 50
462/102B	12/41	Central Asia	1/42	4/42	South
463/103B	12/41	Central Asia	1/42	4/42	SW 6
464/91B	12/41	Transcaucasus	4/42	4/42	North Caucasus
465/242B	12/41	North Caucasus	12/41	4/42	South
466/248B	12/41	Stalingrad	4/42	4/42	SW 6
467/266B	12/41	Stalingrad	1/42	4/42	SW 6
468A/146B	12/41	Moscow	1/42	3/42	West
468B/277B	12/41	Stalingrad	12/41	4/42	SW 38
469/244B	12/41	Stalingrad	1/42	4/42	SW 28
470/73B	12/41	North Caucasus	2/42	4/42	South
471/278B/60G	12/41	Stalingrad	1/42	5/42	SW 38
472/280B	12/41	Stalingrad	1/42	5/42	Bryansk 48
473		Caucasus			Not in order of battle
474/89B	12/41	Caucasus	1/42	8/42	Transcaucasus

Table 6.5 Additional Divisions Formed in December 1941

Division	District	Date Assigned	Front/Army
117B	Moscow	2/42	Kalinin
118B	Moscow	5/42	Moscow Zone, later Stavka 4R
134B	Moscow	2/42	Kalinin
135B	Moscow	2/42	Kalinin
139C	Moscow	5/42	Moscow Zone
140C	Moscow	4/42	Moscow Zone
141B	Moscow	7/42	Voronezh 40
145B	Moscow	2/42	Kalinin 4sh
247B	Kalinin	12/41	Kalinin 31, cadre rifle brigades
41B	Volga	4/42	SW 6
42B	Volga	4/42	West 49
55B	Volga	4/42	NW 11
24B	Archangel	3/42	Kalinin 3sh
412	Archangel		No combat assignment
72B	Leningrad	12/41	Leningrad 55, from 7 Marine Brigade
75B	Transcaucasus	1/42	Iran
124B/50G	South	12/41	SW
126B	Far East	7/42	Stalingrad
193B	Ural	7/42	Voronezh
225	?	12/41	Volkhov 52

New formations continued in January 1942, though at a much slower pace (tables 6.9, 6.10). The newly trained men drafted in the fall of 1941 had been formed into divisions and brigades in December. New formations in January 1942 were odds and ends.

In February 1942, 12 new rifle divisions and nine rifle brigades were formed (tables 6.11, 6.12), but there was explosive growth in new tank brigades.

Table 6.6 Rifle Divisions Formed in January 1942

Division	District	Date Assigned	Front/Army
49B	Moscow	3/42	Moscow Zone
52B	Moscow	7/42	Kalinin 30
2mdno/129B	Moscow	1/42	Stavka 1sh
3mdno/130B/53G	Moscow	1/42	Moscow Zone
131B	Moscow	7/42	Stalingrad 1 Tank
7B Estonian	Ural	7/42	Kalinin 8
20 (north)	Archangel	4/42	Volkhov 59
20 (south)/109A	Crimea	1/42	Crimea Coastal
98B/86G	Far East	8/42	SW 62
28B	Archangel	4/42	Kalinin Reserve

Table 6.7 New Rifle Brigades Formed in December 1941

	Brigade	Date Assigned	Front/Army	Date Abolished
Moscow District	4/212B	1/42	Moscow MD	
	104/297B	2/42	West 61	
	105/110C	5/42	West	
	106/228C	5/42	Bryansk 61	
	107/117Gdrb	5/42	Bryansk 61	
	108/97C	5/42	West	
	109A/5B	5/42	Bryansk	
	110/97C	5/42	West	
	111A/70B	4/42	Bryansk 40	
	112/192B	5/42	West	
	113A/2navalb	5/42	Caucasus	
	166	12/41	Moscow MD	12/41
	170/154navalb	12/41	Moscow MD	
Ural District	101	10/42	Kalinin 39	7/44
	114	3/42	Kalinin	1/44
	115A	2/42	West	9/44
	116A/224B	3/42	NW 1 shock	
	117/96B	3/42	Kalinin	
	124	7/42	Moscow District	1/44
	125/212B	5/42	West	
	126/199B	5/42	NW 11	
	127/150C	5/42	NW 11	
	128/199B	5/42	West	
	129/226B	5/42	West	
	131/316C	3/42	Kalinin	
	132A/49			
	skib/159C	3/42	Kalinin	
	133A	5/42	NW 11	12/42
	151B/150C	5/42	NW 11	
	152/118C	7/42	Moscow District	
Central Asia District	88A	None	Central Asia	2/42
	89	None	Central Asia	2/42
	91A	None	Central Asia	2/42
	92A	None	Central Asia	2/42
	93A	None	Central Asia	2/42
	94	None	Central Asia	7/42
	95A	None	Central Asia	3/42
	96A	None	Central Asia	2/42
	97A	None	Central Asia	2/42
	98A	None	Central Asia	2/42
	99A	None	Central Asia	2/42
	100	None	Central Asia	7/42
	150/173C	5/42	West	
	153/48skib	5/42	West	

(*continued*)

Table 6.7   continued

	Brigade	Date Assigned	Front/Army	Date Abolished
Caucasus District	102Amarine/192A	2/42	SW	
	143A	12/41	Caucasus	6/42
Siberian District	137/321C	3/42	Leningrad 54	
	140A/136C	3/42	Leningrad 54	
	144A/150C	4/42	NW 11	
	145	4/42	NW	1/44
	146/70C	4/42	NW 34	
	147/197C	4/42	NW 34	
	148/157B	5/42	West	
	194	None		12/41
Stalingrad District	135A/81B	8/42	Bryansk 48	
	138A	5/42	North Caucasus	7/42
	139	4/42	Crimea	11/42
	141	4/42	Bryansk 40	10/42
	142A	5/42	North Caucasus	7/42
Volga District	118A/41C	5/42	Bryansk 48	
	119/30B	5/42	Bryansk 40	
	120A/50lrb	5/42	West	
	121/95C	3/42	NW 1sh	
	122A/73C	5/42	Bryansk 48	
	123	2/42	West 16	9/43
	134A/74B	5/42	Bryansk 3	
	136/153C	3/42	Kalinin 30	
Leningrad District	261A	12/41	Leningrad 55	12/41
	267	12/41	Leningrad 55	12/41
	289A	12/41	Leningrad 55	?12/41

Production of new tanks must have finally caught up with losses and made possible the new formations. Eight of the rifle divisions were sent to Stalingrad in July and August. Only two were sent to the Kalinin Front for the planned offensive there.

An amazing total of 50 new tank brigades was formed in February (table 6.13). The table of organization of tank brigades in 1942 included 32 T-34 tanks and 21 T-70 tanks, a total of 53 tanks and 2,650 tanks in 50 brigades, a clear signal that Soviet tank production was in full swing. Most of the tank brigades were assigned in April, May, June, and July to the Kalinin, Bryansk, and West fronts in the center and the Southwestern and Stalingrad fronts in the south. Only four were left unassigned in August.

The rapid expansion of the Red Army tank forces continued in March, along with substantial increases in rifle divisions and brigades. All but 3 of the 16 rifle divisions went to the Stalingrad area (table 6.14). The conversion of rifle brigades

Table 6.8 New Tank Brigades Formed in December 1941

District	Brigade	Date Assigned	Front/Army
Volga	50/30G	4/42	Bryansk
Volga	51/47G	3/42	Volga
Moscow	80	1/42	Bryansk
Stavka	68	1/42	West 61
Stavka	71/30tr	1/42	Kalinin
Stavka	70	1/42	Kalinin
Stavka	69	1/42	NW
Caucasus	52/34G	8/42	Transcaucasus

also began in March, with the 55th Brigade being reformed as the 260B Rifle Division. Ten new rifle brigades were formed in the Stalingrad area but dissolved shortly after, as the men were sent forward as replacements. Seven new brigades were formed in the east and two in Archangel, neither of which had an impact on the eastern front (table 6.15).

In March 1942, another 39 tank brigades were formed (table 6.16), bringing the total for February and March to 89 brigades, with 4,717 tanks. Most of the brigades were assigned to the Moscow and Stalingrad areas by July.

In April there occurred a major change in the mobilization of rifle divisions. Rather than starting from scratch, the Soviets upgraded existing rifle brigades to divisions (table 6.17). This change indicates that the crisis had passed with regard to artillery and service units, which had been in short supply previously. The new rifle divisions were able to take advantage of the unit spirit developed by the rifle brigades, which served as cadres. Most of the upgrades took place in the Moscow District. The two divisions that were not formed from brigades were not assigned until August and October. All the other new divisions were assigned by August 1942, indicating that the time for forming a division from a brigade was four months or less.

Only a few rifle brigades were formed in April, taking advantage of available manpower. But they were not part of an overall mobilization plan (table 6.18). On

Table 6.9 New Rifle Brigades Formed in January 1942

District	Brigade	Date Assigned	Front/Army
Black Sea	8Bnaval	1/42	?
North	74B/56G	4/42	NW 11
Central Asia	87/76B	10/42	Moscow Zone
North Caucasus	103	5/42	North Caucasus 47
Siberia	149/92G	5/42	Moscow Zone
Moscow	154naval/15Gnavalb	1/42	Moscow Zone

Table 6.10   Tank Brigades Formed in January 1942

Army	Brigade	Date in Combat	Front/Army
West 50	112td/112b/44Gb	1/42	West 50
Stavka 1sh	83	2/42	NW 1sh
Stavka 1sh	81/81tr	2/42	Kalinin 30
Stavka 1sh	79	2/42	Bryansk 3
Stavka Reserve	78	2/42	Kalinin 4sh
Kalinin	58td/58b/253tr	1/42	Kalinin

the other hand, the formation of new tank brigades continued at a brisk pace as a result of new tanks coming out of the factories around Moscow and Stalingrad (table 6.19). The Far East tank brigades most likely were equipped with obsolescent light tanks that were being phased out on the eastern front. Six of the new brigades were sent to the Stalingrad area, while only four were sent to Moscow-area fronts. Seven of the brigades were formed in the east and one for use in Iran. The tank brigades sent south in May and June were an attempt to counter the rapid German advances in Ukraine.

In May, the mobilization process slowed as most of the recruits drafted in late 1941 were trained and assigned to units. Most of the rifle divisions formed in May were upgrades of brigades and regiments (table 6.20). Only eight rifle brigades were formed in May, and most remained in the area in which they were formed (table 6.21). Ten tank brigades were formed, but half of them were in the Far East, which had little impact on events on the eastern front (table 6.22).

The month of May seems to have been a matter of tidying up loose ends rather than part of a major plan. A total of 143 rifle divisions, 118 rifle brigades, and

Table 6.11   Rifle Divisions Formed in February 1942

Division	District	Date Assigned	Front/Army
64	Moscow	8/42	Stalingrad 1 Guard
78B	Moscow	7/42	Kalinin 30
120B/69G	Moscow	8/42	Stalingrad 66
231A	Ural	8/42	Stalingrad 66
233B	Ural	5/42	Moscow (cadre 34rb)
249B	Ural	11/42	Kalinin 8 Reserve
100B	Archangel	7/42	Voronezh 40
127B/62G	Volga	7/42	Stalingrad 63
181B	Stalingrad	7/42	Stalingrad 62
96B/68G	Far East	8/42	Stalingrad 31
87C	Far East	7/42	Stalingrad
422B/81G	Far East	7/42	Stalingrad

Table 6.12 Rifle Brigades Formed in February 1942

Brigade	District	Date Assigned	Front/Army	Date Abolished
111A/47rb	Moscow	4/42	Moscow Zone	
157A/299B	Moscow	3/42	Moscow Zone	
256/304B	Moscow	3/42	Moscow Zone	
20mtn	Archangel	8/42	Stavka Reserve	10/42
227	South Ural	?	Transbaikal 17	6/43
246	Far East	2/42	East 1	12/44
247	Far East	2/42	East 25	11/44
259	Far East	2/42	East 25	12/44
132A/49Bskib/159C	?	3/42	?	

Table 6.13 Tank Brigades Formed in February 1942

	Brigade	Date Assigned	Front/Army
Moscow District	53	5/42	Bryansk
	59	4/42	Bryansk 5
	60	4/42	NW 34
	64	3/42	SW 6
	82	2/42	Kalinin 22
	87	4/42	Kalinin
	92	6/42	Kalinin 31
	95	5/42	West
	100	5/42	West
	101	6/42	Kalinin 31
	113	8/42	West 3 Tank
	114	5/42	SW 38
	168	5/42	SW 38
	198	5/42	SW 6
	199	4/42	SW 6
	200	5/42	West
	201	4/42	Bryansk 61
	202	4/42	Bryansk
Stavka Reserve	63B	3/42	South 56
	98	3/42	Leningrad 54
Volga District	107	6/64	Bryansk
	109	6/42	Bryansk
	110	7/42	Voronezh 60
	111	7/42	Voronezh 60
	115	6/42	Voronezh
	116	6/42	Voronezh
	120	6/42	West 20

(continued)

Table 6.13   continued

	Brigade	Date Assigned	Front/Army
	134	7/42	Stalingrad 63
	135	7/42	Stalingrad 51
	153	7/42	Kalinin 58
	155	7/42	Stalingrad 51
	169	7/42	Stalingrad 1 Tank
	175	7/42	Stalingrad 4 Tank
	176	6/42	SW
	189	7/42	Stalingrad 1 Tank
	193	7/42	Stalingrad 63
Ural District	86	7/42	Bryansk
	96	7/42	Bryansk
	97	8/42	West 3 Tank
	99	7/42	Stalingrad 1 Tank
	105	8/42	West 3 Tank
	106	8/42	West 3 Tank
	117	6/42	NW 11
	118	7/42	Bryansk
	119	7/42	Kalinin 29
	166	7/42	Stalingrad 1 Tank
Stalingrad District	84	4/42	SW 28
	85	6/42	SW 21
Kharkov District	36	4/42	SW 38
Far East	Provisional	2/42	East 35

130 tank brigades were formed from December 1941 to May 1942, and most were assigned to combat formations by August 1942. The divisions and brigades were assigned to the areas where they were either needed immediately to block a route, as in Ukraine, or to areas where major operations were planned. The divisions first assigned in March, April, and May went to the center, to the Western Front and the Stavka Reserve, but some to the north, the Volkhov and Northwestern fronts, and the south, the Bryansk and Southwestern fronts. In April, most of the divisions went to the south to support the effort at Izyum. Those assigned in June and July went to the Stalingrad Front for the obvious reason that the Germans were approaching that city. The Voronezh and Western fronts also received divisions in July in anticipation of the attack to be launched there.

While only 9 Soviet divisions were lost in the first five months of 1942, 79 were destroyed in the remaining seven months. Six of the lost divisions were not officially abolished until months after they disappeared from the order of battle. The carnage began in August, with 12 divisions lost in the south (table 6.23). As the Germans approached Stalingrad in September, the rate of destruction of divisions guarding the city dropped to a minor level. In the grinding battle that

Table 6.14   Rifle Divisions Formed in March 1942

Division	District	Date Assigned	Front/Army
1A/58G	Volga	7/42	Stalingrad 63
153B/57G	Volga	7/42	Stalingrad 53
197B/59G	North Caucasus	7/42	Stalingrad 63
203	North Caucasus	7/42	Stalingrad 63
414	Transcaucasus	3/42	Transcaucasus
416B	Transcaucasus	3/42	Transcaucasus
417	Transcaucasus	5/42	Transcaucasus
403	Central Asia	None	
405	Central Asia	None	
221A	Ural	8/42	Stalingrad 24
55Arb/260B	Ural	5/42	Moscow Zone
184C	Stalingrad	7/42	Stalingrad 62
315	Siberia	8/42	Stalingrad 1 Guard
321B/82G	Transbaikal	7/42	Stalingrad 21
399B	Transbaikal	7/42	Stalingrad 1 Tank
136B/63G	Leningrad	3/42	Leningrad 34

followed, few divisions were lost as daily casualties were replaced by new men (table 6.24).

After November 1942, only one division was abolished by the Red Army for the rest of the war. In 1944, Rifle Division 55B in the 61st Army of the 3rd Baltic Front was abolished. All of the remaining divisions were maintained with replacements, although many changed their numbers.

When the Germans launched their drive on Stalingrad and the Caucasus, the Red Army had enormous reserves, but the units lacked combat experience. The 143 divisions formed since December 1941 were becoming more proficient, even though a few were lost earlier in the year.

In May 1942, 10 new reserve armies numbered 1 through 10 appeared in the Soviet order of battle. The armies had an average strength of six rifle divisions, each with 7,000 men. The 1st Reserve Army formed at Tula in April 1942. On July 1, 1942, it included the 18th, 29th, 112th, 131st, 164th, 214th, and 229th divisions. In July the army, redesignated the 64th, went to Stalingrad. In August, after intense combat, the 64th Army had only the 29th Division remaining of the original reserve army.

The 2nd Reserve Army formed at Vologda in April 1942 and was redesignated the 1st Guard Army in July. The army then included the 37th, 38th, 39th, 40th, and 41st guard divisions formed in June and July from airborne corps and the 397th Rifle Division. These divisions had superior manpower but were short on infantry unit training. On July 1, 1942, the army had the 25th Guard Division and the 52nd, 100th, 111th, 237th, and 303rd rifle divisions. The army traveled from Vologda to Stalingrad in early August.

Table 6.15 Rifle Brigades Formed in March 1942

Brigade	District	Date Assigned	Front/Army	Date Abolished
229/230B	Transbaikal	7/42	Bryansk	
173	Volga	None		3/42
174	Volga	None		3/42
175	Volga	None		3/42
176	Volga	None		3/42
177	Volga	None		3/42
178	Volga	None		3/42
179	Volga	None		3/42
180	Volga	None		3/42
181	Volga	None		3/42
182	Volga	None		3/42
226	Transbaikal	3/42	Transbaikal	6/43
229/230B	Transbaikal	3/42	Transbaikal	
161/119C	Moscow	3/42	Moscow Zone	
257/51skib	Moscow	3/42	Moscow Zone	10/42
188	Far East	3/42	East Operating Group	
248	Far East	3/42	East 25	12/43
250/98C	Far East	3/42	East	
253/297B	Far East	7/42	Bryansk	
258	Far East	3/42	East 2	11/44
263	Far East	3/42	East 1	8/42
3light/32skib	Archangel	5/42	Karelian	
4light/32skib	Archangel	5/42	Karelian	

The 3rd Reserve Army, formed at Tambov in April 1942, included the 107th, 159th, 232nd, 237th, 195th, and 303rd divisions. Redesignated the 60th Army, in July it went to the Voronezh Front with the 107th, 159th, 161st, 167th, 193rd, 195th, and 232nd divisions. The 237th Division was sent to the Southwestern Front, while other divisions were added to the 60th Army.

The 4th Reserve Army, formed at Kalinin, included the 165th, 167th, and 169th divisions and the 242nd Rifle Brigade, among other units. The 167th had been redesignated from the 438th Division formed in Magnitogorsk from Communist volunteers. The army headquarters formed a new 38th Army Headquarters, but few, if any, divisions went to the 38th Army. On July 1, 1942, the 4th Reserve Army had the 78th, 88th, 118th, 139th, 274th, and 312th divisions. In August, the 38th Army had the 237th from the 3rd Reserve Army, the 296th from the 9th Army, the 193rd and 340th from the 40th Army, the 240th and 284th from the 48th Army, and the 167th from the 60th Army.

The 5th Reserve Army formed at Novo Annenski on the Don, northwest of Stalingrad in April 1942, including the 1st, 127th, 153rd, 181st, 184th, and 196th divisions. In July it was redesignated the 63rd Army. Three divisions stayed with the 63rd Army and two went to the 62nd Army at Stalingrad. On July 1, 1942, the

Table 6.16 Tank Brigades Formed in March 1942

	Tank Brigade	Date Assigned	Front/Army
Moscow District	62	3/42	Moscow District
	91	6/42	SW 28
	94	3/42	West 16
	161	7/42	West 5
	163	7/42	Stalingrad 1 Tank
	170	5/42	Bryansk 40
	177	5/42	NW 53
	178	5/42	West
	179	8/42	West 3 Tank
	183	5/42	West
	184	5/42	Kalinin 3 Shock
	185	5/42	Volkhov 4
	186	5/42	West
	187	5/42	West
	192	5/42	Bryansk 6
	195	5/42	Volkhov 4
Stalingrad District	6B	4/42	Stalingrad District
	65	6/42	SW 28
	66	6/42	Bryansk
	67	6/42	Bryansk
	88	6/42	SW
	89	4/42	Bryansk
	90	4/42	SW 28
	93	3/42	Stalingrad District
	102	4/42	Bryansk
	180	7/42	Voronezh 60
	181	7/42	Voronezh 60
	191	7/42	Transcaucasus
North Caucasus	136	6/42	North Caucasus
	137	5/42	North Caucasus 51
	138	6/42	SW
	139	6/42	SW
	140	6/42	South
Volga District	154	8/42	West
	164	6/42	Bryansk
Archangel	103	3/42	Archangel District
	104	5/42	Kalinin 3 Shock
Ural District	197	7/43	Bryansk 4 Tank
Far East	203	3/42	East 15

Table 6.17 Rifle Divisions Formed in April 1942

	Division	*Cadre*	*Date Assigned*	*Front/Army*
Moscow District	18C	16rb	7/42	Stalingrad 4 Tank
	88B	39Arb	7/42	West 31
	107B	11rb	7/42	Voronezh 60
	111B	50rb	7/42	Kalinin 30
	119B/54G	51Arb	5/42	Moscow
	133	56Arb	8/42	West 31
	258B/96G	43Arb	5/42	Moscow Zone
	274B	30Arb	5/42	Moscow Zone
	306B		10/42	Kalinin 43
Volga District	161B	13rb	7/42	Voronezh 60
Stalingrad District	192A	103rb	7/42	Stalingrad 62
Ural District	264B/48G	17Arb	5/42	Moscow Zone
Siberia District	308B/120G		8/42	Stalingrad 24
Far East	187B		4/42	East 1
	190B		4/42	East 25

5th Reserve Army had 11th/4th Guard, 1st, 127th, 153rd, 197th, and 203rd divisions.

The 6th Reserve Army, formed on the Don River northwest of Stalingrad in April, included the 141st, 160th, 206th, 212th, 219th, 309th, and 350th divisions. The 6th Reserve was redesignated the 6th Army on the Southwestern Front in June 1942 and four of the divisions stayed with it. On July 1, 1942, the army included the 99th, 141st, 174th, 206th, 219th, 232nd, and 309th divisions.

The 7th Reserve Army formed at Stalingrad in May 1942 with the 147th Division and possibly the 62nd, 98th, 147th, 192nd, 214th, and 308th divisions and the 124th and 149th brigades. On July 1, 1942, the army included the 33rd Guard Division and the 147th, 192nd, 206th, 219th, 232nd, and 309th divisions. In July, the army was redesignated the 62nd Army. After heavy fighting in the Don basin, only the 98th and 192nd divisions from the reserve army remained; the others were replaced by new divisions.

The 8th Reserve Army formed at Saratov in April and included the 49th, 120th, 231st, and 315th divisions. On July 1, 1942, the army contained the 64th, 120th,

Table 6.18 Rifle Brigades Formed in April 1942

District	*Brigade*	*Date Assigned*	*Front/Army*
Leningrad	13/201B	7/42	Leningrad
Black Sea	113A/2marineb	5/42	?
Central Asia	153A/207C	5/42	?
Far East	262	4/42	East 25, abolished 12/44

Table 6.19 Tank Brigades Formed in April 1942

	Brigade	Date Assigned	Front/Army
Moscow District	57	5/42	SW 6
	156	5/42	SW 38
	158	6/42	SW
	159	6/42	SW 38
	160	5/42	Bryansk
	167	6/42	SW 21
	188	6/42	West 20
	196	7/42	Kalinin 30
Stalingrad District	173	7/42	Stalingrad 4 Tank
	174	6/42	Bryansk
Far East	3 East	4/42	East 15
	4 East	4/42	East 1
	5 East	4/42	East 1
	6 East	4/42	East 1
Transbaikal	205	4/42	Transbaikal
	206	4/42	Transbaikal
Transcaucasus	207	7/42	Transcaucasus Iran

221st, 231st, 308th, and 315th divisions. In August, redesignated the 66th Army, it went to Stalingrad. There additional divisions joined the army, including the 42nd from the Northwestern Front 34th Army, the 99th from the Southwestern Front 6th Army, and the 316th from the 9th Reserve Army.

The 9th Reserve Army was formed with 10 rifle brigades from the Gorki, Ivanovo, and Vladimir oblasts of the Moscow District as cadres. The 10 brigades became the 32nd, 93rd, 180th, 207th, 238th, 279th, 292nd, 299th, 306th, and 316th divisions. The eastern oblasts of the Moscow District, the Caucasus, and Central Asia provided 200 companies of replacements (20,000 to 40,000 men) to reinforce the new divisions. On July 1, 1942, the army included the 32nd, 93rd, 238th, 279th, and 316th divisions. In July, five of the divisions plugged gaps in the Southwestern Front. On August 27, 1942, the army headquarters,

Table 6.20 Rifle Divisions Formed in May 1942

District	Division	Cadre	Date Assigned	Front/Army
Moscow	32B		10/42	Kalinin 43
Moscow	180B	41Arb	8/42	West 31
Moscow	418		5/42	Moscow
Kalinin	215B	48rb	5/42	Kalinin
Ural	174B/46G	6Brb	7/42	Voronezh 6
Far East	393B	175, 1407ir	5/42	East 25

Table 6.21 Rifle Brigades Formed in May 1942

District	Brigade	Date Assigned	Front/Army
Transcaucasus	9A/257C	5/42	Transcaucasus
Transcaucasus	10B/29C	5/42	Transcaucasus
Transcaucasus	155	6/42	Transcaucasus 46
North	27B/127Crd	6/42	NW 1 Shock
Volga	52B/127Crd	9/42	Stalingrad 28
Ural	120A/50lrb	5/42	?
Archangel	2 (32 Army)/33lrb	5/42	Karelian 32
Archangel ?	8light/1strb/32lrb	5/42	Karelian ?

redesignated the 24th Army, went to the Stalingrad area, but its five divisions were sent to other fronts. Of the five divisions assigned to the 9th Reserve Army before August 27, 1942, the 32nd and the 279th went to the Western Front, 43rd Army; the 93rd went to the Kalinin Front, 41st Army, and the 316th went to the Don Front, 1st Guard Army. The 238th was with the 30th Army. The dispatch of the four divisions of the 9th Reserve Army to the Moscow area revealed a continued interest in offensive action at Rzhev.

The new 24th Army entered the front line and took control of the 173rd, 207th, 221st, 292nd, and 308th divisions plus the 217th Tank Brigade. Of these divisions, the 207th, 292nd, and 308th had been in the original 9th Reserve Army. The 221st had been part of the 8th Reserve Army and the 173rd came from the 10th Army on the Western Front.

The 10th Reserve Army, formed at Ivanovo in April, was redesignated the 5th Shock Army in July and took part in the Stalingrad offensive. On July 1, 1942, the army included the 133rd, 180th, 207th, 292nd, 299th, and 306th divisions.

The assignments of the reserve armies and their divisions revealed the many demands on the Red Army in 1942. The crushing defeats in the south in the

Table 6.22 Tank Brigades Formed in May 1942

District	Brigade	Date Assigned	Front/Army
Moscow	157	7/42	Moscow District
Moscow	162	7/42	Voronezh 60
Leningrad	152	5/42	Leningrad
Bryansk Front	130B	6/42	Bryansk
Transcaucasus	151	12/42	Transcaucasus
Far East	165	5/42	East 15
Far East	171	5/42	East 15
Far East	208	5/42	East 1
Far East	209	5/42	East 1
Far East	210	5/42	East 1

Table 6.23 Divisions Lost in August 1942

	Army	Division
North Caucasus	12th	4A, 230A
	24th	335A
	37th	74A, 462/102B
	Reserve	261
Transcaucasus	9th	81mtr/A, 106Ab, 140C, 225A
Volkhov Front	2nd Shock	46B, 92A, 267A
	52nd	305A
Other fronts	Stalingrad 4th Tank	205A
	Southeast 62nd	192A
	Bryansk 38th	296A

summer of 1942 created a crisis requiring the employment of reserve armies before their training was complete. The overwhelming majority of the divisions of the reserve armies went to the south, most as early as July. The Red Army reserves had grown from 24 divisions in April to 40 in June and 62 in July. In June the high command began to commit the reserve divisions in the south, and by August the reserves decreased to only 23 rifle divisions, one rifle brigade, and two mechanized corps. By September most reserves had been absorbed in the battles in the south and only 17 divisions remained in reserve in October.

In June 1942, the Soviets continued to form new divisions, mostly from existing rifle brigades at a moderate scale (table 6.25). Six of the new divisions went to the south, five remained in the center, and one was formed in the north and went to Leningrad. Only one rifle brigade was formed in June, the 3/157rb/301C brigade, assigned in July 1942 to the Transcaucasus Front reserve.

A half dozen new tank brigades were formed in June (table 6.26). The tank brigades appear to be the result of gathering up available manpower and tanks and giving them brigade numbers rather than a concerted effort to create new

Table 6.24 Divisions Lost, September–November 1942

	Front	Army	Division
September	Stalingrad		181B
October	Don Front	24th	207B, 221A, 231A, 292A, 316B
	Other fronts	Transcaucasus 9th	51A
		Stalingrad	208A
		Southwest 5th Tank	228
		Caucasus 18th	408
November		Don 66th	62B, 212mtr/A
		Northwest 11th	384A
		Transcaucasus 58th	319B

Table 6.25 Rifle Divisions Formed in June 1942

	Division	Cadre	Date Assigned	Front/Army
Moscow District	63A/52G	8nkvdrd	7/42	Stalingrad 21
	82	64mtnb	6/42	West 20
	93B		8/42	Kalinin
	207B	52 rb	9/42	Don 1 Guard
	238B		10/42	Kalinin 41
	279B		9/42	Kalinin 43
	292B	74mtnb	8/42	Stalingrad 24
	299B	157rb	8/42	Stalingrad 66
	316B	27rb	8/42	Stalingrad 66
	338B	18rb	6/42	West 43
Southwest Area	318mtn	78mtnb	6/42	SW 9
Archangel District	224B	116Amtnb	12/42	Leningrad

forces. All of the brigades were assigned immediately to units in the area where they were formed.

The German threat in the south caused a flurry of creating eight new divisions there, but elsewhere only five divisions were formed in various areas (table 6.27). None of the divisions formed in the south had cadres; they were assembled from reserves and newly trained recruits.

Given the German threat in the South, most of the Red Army reserves were directed there, but a substantial number also went to the Rzhev salient. To create additional reserves quickly, 23 new rifle brigades were formed in July 1942 (table 6.28). Three rifle divisions (126B, 205A, and 208B) were sent from the Far East to the Stalingrad Front in July, one each going to the 4th Tank Army, the 64th Army, and the Stalingrad Front reserve. To replace these divisions, eight new rifle brigades were formed in the east. Another three new brigades were formed in the Caucasus. The remaining brigades were formed in scattered areas. All but 6 of the 23 new rifle brigades were later upgraded to divisions, so this was merely a temporary measure to provide more manpower for the front.

Table 6.26 Tank Brigades Formed in June 1942

District	Brigade	Date Assigned	Front/Army
Moscow	34	6/42	West 49
Leningrad	220	6/42	Leningrad 55
Orel	7B	6/42	Bryansk 6
Far East	11	6/42	Transbaikal
Far East	125	6/42	East 35
Far East	172	6/42	East 35

Table 6.27 Rifle Divisions Formed in July 1942

	Division	Date Assigned	Front/Army
North Caucasus District	248C	9/42	Stalingrad 28
	276B	8/42	Transcaucasus
	317B	8/42	North Caucasus 58
	319B	9/42	North Caucasus 58
	320B	11/42	North Caucasus 58
	328B	8/42	North Caucasus 58
	337B	8/42	North Caucasus 58
	351B	8/42	Transcaucasus
Siberia District	150B/22G	10/42	Kalinin 22
Archangel District	270B	10/42	Voronezh 6
Kalinin Front	47	7/42	Kalinin 4 Shock, Cadre 21rb
Far East	103C	7/42	Transbaikal
	388B	7/42	East 15

Table 6.28 Rifle Brigades Formed in July 1942

District	Brigade	Date Assigned	Unit	Date Abolished
Leningrad	3/50Brb/11Brd	7/42	Leningrad Coastal Group	
Leningrad	56B/124Crd	7/42	Leningrad Coastal Group	
Moscow	116B/110Crd	9/42	Moscow Zone	
Caucasus	3/157Brd/301Crd	7/42	Transcaucasus	
Caucasus	229/43Brb/304rd	7/42	Transcaucasus	
Caucasus	239/51Brd/218Brd	7/42	North Caucasus	
Siberia	75B/65Grd	10/42	Kalinin 22	
Siberia	78B/65Grd	10/42	Kalinin 22	
Central Asia	90A	10/42	Moscow Zone	1/43, remnant to 60Gd
Central Asia	94A	10/42	Moscow Zone	1/43, remnant to 266
Central Asia	100/1Brd	10/42	Kalinin 39	
Ural	93B/12Grb	10/42	Stalingrad 64	
Transbaikal	39B	7/42	Transbaikal	6/43
Far East	12/366rd?	7/42	East 1	
Far East	17/ ?rd	7/42	East 2	
Far East	18B	7/42	East	11/44
Far East	29B/365	7/42	East 1	
Far East	30B/30C	7/42	East 35	
Far East	38B/ ?rd	7/42	East 15	11/44
Far East	41B/ ?rd	7/42	East 2	12/44
?	229/43Brb/304B	7/42	?	
?	238	7/42	?	?10/42
?	239/51rb/218B	7/42	?	

Table 6.29 Tank Brigades Formed in July 1942

	Brigade	*Date Assigned*	*Front/Army*
Moscow District	144B	None	Moscow District
	216	9/42	Bryansk 5 Tank
	217	9/42	Don
	219	9/42	Kalinin
	224	None	Moscow District
	229	None	Moscow District
	234	None	Moscow District
	241	None	Moscow District
	246	8/42	Stalingrad 66
	248	8/42	West 33
Kalinin Front	236	7/42	Kalinin 30
	238	7/42	Kalinin 30
	240	7/42	Kalinin 30
	255	7/42	Kalinin 30
	256	7/42	Kalinin 30
Western Front	212	8/42	West
	213	7/42	West 20
Stalingrad Front	254	7/42	Stalingrad
Volga District	239	None	Moscow District
	249	None	Moscow District
Leningrad	61	7/42	Leningrad
North Caucasus Front	NCF	7/42	North Caucasus
	132B	7/42	North Caucasus 9

The formation of new tank brigades continued at a rapid pace, though most of the units were formed in the Moscow area and remained there (table 6.29). Only three of the brigades went to the Stalingrad area, and one of those was formed in Stalingrad. An additional two brigades were formed by the North Caucasus Front and remained there. Five tank brigades formed in the Moscow District and two formed in the Volga District were never assigned. These brigades were most likely training brigades for crews who would later pick up new tanks as they were produced. Most likely these brigades were given obsolete and lend-lease tanks for training purposes.

The formation of 23 tank brigades indicates the availability of at least 1,300 new tanks in July over and above those required for replacements in existing units. Although some of the brigades were most likely below the authorized strength, tank units sent to the front tended to begin with a complete table of organization and equipment. Otherwise, what would have been the point of forming them? An oddity in the July formations was that while the Far East was busy forming new rifle brigades, it did not form a single tank brigade. Perhaps the supply of obsolete tanks had been exhausted.

Table 6.30 Rifle Divisions Formed in August 1942

District	Division	Date Assigned	Front/Army
Leningrad	1nkvd/46c	8/42	Leningrad Neva Group
Leningrad	20nkvd/92B	8/42	Leningrad 23
Leningrad	21nkvd/109B	8/42	Leningrad 42
Transcaucasus	228	8/42	Transcaucasus 45
Volga	253C	10/42	NW
Volga	266C	11/42	SW 1 Guard

The new formations indicated that the crisis in the south continued to mount as the Germans closed in on Stalingrad. The available resources had been used in July and few were left in August. Of the six divisions that were formed, three were NKVD divisions taken from internal security duties, transformed into rifle divisions, and sent to Leningrad (table 6.30).

In August, 13 brigades were formed (table 6.31). The four formed in the east organized available personnel, and two of these were abolished in November 1944 because the soldiers were used as replacements. The two brigades formed in Leningrad took advantage of available troops. One of these brigades was formed with sailors from the blockaded warships. Five brigades were formed in the south and two more in the center. Of the 13 brigades, 5 were later reformed as divisions.

Seven tank training brigades were formed in the Moscow District in August, revealing a program for training mass numbers of tank crews in anticipation of the increased production in the coming months. The 149th, 221st, 223rd, 225th,

Table 6.31 Rifle Brigades Formed in August 1942

District	Brigades	Date Assigned	Front/Army	Date Abolished
Leningrad	5marinel/ 71Bmarineb	8/42	Leningrad Coastal Group	
Leningrad	55B	8/42	Leningrad	9/43
Southeast	138B/124C	9/42	Moscow Zone	
Southeast	10C/150rb/96C	8/42	Stalingrad 62	
Transcaucasus	164	8/42	Transcaucasus	5/43
North Caucasus	156/130C	12/42	South 28	
Ural	96B/94G	10/42	Stalingrad 64	
Siberia	91B/56G	10/42	Kalinin 22	
Far East	21	8/42	East 25	11/44
Far East	88B	8/42	East	
Far East	95B	8/42	East 1	
Far East	158	8/42	East 25	11/44
Black Sea	1marine/255marine	9/42	Transcaucasus 47	

Table 6.32 Rifle Divisions Formed in September 1942

District	Division	Date Assigned	Front/Army
Moscow	172C	9/42	Moscow Zone
Moscow	267B	9/42	Moscow Zone
Stalingrad	95B/75G	9/42	Stalingrad 62
Transcaucasus	261B	9/42	Transcaucasus Turkish border

228th, 232nd, and 252nd tank brigades were formed in August 1942, all in the Moscow District, where they remained. Seven additional brigades would have needed some 350 tanks. Added to the thousand in the previous months, the Red Army had a major investment in a tank training program that would ensure crews for the thousands of new tanks coming out of the factories.

Formation of new units slowed considerably in September. Only four rifle divisions and five tank brigades were formed (table 6.32), although new rifle brigades continued to be created at a brisk pace (table 6.33). A new class of a million recruits was being trained, and the brigades formed a convenient home once they had completed their basic training. Most of these brigades were later upgraded to divisions. All were assigned immediately, indicating that most likely they consisted of previously existing regiments or battalions that were gathered up into divisions for better control.

Table 6.33 Rifle Brigades Formed in September 1942

District	Brigade	Date Assigned	Front/Army
Leningrad	162/98Crd	9/42	Leningrad
Transcaucasus	2/34Brb/157B	?	Transcaucasus
Black Sea	2/83Bmarinerb	10/42	Transcaucasus 46
Caucasus	159/130Crd	9/42	Stalingrad 28
Transcaucasus	163A	9/42	Transcaucasus 47
Transcaucasus	165/218D	9/42	Transcaucasus
Volga	143B/14Gdrb	10/42	Stalingrad 57
South	228/111Crb/92Brb/93G	9/42	Stalingrad 62
Moscow	102B/124C	9/42	Moscow Zone
Moscow	142B/120C	9/42	Moscow Zone
Central Asia	64B/192B	7/43	?
Central Asia	98B/127C	12/42	South 28
Central Asia	99B/99B	12/42	South 28
Ural	97B/13Gdrb	10/42	Stalingrad 64
East	113B	9/42	East
South	2 South/165rb	?	Abolished 11/42, remnant to 165rb
?	48skib/153Brb/207C	1/43	West

Table 6.34 Tank Brigades Formed in September 1942

District	Brigade	Date Assigned	Front/Army
Moscow	235	10/42	Stalingrad
Moscow	215	None	Moscow
Leningrad	222	12/42	Leningrad
Far East	214	9/42	East
Far East	218	9/42	East 25

The new rifle brigades were in a wide range of districts and most were sent quickly to the Stalingrad area, reflecting the heavy losses sustained there and the need for units to delay the German advance. Most of the brigades were assigned quickly to the Southern Front, reflecting the need for additional units to delay the German advance. Only five tank brigades were formed (table 6.34). Two were formed in the Far East and one was a training brigade in Moscow.

In October a handful of rifle divisions and rifle brigades were formed (table 6.35), but no new tank brigades. With intense fighting both in the center and in the south at Stalingrad, the emphasis was on replacement regiments to fill out worn-down units. In addition, Stalin was planning the counteroffensive in the south and building up the units that would participate. Six rifle divisions were simply upgrades of rifle brigades, four being upgraded by the Bryansk Front. The 75th UR (fortified region), also upgraded to a division, was a brigade-sized unit with older men heavily armed with machine guns and artillery used to defend a quiet sector of the front line. These formations did not make a major addition to the Red Army, as the former rifle brigades were simply given a replacement regiment, an artillery regiment, and some service units and renumbered as a division. The upgrading did reflect the availability of 40,000 replacements.

In October a few rifle brigades were formed in the south, two of which later were upgraded to divisions and the other abolished in December 1942 (table 6.36). For the remainder of 1942, very few rifle units were formed. The major role

Table 6.35 Rifle Divisions Formed in October 1942

District	Division	Cadre	Date Assigned	Front/Army
Transcaucasus	77B		10/42	Transcaucasus
Transcaucasus	402		?	?
Ural	5B	109Arb	10/42	Bryansk 3
Ural	41C	118rb	10/42	Bryansk 48
Bryansk	73C	122Arb	10/42	Bryansk 48
Bryansk	74B	134Arb	10/42	Bryansk 13
Bryansk	81B	135rb	10/42	Bryansk 48
Bryansk	305B	75 UR	10/42	Voronezh 60

Table 6.36 Rifle Brigades Formed in October 1942

District	Brigade	Date Assigned	Front/Army
Central Asia	79B/221B	12/42	South 28
North Caucasus	86	10/42	Transcaucasus 18, abolished 12/42
Transcaucasus	408/7rb/23B	10/42	Transcaucasus

of the GUF was providing replacement regiments to rebuild decimated divisions and converting brigades to divisions. Three NKVD divisions were restructured as rifle divisions (table 6.37), and two new rifle brigades were formed (table 6.38). No tank brigades were formed.

In December, the only new units were three rifle brigades (table 6.39). The 28B Rifle Division may have been formed in the Archangel District in December 1942 but first appeared in the order of battle in April 1943 on the Kalinin Front.

During the period from June to December 1942, 47 rifle divisions, 62 rifle brigades, and 44 tank brigades, including rifle brigades upgraded to divisions and tank training brigades, were formed, compared to the preceding six months when 143 rifle divisions, 118 rifle brigades, and 130 tank brigades were created. This was a dramatic turnaround. The loss of only 31 rifle divisions in the last half of 1942 indicated that the Germans were no longer surrounding and destroying large numbers of Soviet divisions. As a result, the GUF was primarily concerned with providing individual replacements for the divisions in the south.

The poor performance of the Red Army in the spring and summer of 1942 resulted from inexperienced commanders and premature commitment of new rifle divisions and tank brigades to offensive action. The divisions sent to withstand the German offensive in the summer of 1942 were new and few had prior combat experience. The older divisions remained in the center and in the north. After August, few of the newly formed divisions entered combat prematurely, as Stalin released only enough divisions to delay the Germans at Stalingrad. Most of the new rifle divisions and tank brigades were reserved for the counteroffensives at Stalingrad and Rzhev planned for December.

The new divisions arrived at the front from three to four months after formation. Seven divisions from the Far East, Transbaikal, and Siberia were sent to Stalingrad in July and August. The 399th formed in Transbaikal in March 1942;

Table 6.37 Rifle Divisions Formed in November 1942

District	Division	Date Assigned	Front/Army
Ural	Ural nkvd/175C	11/42	Stavka 70
Far East	FE nkvd	11/42	East
Sabjaikal	Sab nkvd/106B	11/42	Stavka 70

Table 6.38 Rifle Brigades Formed in November 1942

District	Brigade	Date Assigned	Unit
Caucasus	109B/138B	5/43	Caucasus?
Transcaucasus	111B	11/42	TCA 45, abolished 5/43, remnant to 318rd

the 321st and 422nd from the Far East in April; the 204th from the Far East in June; and the 126th, 205th, and 208th from Siberia in June 1942. None of these divisions had appreciable unit training, five arriving in Stalingrad a month after formation.

By November 1942, the new divisions had six or more months' experience. Russian historians refer to November 1942 as the beginning of the Second Period of the war. The remarkable aspect of the 1942 rebuilding program was its responsiveness to tactical and strategic lessons learned since the beginning of the war. The previous two rebuilding programs in 1941 and early 1942 emphasized rifle and light tank units because of the shortage of weapons, not poor doctrine. The third rebuilding in mid-1942 reflected the new strategy and tactics. Experience was translated into doctrine that, in turn, determined production schedules and mobilization. The increased production of weapons, tanks, artillery, and automatic weapons and the formation of a wide variety of units was not haphazard but rather part of a comprehensive plan.

For the remainder of the war, except in a few months, the Russians had a substantial reserve that could be used to obtain local superiority anywhere on the line. The Germans, on the other hand, seldom had many reserves and had to thin out less threatened sectors when troops were needed to counterattack. In the time the Germans required to accomplish the thinning process and move the divisions to the threatened area, the Russians made substantial gains.

Few new rifle divisions were created after 1942 (table 6.40). Additional new divisions were formed by reorganizing existing units.

At the end of 1942, the Red Army had roughly the number of rifle divisions that it needed to complete the war. In 1942 the problem became one of moving the weapons and troops to the south, which was hampered by limited rail capacity. When the Nazis drove into the Caucasus, sweeping aside the Russian defenders, the Soviets had to deploy newly formed units before they were ready

Table 6.39 Rifle Brigades Formed in December 1942

District	Brigade	Date Assigned	Front/Army
Volga	25B/174C	None as a brigade	
Caucasus	40B/38C	12/42	Transcaucasus 18
Central Asia	118B/136C	None as a brigade	

Table 6.40   New Rifle Divisions by Year, 1941–45

	1941	1942	1943	1944	1945	Total
From brigades	3	15	41	5	0	64
From NKVD	0	8	1	0	0	9
Ethnic divisions	1	1	0	0	0	2
Total	4	24	42	5	0	75

and arm them with whatever weapons were at hand. On August 27, 1942, the Stavka sent the 1st Guard, 24th, and 66th armies to defend Stalingrad. Because of the transportation problem, the armies were poorly equipped and short of fuel and ammunition. In the 9th Army in August 1942 defending the Caucasus, the recently formed 417th Rifle Division had only 500 rifles. The 151st Rifle Division of the same army equipped half of its men with foreign rifles. Only 30 percent of the men of one infantry brigade were armed using foreign rifles, and there were no machine guns or artillery. These problems were caused by lack of transportation facilities rather than availability. The nearest railroad to Stalingrad available to the Russians was many miles east of the Volga River. Troops had to march and supplies were carried in horse-drawn wagons to the front.

The supply of weapons improved greatly by the fall of 1942 (table 6.41). Weapons for the entire Red Army were more than sufficient. The inventory of heavy weapons on hand had increased dramatically compared to the year before. These totals exceeded the number of weapons in the hands of the Germans and their satellite forces on the eastern front in November 1942. By January 1942, the manpower situation and hand weapons crisis had turned the corner. The rifle division was increased to 11,626, with 582 machine pistols and 359 machine guns. During 1942, the number of riflemen in the division was reduced as the number of automatic weapons was increased. The Soviet rifle division in December 1942 had a table of organization of 9,435 men, 727 machine pistols, 605 machine guns, and 212 antitank rifles. With only about two-thirds of the men compared to the 1941 division, the new division had more machine guns than the prewar division. The rifle company had 12 machine pistols and 12 light machine guns, double the number in December 1941. The supply of antitank rifles was ample. The Russians were winning the production battle by the end of 1942. Rifle divisions were smaller but more heavily armed.

Table 6.41   Comparative Numbers of Weapons in Late 1941 and 1942

Weapons	December 1941	November 1942
Guns and mortars	22,000	77,851
Tanks	1,954	7,350
Combat aircraft	2,238	4,544

Finding the necessary equipment for the new divisions had been a severe strain. From December 1941 to May 1942, the Russians manufactured 129,683 guns and mortars. Despite serious setbacks that cost 108,043 in lost weapons, the total on hand increased from 22,000 in December 1941 to 43,640 guns and mortars in May 1942. The new guns included a modernized version of the 45 mm antitank guns and the improved ZIS-3 76 mm gun. The number of guns 76 mm or greater doubled from 1941 to 1942, from 15,856 to 33,111. Production of 82 mm and 120 mm mortars increased more than five times.

From May to November 1942, production of guns and mortars increased nearly 50 percent from the prior six months, to 182,433. The heavy losses of the summer had reduced the stock by 153,753, but because of increased production the inventory grew from 43,640 to 72,500, the greatest increase of any period in the war, despite the heavy losses. In the second half of 1942, rifle and carbine production increased to 1,943,000, machine pistols to 524,000, antitank rifles to 114,370, and machine guns to 150,000. These numbers were the highest for any six months in the war.

Production of artillery peaked in 1942 and declined steadily during the remainder of the war, as production of mortars and 45 mm antitank guns was sharply curtailed. The light and medium mortars and the 45 mm gun were obsolete after 1942. These weapons made up 250,800 of the total of 287,700 in 1942 and only 6,100 of the total of 43,300 in 1944. The total of all other guns and mortars in 1942 was 36,900, compared to 37,200 in 1944.

After June 1941, the Russians developed new guns to replace the heavy losses in the first six months of the war (table 6.42). To build the powerful artillery arm called for by Russian tactics, new guns were needed.

In 1942, the Soviets favored massive bombardments to reduce German resistance, which required stupendous amounts of munitions. The Soviets developed their chemical industry under the Five-Year Plans to prevent a shortage of explosives in any future war. In 1939 construction of new plants began and old plants were modernized. In 1940 production of shells had increased by 50 percent over 1939, and in 1941 production was increasing again.

However, shortages did develop because many plants were in Ukraine and the Donbas, areas overrun by the Germans. In the second half of 1941, 303 ammunition

Table 6.42 Guns and Mortars Introduced during World War II

Weapon	Weight (kg)	Muzzle Velocity (m/s)	Shell (kg)
45 mm antitank gun M1942	570	820	1.43
57 mm antitank gun ZIS-2	1,150	990	3.14
M1943 76 mm divisional gun ZIS-3	1,115	680	6.2
M1942 76 mm regimental gun OB-25	600	262	6.2
100 mm gun BS-3 M1944	3,650	887	15.6
MT-13 152 mm howitzer M1943	3,600	510	39.9

plants with a capacity of 100 million artillery shells and 32 million mortar bombs ceased to operate. Added to this loss was the unexpectedly large quantity needed to break through German defenses.

Among the factories producing shells was Munitions Plant No. 22 at Seredovina near Kuibyshev, the second largest munitions plant. The factory employed 20,000 workers in September 1942, working two 11-hour shifts. The factory had been built in 1905 and occupied a site of nearly 50 square kilometers. The daily production was more than 30,000 76 mm shells, 50,000 45 mm shells, 60,000 37 mm shells, and shells for 122 mm, 152 mm, and heavier guns. A factory near Chelyabinsk, which had been a railroad car repair works before the war, received workers and machinery evacuated from Bessarabia in late 1941. In 1943 the plant made 76 mm and 122 mm gun ammunition. Plant No. 45 in Tashkent received machinery and workers from the Kaganovitsch railroad repair works at Dnepropetrov in 1941. Tashkent became the major locomotive repair works in central Asia, repairing 30 locomotives per month and overhauling 23 more. The plant also made 122 mm shells. The plant had 7,000 workers, 60 percent women and 15 percent youths working two 12-hour shifts.

Plant No. 62 at Schirschni near Chelyabinsk, evacuated from Yaroslavl in October 1941, employed 800 men working two 12-hour shifts making parts for antiaircraft guns and 12,000 shells per day using American copper. Plant No. 259 in Ziatoust near Chelyabinsk was built in 1917. It had 20,000 workers in 1942 after it had been expanded by evacuated machinery and workers in 1941. In 1942 it was producing rifle and artillery ammunition. Plant No. 318 in Baku, which made machinery for the oil industry before the war, by December 1942 was making 96,000 152 mm shells per month.

In summary, the more one studies the details of mobilization of the Red Army, the more impressive is the magnitude of the accomplishment. The Red Army in June 1941, in the midst of expansion, was poorly trained, equipped with obsolete weapons, and led by inexperienced commanders. That month the army was surprised despite the warnings and was destroyed at the frontiers in the opening months of the war. New armies were hastily but efficiently mobilized between July and December 1941. The new divisions, despite anecdotes of cavalry without saddles and shortages of all kinds, halted the vaunted Germany Army at the gates of Leningrad, Moscow, and Rostov. Most of these divisions had less than six months' training or had provided cadres for other divisions. The Red Army switched from defense to offense in the winter offensive of 1941–42.

Ground down by the winter offensive, the Red Army reformed a second time beginning in March 1942 but suffered serious defeats during the German summer offensive of 1942. By November 1942, a third program had developed a powerful force that defeated the Germans at Stalingrad and went on to victory.

Chapter 7

Hitler's Last Hurrah: Kursk, 1943

IN THE SPRING of 1943, after cleaning up Stalingrad and halting Marshal Erich von Manstein's counteroffensive in Ukraine, the Soviet general staff set about reconstructing the Red Army to a level comparable to that of early 1942. At the same time, new tank and artillery formations were added to the Red Army, among other major improvements, causing a rebirth of the Red Army in 1943. The Soviet military potential was renovated in four areas: leadership, organization, logistics, and weapons production. Improvements in each of these areas produced an army capable of meeting the Germans at any time or place and inflicting a crushing defeat, denying the Germans the initiative for the remainder of the war. The summers would no longer belong to the Germans; after the battle of Kursk in July 1943, the Soviet offensives continued to roll on 12 months of the year, halted only by the need to move the logistical tail forward, rather than any effort on the part of the Nazis and their satellites.

Two years of combat experience was the major factor that improved leadership. Inept generals were weeded out and talented junior commanders were promoted to higher commands. Thousands of junior-grade officers were trained in schools to command companies and battalions. Advanced officer training courses were expanded and the military academy course was extended from one to two years. In addition, more than 250,000 wounded officers returned to duty in 1943, ending the officer shortage that plagued the Red Army in 1942. Zhukov in his memoirs stated that the Russians had 93,500 officers in reserve in 1943.

Generals at the division and army level had more experience and a better understanding of their roles. In 1942 Stalin, not trusting his advisors, opposed them and insisted that they go ahead with the abortive attack at Izyum in the spring.

During the setback in Ukraine in the spring of 1942, the local commanders, aware of the overextension of their forces, requested time to rehabilitate their troops and equipment before advancing into the Nazi trap. However, their caution was overridden by Stalin, who was eager to close another noose around the German Army in Ukraine. Before Kursk in 1943, Stalin deferred to the opinion of his generals to wait for the Germans to attack first. From the very top to the platoon level, the leadership of the Red Army matured and gained Stalin's trust in 1943.

In the all-important area of logistics, the reoccupation of some of the territory lost during the summers of 1941 and 1942 partially restored the economy and the infrastructure. Two major logistical crises in 1942 were the oil supply and poor rail connections. The severe shortage of fuel in 1942 resulted from the German drive into the Caucasus, which had cut pipeline and rail connections with other areas of the country. In 1941, 33 million tons of oil were produced (86% in the Caucasus), with 15.7 million produced in the last six months, a rate of 2.5 million tons per month. In the first six months of 1942, 11.7 million tons were produced, less than 2 million tons per month. The reduction in production, only 10 million tons in the last six months (1.7 million tons per month), was barely adequate for military demands.

The major issue was moving the oil. Before the war, half the oil moved from the refineries in Baku on the west coast of the Caspian Sea via pipeline across the Caucasus, either to Rostov for rail shipment or to the Black Sea and then by ship to Odessa, Sevastopol, and other Black Sea ports. The other half, 9 million tons, moved by barge up the Volga River. Only limited supplies were sent by the Caspian Sea to Astrakhan for a tortuous roundabout rail trip to the north. The Black Sea, the rail routes, and the Volga route were all cut by the summer 1942 campaign.

The Russians destroyed the oil-producing facilities before the Germans occupied the Grozny wells in the Caucasus. As a result, the Germans were unable to return the wells to production, despite vigorous attempts by technicians. When the Germans evacuated the Grozny area, they too made every effort to prevent the Russians from reopening the oil fields. Not surprisingly, Soviet production of oil never returned to the 1941 level. Production rose slowly from 18 millions tons (1.5 million tons per month) in 1943 to 18.3 million tons in 1944 and 19.4 million tons in 1945. Nevertheless, the amount was adequate for the Soviet war effort. With the reopening of the Volga route and the availability of the rail route through Rostov after the winter of 1942–43, distribution improved immensely. The Soviet shortage of fuel for military purposes had ended by the spring of 1943.

In early 1943, the all-important railroads were repaired quickly in the liberated areas, and the supply depots were moved forward. The newly won territory provided at least one additional north-south and east-west rail line for each front. These new lines ended the long detours to the east, northwest to Moscow, and then southeast to the battle area. The line through Novy Oskol and Valuiki with branches to Kastornoie-Kursk, Kupyansk-Lisitschansk, and Starobelsk-Voroshilovgrad was an important asset, providing direct rail access to the Kursk salient from Moscow and Stalingrad. In July 1943, the Red Army was able to create vast reserves of supplies in and about the Kursk salient, adequate not only for the defensive phase but for the support of the counteroffensives that followed.

To enable the Red Army to launch offensives, the tables of organization of units were changed in late 1942 and early 1943. Additional artillery units were formed to give the infantry and the armored forces more firepower and support. Large numbers of SU regiments, a generic Soviet term that included mechanized artillery, assault guns, and self-propelled tank destroyers, were formed to counter the increasing power of the new German tanks. The emphasis was not on new rifle divisions, rifle brigades, and tank brigades but rather on refitting existing units, which were reinforced, trained, and equipped with vastly improved equipment during 1943.

The primary building block of the Red Army was the rifle division. The authorized size of the division had been reduced in 1942 to 9,435 men in three rifle regiments, an artillery regiment, and other support units. In June 1943, the division organization again was reduced, dropping to 9,380 men, but retaining the thirty-two 76 mm guns, twelve 122 mm howitzers, 160 mortars, forty-eight 57 mm antitank guns, 212 antitank rifles, 434 light machine guns, 111 heavy machine guns, 124 vehicles, and 1,700 horses. However, the number of rifles was reduced by 200 and replaced by an increase in machine pistols from 727 to 1,048. The latter change was a major improvement in the firepower of the rifle companies. One out of seven men was armed with an automatic weapon.

Most Soviet rifle divisions were near authorized strength in the summer of 1943. A German report estimated that Soviet rifle divisions on the Leningrad Front had 8,000 men, with 1,900 men in each of the three rifle regiments. The rifle company had 120 men and the rifle battalion 513 men. The total for nine battalions was 4,617 men. The remainder were in the supporting units. Rifle divisions on the Voronezh Front were increased to between 8,000 and 9,000 men in the first half of 1943, while the Central Front divisions were raised to 7,000 to 7,500. In May 1943, for example, 3,000 men from the 15th, 19th, and 23rd replacement training regiments in Chelyabinsk were transported by rail to the 42nd Guards Rifle Division in the Kursk area. Additional smaller replacement groups with from 30 to 50 men continued to arrive in June.

After the heavy fighting in July and August 1943, divisional strength dropped below 6,000 as the Soviets diverted much of the available manpower to combat support units, tank brigades, artillery regiments, and tank destroyer brigades.

A massive restructuring occurred in 1943 as, for example, two existing rifle brigades were joined to form a new rifle division or a rifle brigade was reinforced with a replacement regiment and some artillery battalions to form a new division (tables 7.1–7.8). This reorganization began in earnest in May 1943. In some instances, the new division was immediately assigned to a field army; in others a few months elapsed before the new division was moved into a field army.

Table 7.1 Rifle Divisions Created in February 1943

Division	Military District	Date Assigned	Front/Army
4B	Moscow	7/43	Bryansk 11
Siberiankvd/140D	Siberia	2/43	Center 70
CenAsiankvd/162C	Central Asia	2/43	Center 70
10nkvd/181C	?	2/43	Center 70

A total of 72 rifle divisions were created in 1943, but many were held back in reserve. On January 1, 1943, there were 369 rifle divisions at the front, 8 in reserve, and 30 in the military districts and the Far East, for a total of 407. On July 1, 1943, there were 376 at the front, 58 in reserve (an increase of 50), and 28 in the districts and the Far East, for a total of 462—a total increase of 55. New divisions were formed by upgrading brigades to divisions. The number of rifle brigades declined from 177 on January 1, 1943, to only 98 on July 1. The number of brigades at the front declined from 134 to only 66 as many were upgraded to divisions. Two of the four rifle battalion brigades were roughly equal to one 9-battalion division, so the loss of 79 brigades (equal to 39.5 divisions) reduced the impact of the net gain. However, in the reorganization, many understrength rifle brigades emerged as rehabilitated rifle divisions with 9,000 men. Most of the new divisions were created by reinforcing worn-out brigades.

The new divisions were of high quality, with young men. An example was the 226th Rifle Division. The third division to bear this number was formed in Lgov in July 1943 using the 129th Rifle Brigade as a cadre. Lgov is located directly west of Kursk on the Seim River, which was slightly more than 20 miles from the front line, so this reformation occurred just behind the front. The previous 226th Rifle Division had been redesignated the 95th Guards Rifle Division in May 1943.

The men in the new 226th Division ranged in age from 21 to 46, but 70 percent were ages 21 to 27. Russians made up 90 percent of the men. Based on the age and nationality of the men, the 129th Brigade received an influx of new young men when the division was formed. Apparently the four rifle battalions of the brigade were divided to form cadres for the nine battalions of the division, and new recruits came in to fill out the new battalions. The transition happened very

Table 7.2 Rifle Divisions Created in March 1943

Division	Military District	Date Assigned	Front/Army	Cadre
63B	Moscow	7/43	West 21	45rb
70B	Moscow	7/43	West 21	86Arb
96C	Northwest	7/43	Bryansk 11	160, 117rb
119C	Moscow	7/43	West 21	161rb

Table 7.3   Rifle Divisions Created in Moscow and Archangel Districts in April 1943

	Division	Date Assigned	Front/Army	Cadre
Moscow	23B	4/43	Steppe 47	7rb, 76marineb
	29C	4/43	Steppe 47	10Brb, 68rb
	30B	4/43	Steppe 47	16rb, 119rb
	38C	7/43	Steppe 47	40rb
	45B	4/43	Karelian 26	67marineb, duplicate 186rd
	51B	7/43	West 21	15rb
	62C	7/43	West 21	44rb
	76B	7/43	West 21	87rb
	95C	7/43	West 21	121rb
	97C	4/43	Bryansk 61	108rb, 110rb
	98C	4/43	Leningrad 55	162rb, 250rb
	120C	4/43	Leningrad 67	11marineb, 142marineb
	124C	4/43	Leningrad 67	138rb, 56Brb
Archangel	25B		No field army assignment	

quickly as the brigade still appeared in the 60th Army in the Soviet order of battle on July 1, 1943, and on August 1 the division appeared in the 24th Corps. The Germans continued to identify the unit as the 129th Brigade in the 24th Corps in early July. The 24th Corps was in the 60th Army reserve in July 1943, located at the tip of the Kursk bulge where little activity was expected.

Fourteen new tank brigades were created in 1943, a rather small number considering the activity in 1942 and the enormous numbers of tanks coming off the assembly lines (table 7.9). Only five of the new tank brigades were assigned to active fronts, two each to the Bryansk and Voronezh fronts and one to the Western Front.

Beginning in January, 12 rifle brigades were formed in 1943 (table 7.10). Five of these brigades were later upgraded to rifle divisions and four were abolished within a few months. Only three survived to the end of the war in central Asia and the Far East. Only two additional rifle brigades were formed during the remainder of the war: the 8th East Brigade, which was formed by the East 25th Army in October 1944 and abolished in December 1944; and the 31st Mountain Brigade, which was formed in the Stavka Reserve in January 1945 and assigned to the 4th Ukrainian Front in February 1945. The Red Army was definitely moving away from the rifle brigade organization.

While the rifle divisions were being reinforced and rifle brigades were being transformed into divisions, major increases also were made in the combat support units. This restructuring was made possible by a torrent of new weapons. Soviet

Table 7.4 Rifle Divisions Created in May 1943

Division	Date Assigned	Front/Army	Cadre
118C	5/43	South 28	152rb
130C	5/43	South 44	156rb, 159rb
99B	5/43	South 51	99Brb
127C	5/43	South 5sh	52Brb, 98Brb
199C	7/43	Bryansk 11	120B, 147rb
110C	5/43	Bryansk 61	105mb, 116mb
204B	5/43	Voronezh 38	37rb
136C	8/43	Voronezh 52	118Bmb, 140Arb
138B	5/43	Stavka 52	6mb, 109Brb
173C	7/43	West 5	150rb, 135Brb
174C	7/43	West 21	28, 25Brb
153C	7/43	West 68	122B, 136rb
154B	7/43	West 68	130rb, 82mb
156B	7/43	West 68	26rb, 163rb
157B	7/43	West 68	148rb, 34Brb
159C	7/43	West 68	20Brb, 49 skib, 132rb
192B	7/43	West 68	112rb, 64rb
199B	7/43	West 68	126rb, 128rb
201B	5/43	Leningrad	23rb, 27rb, 13rb

factories were turning out ample supplies of all kinds of weapons to equip the new troops. After the disaster of 1941 and the hurried evacuation of many factories, Soviet industry was back in stride by mid-1942, but in 1943 production reached a point that available stocks exceeded demand and in 1944, production of some weapons either leveled off or was reduced.

Beginning with the basic weapon, the rifle or carbine issued most widely to troops, production in 1942 reached 4 million. Production was reduced to 3.4 million in 1943 and further reduced to 2.4 million in 1944. The Red Army lost

Table 7.5 New Divisions Formed in June 1943

Division	Date Assigned	Front/Army	Cadre
257C	7/43	North Caucasus	56, 90, 62mb, ?9Brb, 60rb
205B	6/43	Karelian 26	186Wrd, 60rb
221B	6/43	South	5sh, 79Brb
228C	6/43	Southwest 6	106rb
230B	6/43	Southwest 1G	229rb
207C	6/43	West 5	40rb, 153Brb
208B/435rd	6/43	West 5	35rb, 49rb
212B	6/43	West 50	4rb, 125rb
218B	7/43	Voronezh 47	51Brb, 165rb

Table 7.6   New Rifle Divisions Formed in July 1943

Division	District	Date Assigned	Front/Army	Cadre
231B	Far East	7/43	East 1	154 rifle reg
255B	Far East	7/43	East 15	
258C	Far East	7/43	East 25	157 East rifle reg
264C	Far East	7/43	East 35	
275B	Transbaikal	7/43	Transbaikal	
278C	Transbaikal	7/43	Transbaikal 36	
284C	Transbaikal	7/43	Transbaikal 17	
292C	Transbaikal	7/43	Transbaikal	109 East, 35 rifle reg
293B	Transbaikal	7/43	Transbaikal	
298C	Transbaikal	7/43	Transbaikal 36	
296B	Transcaucasus	7/43	Transcaucasus	
301C	Steppe Front	8/43	South 5sh	34B, 157rb
297B		7/43	Southwest 8G	104, 253rb
226B		7/43	Center 60	42, 129rb

only 198,000 rifles and carbines in the Voronezh and Kharkov operations in March 1943, compared to 1,764,000 in the Kiev disaster in 1941.

The downward trend in rifle production reflected not only fewer losses, but also a movement toward more automatic weapons in the rifle company. The number of machine pistols in the rifle regiment increased from 216 in 1942 to 450 in the summer of 1943. One-fourth of the men in the rifle companies had machine pistols. Production of machine pistols increased from 1,560,000 in 1942 to 2,060,000 in 1943. The stock on hand increased from 100,000 on January 1, 1942, to 2,640,000 on January 1, 1944. The ratio of rifles to machine pistols changed from 37 to 1 in January 1942 to 5 to 1 in January 1943. Providing the rifle company with an ample supply of machine pistols increased the firepower of the company, both on defense and offense.

The rifle companies also received more light machine guns, the most effective weapon in delivering a high volume of fire both in defense and offense. Light machine gun production increased from 173,000 in 1942 to 250,000 in 1943, increasing the number on hand at the end of 1943 to 344,000 from 177,000 at the beginning of the year. By July 1943, there were ample stocks to fill the needs of the infantry. A similar increase took place in heavy machine guns: Production increased from 58,000 in 1942 to 90,500 in 1943, and in 1943 the stock increased

Table 7.7   New Rifle Divisions Formed in August 1943

Division	Date Assigned	Front/Army	Cadre
227B	8/43	North Caucasus 9	19rb, 84mb
304B	8/43	North Caucasus 9	43Brb, 256rb

Table 7.8 New Divisions Formed in September and October 1943

	Division	District	Date Assigned	Front/Army	Cadre
September	300B	Far East	9/43	East	
	386B	Far East	9/43	East 25	Rifle brigade
	316C	?	9/43	North Caucasus 9	57rb, 131rb
	1B	?	9/43	2 Baltic 6G	31rb, 100rb
	150C	?	9/43	Northwest 34	127, 144, 151rb
October	319C		10/43	2 Baltic 22	32, 33, 46rb

from 63,500 to 133,000, more than double. This immense outpouring of weapons from Soviet factories provided the new and rebuilt units with ample supplies. All of the prisoners taken by the Germans at Kursk reported that the rifle companies were fully equipped.

By June 1943, the allotment of machine pistols to the rifle division increased to 1,500 and machine guns to 666. The rifle company then had 35 machine pistols, 18 light machine guns, and one heavy machine gun. Some divisions had more than the authorized number. The 112th Guard Rifle Regiment in July 1943 had 745 machine pistols, compared to the authorized 450. The 5th Company of the 574th Rifle Regiment had 70 machine pistols instead of the authorized 35. These are only two of the many examples of supplies of automatic weapons exceeding the established number.

Russian production of artillery came into full swing in 1943. Between November 1942 and July 1943, the Russians produced 175,067 guns and mortars but lost 148,177 in the costly defeats in Ukraine. Still, the total stock grew from

Table 7.9 Tank Brigades Created in 1943

Date Formed	Brigade	District/Army	Date Assigned	Front/Army
1/43	230	Transcaucasus Front	1/43	Transcaucasus
2/43	226	Transcaucasus 45	2/43	Transcaucasus 45
2/43	227	Transcaucasus 45	2/43	Transcaucasus 45
3/43	244	Ural	7/43	Bryansk 4T
3/43	243	Ural	7/43	Bryansk
4/43	233	Steppe Front	7/43	West
4/43	USSUR	East 1	4/43	East 1
4/43	Coastal	East	4/43	East 25
4/43	Birski	East	4/43	East 15
5/43	237	Voronezh 1T	5/43	Voronezh 1T
5/43	242	Voronezh 1T	5/43	Voronezh 1T
7/43	257	East 1	7/43	East 1
7/43	258	East 2	7/43	East 2
7/43	259	East 25	7/43	East 25

Table 7.10 Rifle Brigades Formed in 1943

	Brigade	Military District	Date Assigned	Front/Army	Date Abolished
January	120B/197C	Volga	5/43	Volga District	
	122B/153C	South Ural	5/43	Ural District	
	132B/159C	South Ural	5/43	Ural District	
	134B	South Ural			3/43
	163B	Volga			4/43
February	90B/257C	Transcaucasus			
	94B	Transcaucasus			3/43
	133B	Transcaucasus			3/43?
	135B/173C	Archangel	5/43	Moscow District	
March	93C	Central Asia	3/43		
	105	Central Asia	3/43		
July	285	East	7/43		

72,500 in November 1942 to 98,790 in July 1943, the greatest number of guns and mortars on hand during the war. Subsequent reductions in production leveled the supply at 90,000. The Russian production battle had been won, and there would be no shortages of weapons in the future.

The program to reinforce the combat support units was evident in early 1943, as units assigned to the field armies increased dramatically. In 1942 the number of artillery, mortar, and antitank regiments assigned to army commands had been more or less arbitrary, depending on the mission of the army. In 1943 the armies received a minimum assignment of supporting units to be supplemented from the Stavka Reserve, as dictated by the role of the army in a particular operation.

In 1943, each field army was assigned an antiaircraft regiment, a gun artillery regiment with 152 mm guns, a mortar regiment with thirty-six 120 mm mortars, and a tank destroyer regiment with twenty-four 76 mm antitank guns. In April 1943, each army was authorized an additional 37 mm antiaircraft regiment. The field army in 1943 had over 2,000 guns and mortars.

The artillery was reorganized in 1943. The artillery divisions, formed in October 1942 to provide centralized control for the large numbers of guns used to break through the German defenses, had proved successful in the Stalingrad operation. However, the eight independent regiments with 168 guns were difficult to control, especially as the various types of regiments had differing roles in a battle. In December 1942, the regiments were divided into brigades by type, and in April 1943 the artillery division was reinforced with additional brigades.

The April 1943 organization called for a light artillery brigade with three 76 mm gun regiments, a howitzer brigade with three 122 mm howitzer regiments, a heavy howitzer brigade with three 152 mm howitzer regiments, a gun brigade with three 152 mm gun regiments, a long-range howitzer brigade with four

203 mm howitzer battalions, and a mortar brigade with three 120 mm mortar regiments. The 1943 artillery division had seventy-two 76 mm guns, eighty-four 122 mm howitzers, thirty-two 152 mm howitzers, thirty-six 152 mm guns, twenty-four 203 mm howitzers, and one hundred eight 120 mm mortars, for a total of 356 guns and mortars, compared to 168 in the 1942 division. The addition of heavier guns almost doubled the firepower of the artillery division.

When the Red Army moved to the offensive, more sophisticated guns and howitzers were required. Light and medium mortar production declined by the end of 1942. The heavier mortars were special-purpose artillery pieces, and their numbers grew in the final years. During the war new types were introduced, the M1941 82 mm, the M1943 120 mm, and a heavier model, the M1943 160 mm. Production of 82 mm and 120 mm mortars increased in 1942. In the first half of the year, 45,485 82 mm mortars and 10,183 120 mm mortars were made; in the second half, 55,378 82 mm and 15,164 120 mm mortars. In 1943 the production of all types of mortars declined to 69,500, and in 1944 only 7,100 were made. Losses on the battlefield were apparently minor. The new mortar regiments used heavy mortars. Later mortar production also provided rifle divisions with heavier mortars and replaced losses. Total production from 1941 to 1945 was 351,800, compared to 79,000 produced by the Germans.

The number of artillery divisions increased from 25 on January 1, 1943, to 28 on April 1 and then declined to 25 on July 1. The guards mortar divisions with rocket launchers remained at 7. Some 17 new independent artillery brigades were formed, but the number of independent artillery regiments declined from 271 on January 1, 1943, to 234 on July 1, the result of converting many artillery regiments to the role of tank destroyers or combining them into the new brigades.

One artillery role that was completely overhauled was the tank destroyer function. In 1942, the antitank guns were formed into destroyer brigades with two or three mixed regiments of 76 mm, 45 mm, and 37 mm guns plus a rifle battalion armed with antitank rifles. Three of these brigades were at times joined to form a destroyer division. The division was too large to control, and the mixture of guns in the regiments was a challenge to the regimental commander. In April 1943, the destroyer division was eliminated, and some destroyer brigades were reorganized as tank destroyer brigades containing two 76 mm gun regiments and one 57 mm or 45 mm gun regiment.

The most crucial factor in the defense at Kursk was the distribution of the antitank guns. In Zhukov's proposal to Stalin on April 8, 1943, he stressed the need to strengthen the antitank defense of the Central and Voronezh fronts by moving units from other sectors. To control the increased number of antitank guns, new tank destroyer brigades were activated, providing central control of 60 to 72 guns. By July 1, 1943, 27 of the brigades (including 81 regiments) had been formed and 24 were at the front. A few of the old-type destroyer brigades continued in action at Kursk. The tank destroyer brigades played an incredibly significant role. The brigade commander controlled the antitank defense of a sector, creating antitank strong points with four or more guns and with interlocking fire with other strong points. The brigade commander held a reserve that could move swiftly (the guns were drawn by trucks, not horses) to any threatened point. The front commander could also hold a brigade or more in reserve to counter any tank penetration of the first line of defense. A brigade with 60 guns was sufficient to stop a panzer division, though the brigade might lose most of its guns in the process if the Germans used Tiger tanks to combat the antitank guns.

Beginning in April 1943, the Soviets formed 30 antitank battalions to be assigned to the tank and mechanized corps. The battalions were armed with 85 mm towed antiaircraft guns on special mounts with crews trained as antitank gunners. The 85 mm gun was a match for the 88 mm gun on the Tiger. Many, although not all, of the tank and mechanized corps at Kursk had been reinforced with 85 mm antitank battalions. Other battalions were still in training in the Moscow Military District.

The Russians continued to have faith in the antitank rifle, a long high-velocity weapon firing a 14.5 mm projectile. The Degtyarev antitank rifle had a muzzle velocity of 1,010 meters per second and could inflict damage on the Panzer III or on the tracks of the heavier German tanks. An example of the antitank rifle organizations was the 121st Independent Antitank Battalion established in March 1943 near Moscow. The men had been inducted in the winter of 1942–43 from the classes of 1923, 1924, and 1925 and were 18 to 20 years old. The enlisted men came through the 131st Replacement Regiment and the officers from a school at Pokrov near Moscow. The battalion had three companies, each with 70 men and 18 to 20 antitank rifles. On April 5, 1943, less than a month after being formed, the battalion was sent by rail to Staryi Oskol and from there marched to Korotscha. Later the battalion was assigned to the 69th Army.

The antiaircraft forces with the field army increased in number in the first six months of 1943, probably as a result of the heavy losses to air attack in early 1943. The number of antiaircraft divisions with the field armies and training in the districts increased from 27 on January 1, 1943, to 48 on July 1. These antiaircraft divisions had three regiments with 37 mm guns and one regiment with 85 mm guns that also could serve as heavy antitank guns in the same way that the Germans used their 88 mm antiaircraft guns. The Russian 85 mm gun was a close relative of the German 88 mm gun, with many common design characteristics. The antiaircraft division had a total of forty-eight 37 mm guns and sixteen 85 mm guns.

The number of independent antiaircraft regiments increased from 123 on January 1, 1943, to 183 on July 1, including 24 in the PVO, the home antiaircraft defense command. The total of 109 independent antiaircraft battalions remained stable, with more than half the battalions at the front. Each cavalry, tank, and mechanized corps had an antiaircraft battalion with four batteries of 37 mm guns and a company of machine guns. An antiaircraft company was added to the armored brigades to protect against German ground attack aircraft. Each of these companies had nine heavy machine guns. The cavalry divisions were given a two-company battalion of 18 machine guns to protect the vulnerable horsemen.

In June 1943, 15 new antiaircraft divisions were formed in the PVO. Over a hundred new battalions and regiments were organized in that month to fill the divisions. Three-fourths of the personnel of these new units were women. This remarkable expansion reflected the increased availability of antiaircraft guns, available personnel, and the recognition that the factories and communications system needed protection from Luftwaffe attacks. Although antiaircraft guns did not destroy a large percentage of attacking aircraft, the very presence of the guns prevented the attackers from flying low and making accurate bomb runs. Even if the guns only damaged German aircraft, the planes required repairs and sometimes were scrapped. Thus the antiaircraft guns were a powerful deterrent to air attacks on Russian cities and railroads.

The increase in artillery, tank destroyer, and antiaircraft units in the first six months of 1943 radically altered the firepower of the Red Army, especially the creation of the 27 tank destroyer brigades and 36 antiaircraft divisions. Both of these units were essentially defensive formations to protect the troops from German tank and air attack. The lessons of 1942 had been well learned. The troops could not be left defenseless in the face of German tanks and aircraft, as happened in Ukraine in the summer of 1942. The Soviet high command saw the problem and applied solutions.

Tank production from November 1942 to July 1943 reached 15,708 and imports were 2,413, making a total of 18,121. The number of tanks in the field armies on the front increased to 9,580 in July 1943, with more in the supply line and depots.

The Russians did not subscribe to the theory that the best antitank weapon was another tank, but they did make major changes in the spring and summer of 1943. Later models of the T-34 had a larger turret to make space for the M1940 76 mm gun with a 41.5-caliber barrel for higher velocity. In 1943 the Russians modified the T-34 by replacing the 76 mm gun with the M1939 85 mm antiaircraft gun, producing the T-34/85. The weight increased to 32 tons, the crew to five, and the armor to 90 mm, but the speed remained at 55 km per hour. The Russians stressed the heavy projectile approach instead of high velocity. The 85 mm gun had a heavier projectile than the 75 mm gun used on the German Panther, but the latter was able to penetrate thicker armor at longer ranges.

The tank forces needed a lighter version of the KV to achieve a better balance between engine power and weight to give greater speed. The KV-1S entered production in August 1942, and by April 1943 the Soviets had built 1,370 for the heavy tank regiments.

In October 1943, a further development of the KV was the KV-85, equipped with the 85 mm antiaircraft gun. Production of the JS-1 heavy tank armed with a 122 mm gun to replace the KVs began in December 1943. The JS-2 weighed 46 tons, had a crew of four, a 122 mm gun, 90–120 mm of armor, and a speed of 37 km per hour.

The Germans estimated the breakdown of monthly Soviet production by factory in 1943. Although these numbers do not coincide exactly with Soviet totals, they do give an approximation of the relative importance of the plants. According to German estimates, the Gorki Molotov plant made 550 T-70s, the GAZ plant made 380 SU-76s, the Gorki Sormovo plant made 300 T-34s, the Kuibyshev plant made 150 T-70s, the Kirov plant made 450 SU-76s, the Nishnij Tagil plant made 550 T-34s, the Chelyabinsk plant made 100 T-34s and 100 KVs, the Omsk plant made 150 T-34s, and the Sverdlovsk plant made 200 T-34s.

The composition and strength of the armored units was increased, although the number remained somewhat constant. The concept of the tank army was revived in early 1943 with a radical change in doctrine, organization, and strength. Previous tank armies had included both tank formations and marching infantry. The new tank armies were completely motorized. Rifle divisions were seldom attached to the tank armies, which gained complete mobility. The 1943 tank army usually had two tank corps, one mechanized corps, a motorcycle regiment, an antiaircraft division (four regiments), a tank destroyer regiment, a howitzer regiment, and a guards mortar regiment of rocket launchers. In support, the tank army had a service regiment, an engineer battalion, a motor transport regiment, two tank repair battalions, and medical and other service units, including a special unit for the evacuation of captured tanks. The tank army had over 600 tanks and 22 battalions of motorized infantry.

The 1943 tank corps had three tank brigades each with two tank battalions and a motorized rifle battalion, a mechanized brigade with three motorized battalions, and a tank regiment especially fitted to carry riflemen, three SU regiments, a mortar regiment, a light artillery regiment, a guards mortar battalion, an armored car battalion, an engineer battalion, and a service battalion. The tank corps had a total of 10,977 men (an increase from 7,800 men in the 1942 corps), 208 T-34 tanks (increased from 98 medium and 70 light tanks in 1942), 49 SUs, 60 guns and mortars, and eight rocket launchers in the guards mortar battalion. In comparison, German panzer divisions had only about 150 tanks and assault guns.

The mechanized corps of 1943 was an even more powerful unit. The corps had three mechanized brigades, each with three motorized battalions and a tank regiment modified to carry riflemen, a tank brigade with two tank battalions and a motorized battalion, three tank regiments, three SU regiments, a mortar regiment, a light artillery regiment, a guards mortar battalion, an armored car battalion, an engineer battalion, and a service battalion. The corps had 15,018 men, 229 tanks and assault guns (including 162 T-34s, 42 light tanks, and 25 assault guns), 108 guns and mortars, and eight rocket launchers.

Independent tank brigades were also brought up to the new tables of organization when possible, but often light tanks and lend-lease tanks were issued to the independent brigades. The independent tank brigades were more often used for infantry support, along with the assault guns. Independent tank regiments were also formed for use with the infantry, and in 1943 a new type of tank regiment equipped with specially modified T-34s to clear minefields was introduced. The mine-clearing tank regiment had 22 T-34s and 18 mine-clearing vehicles.

Four additional tank corps were created in the first six months of 1943, increasing the number to 24. The number of mechanized corps increased from 8 to 13. The number of independent tank brigades declined from 114 to 101 on July 1, 1943, while the number of independent tank regiments increased from 77 to 110. These changes reflected a continuing Soviet allocation of substantial numbers of tanks to direct support of the infantry. At Kursk, half of the available tanks were in tank brigades and regiments assigned to the field armies. There were 211 tank brigades and regiments available to support 462 rifle divisions and 98 rifle brigades on July 1, 1943.

The major change in the armored force was the reorganization of the assault gun or SU regiments in early 1943. In 1942 the Russians realized the need for a mobile 76 mm gun, both as an infantry support gun and as a tank destroyer. A major innovation was the development of self-propelled artillery. The SU-76 was a 76 mm gun mounted on a light tank chassis. The 76 mm gun had greater range than the German 50 mm antitank gun and was equal to the 75 mm antitank gun. The concept of the SU-76 was that it would engage targets (antitank guns, machine guns, and tanks) at distances beyond the effective range of its targets. The SU-76 was best at providing escort artillery fire. It was not successful in the tank role: The open top invited grenades and machine gun fire; the armor was thin; and the SU had no machine gun. Therefore, it could not drive infantry from trenches without riflemen for protection. However, the gun could destroy bunkers and machine gun nests, making the job of the infantry easier. In the escort role, the SU was especially useful in breaking through the German antitank gun line.

The Soviets developed the SU-122 with the 122 mm M1938 M30 howitzer in late 1942 using the T-34 chassis. The howitzer had a muzzle velocity of 500 meters per second, but the heavy weight of the 21.7 kg shell quickly reduced the velocity and its ability to penetrate armor. The gun was a poor antitank weapon except at short range. Without a high velocity at the point of impact, a projectile could not penetrate the armor. However, a heavy projectile had the total energy to blow a turret off a tank.

The SU-85 tank destroyer, developed late in 1943, mounted a D-5S antiaircraft gun on a T-34 chassis. The gun had a muzzle velocity of 880 meters per second, and the high velocity held for a greater distance because of the light weight of the shell. The 85 mm gun performed much better in penetrating armor at long range than the 122 mm howitzer. Beginning in August 1943, the SU-85 regiments had four batteries, each with four SU-85s. The 1438th Mechanized Artillery Regiment, equipped with SU-122s, suffered heavy losses at Kharkov and was sent to Pravda, near Moscow, in late 1943. There the regiment was reequipped with 16 SU-85s plus a T-34 command tank.

The Russians formed seven light mechanized artillery brigades in late 1943 equipped with the SU-57, the Soviet designation for the American T48 half-track mounting an American M2 57 mm antitank gun, the American version of the British 6-pounder. In 1942 the United States mounted the M1 57 mm antitank gun on the basic M3 half-track. The gun had a muzzle velocity of 2,720 feet per second (900 meters per second). The lightweight shell (6.25 pounds, 2.8 kg) would retain this velocity for a considerable distance. The German analysis rated the M2 57 mm gun with a muzzle velocity of 830 meters per second, effective at 800 meters and able to penetrate 70 mm of armor at 300 meters. With front armor on the Mark IV of 85 mm and side armor of only 50 mm on the Panther and only 80 mm on the Tiger, the 57 mm gun was still useful at close range. Mounting the gun on a half-track gave it the mobility to find a desirable hull-down position.

By July 1942, the Russians had developed three prototypes: the SU-76 (a 76 mm gun on a T-60 or T-70 chassis), the SU-122 (a 122 mm howitzer on the chassis of a captured German Mark III), and the AA SU-37 (a 37 mm antiaircraft gun on a T-60 chassis). The Russians decided on December 9, 1942, to produce the SU-76, the AA SU-37, and the SU-122 using a T-34 chassis. But the mixture of the SU-76 and the SU-122 in the same regiment was a failure. The two chassis moved across rough terrain at different speeds, and the guns were not appropriate for the same targets.

SU-76 production began in December 1942 in the factories at Gorki and Kirov that had previously produced the T-70 light tank. The SU-76 used the T-70 chassis and was easy to manufacture. Production of the T-70 continued for a time, then halted so that the factories could devote all their capacity to the SU-76. The SU-76 mounted the comparatively high-velocity gun used as the divisional artillery piece, making it satisfactory for all three roles: infantry support, antitank defense, and indirect fire. An improved model, the SU-76M, was produced in May 1943.

The Germans unveiled the Tiger in November 1942. To cope with the Tiger, the Soviets needed a heavy self-propelled tank destroyer. In reaction to the Tiger tank, the SU-85 and an SU-152 were developed in 1943. Production of the SU-152 began in March 1943 using an ML-20 (Model 1937) 152 mm gun-howitzer on a KV-1S chassis. The ML-20 fired a 43.6 kg shell with a muzzle velocity of 655 meters per second. At short range, the projectile delivered a powerful blow to even the heaviest tank. The JS chassis replaced the KV in 1943, and few of the SU-152s were made.

The SU regiments used the newly developed SU-76 mounted on a light tank chassis. The SU-122 mounted a 122 mm howitzer on a T-34 chassis, and the SU-152 mounted a 152 mm howitzer on the KV chassis. By mid-1943 the Russians had formed three types of SU regiments, having tried unsuccessfully to combine several types in a single regiment. The SU-76 regiment had four batteries of 5 guns plus a command SU for a total of 21 in the regiment. The SU-122 regiment had four batteries of 4 guns, with a total of 16 guns and one T-34 tank. The SU-152s were organized in regiments with four batteries of 3 guns each, for a total of 12 guns and a KV tank. The cadres for the new SU regiments probably came from disbanded tank brigades. Nearly 20 tank brigades disappeared from the Soviet order of battle in May and June 1943. The SU regiments were designed to counter the heavy tanks being developed by the Germans. The Soviets first encountered the Tiger in the Leningrad area in November 1942 and were immediately moved to find an antidote. By eliminating the turret and in most cases the overhead armor, a chassis could carry a much heavier gun. Theoretically, the SU would use its larger gun to destroy its opponent while remaining beyond the range of the gun mounted on the enemy tank.

Most of the SU regiments were attached to tank and mechanized corps, but some were attached to the infantry. The Russians used SUs in four ways: (1) to provide direct support for tank attacks; (2) to establish an antitank gun line behind tanks; (3) to attack strong points, machine gun nests, antitank guns, and tanks; and (4) to provide indirect fire for the infantry in defense.

The Russians had formed 41 of the new SU regiments by April 1, 1943, but only 9 were at the front and 4 in reserve, with the remaining 28 still training in the military districts. By July 1, 21 were at the front and 3 in reserve, with only 17 still training. Independent tank destroyer regiments with 20 or 24 guns of 76 mm or 45 mm were held in front reserve or assigned to army reserves. The number of independent tank destroyer regiments remained static, with 171 in January and 163 in July 1943, despite the rapid increase in the number of regiments assigned to tank destroyer brigades.

Based on the Kursk experience, production of SUs increased in the second half of 1943. The Russians concentrated on a few types of SUs, making thousands of SU-76s by the end of the war, with slight modifications. Of the 21,000 SUs manufactured, 59 percent were light SUs armed with the 76 mm gun; 21.5 percent were mediums with 85 mm guns, 100 mm guns, and 122 mm howitzers; and 19.5 percent were heavy, with 122 mm and 152 mm guns.

The cavalry organization was standardized in early 1943. The role of the cavalry was then clearly defined to work in cooperation with the armored force. There were seven cavalry corps in 1943, each with three divisions, a tank destroyer regiment (24 guns of 76 mm), an SU regiment (20 SU-76s), an antiaircraft regiment, a guards mortar regiment, a heavy tank destroyer battalion, and service units. Each division had a tank regiment with 29 T-34s and 16 T-70 light tanks. The cavalry corps had a total of 117 tanks, approximately equal to the number in a German panzer division at the time. The corps had 21,000 men and 19,000 horses.

Many of the cavalry divisions had been disbanded earlier because of the shortage of horses. In the first six months of 1943, 4 more divisions were disbanded, leaving 21 in the seven corps on the German front and 6 in the Far East. On July 1, 1943, five of the cavalry corps were held in reserve waiting for the counteroffensives to exploit the breakthroughs. After November 1942, the cavalry corps were usually joined with a tank corps to form horse mechanized groups to exploit breakthroughs. The cavalry was more mobile than the truck-mounted infantry in the mechanized corps across country and in mud and snow, making the horse mechanized group preferable in bad terrain.

The airborne forces also witnessed a major expansion. The number of divisions remained stable at 10, all retained in the Stavka Reserve, but 20 new guards airborne brigades were formed in April and May and held in the Stavka Reserve. The men in the airborne divisions were the elite of the Red Army and formed a strong reserve force in the Moscow area to ensure the safety of the capital. The diversion of so many (probably 60,000) excellent troops to the new brigades that performed a reserve activity was another indication of the plentiful supply of manpower in the spring of 1943.

Some of the airborne divisions were used at Kursk. The 9th Guards Parachute Division had been moved by rail from Gorki to Staryi Oskol in May 1943 and on July 9 was ordered to move to Prokorovka as part of the 5th Guards Tank Army. The division was a parachute troop in name only; the men had no jump training or parachute equipment.

During the first half of 1943, the PVO was expanded and reorganized. The previous organization was replaced by two fronts (East and West) and three zones (Far East, Transbaikal, and Central Asia). Corps areas and division areas were named after the cities they defended, usually significant military targets such as the oil fields at Grozny and the tank plants at Saratov and Yaroslavl. The corps and division areas had varying numbers of regiments and battalions, with the Moscow area having the largest contingent. Most PVO antiaircraft divisions had five regiments of twenty 85 mm guns each, a battalion of 37 mm guns, and a searchlight regiment.

The rapid expansion of the total number of units in the Red Army in early 1943 occurred at the same time that battle-worn rifle divisions were being restored to full strength in men and equipment. By July 1943, the Red Army had absorbed a million new recruits, replaced losses in existing units, and formed hundreds of new battalions, regiments, brigades, and divisions. All of this activity compelled the Russian economy to provide enormous quantities of equipment and weapons.

The stocks of artillery grew rapidly in 1943. Production of antiaircraft guns increased from 6,800 in 1942 to 12,200 in 1943, and the stocks on hand increased from 13,100 in January to 24,600 in December, providing the weapons for the explosive growth in the number of antiaircraft units. Field artillery production declined from 30,100 in 1942 to 22,100 in 1943 as production facilities were diverted to tank guns, antiaircraft, and antitank gun production. Losses were minuscule (only 5,700 guns in 1943), and the number of pieces on hand increased in 1943 from 36,700 in January to 53,100 in December. Production was reduced because more guns were available than were needed.

Tank and SU deliveries leveled off in 1943, with only 22,900 received compared to 27,900 in 1942. Total Soviet tank and SU receipts included both production and lend-lease tanks, with no breakdown in the Soviet sources. About 4,000 tanks came from the United States and Great Britain in 1943. The decline in tank production resulted from the beginning of SU production, which increased from less than 100 in 1942 to 4,400 in 1943. Production was also shifted to heavier tanks. The receipts of light tanks declined from 11,900 to 5,700 in this period as production was diverted to produce the SU-76, and lend-lease provided more medium tanks instead of the light tanks provided in 1942.

Receipts of medium tanks increased from 13,400 to 16,300 as more T-34s were built and the West delivered more medium tanks. Production of the KV dropped from 2,600 to only 900 as the Russian engineers sought ways to produce a more effective heavy tank.

The total stock of tanks and SUs on hand decreased slightly from 28,000 as production matched the numbers of tanks lost on the battlefield. Soviet statistics published prior to 1995 vary considerably from these totals because only the authorized number of tanks in units at the front were included. Tanks in depots, training schools, and units in the military districts were omitted. Red Army tank units after June 1943 often went into battle with large numbers of replacement tanks and crews on the fronts and in army replacement regiments. These tanks were able to replace losses quickly, while the tank replacement regiments were refilled from tank depots located at the major tank factories.

The expansion of the Red Army in early 1943 also benefitted from increased deliveries of lend-lease supplies. The improvement of port facilities and railroads in Iran made possible major lend-lease deliveries, especially trucks so necessary to improve the Red Army supply system. In 1942 the United States delivered 2,740,000 tons of supplies to the Soviet Union, but only 790,000 came through Iran. More than a million tons came through Murmansk and Archangel as the Germans did not block the northern route until June 1942. The remaining million tons in 1942 were delivered to Vladivostok. In 1943, 1,800,000 tons came by way of Iran, while only 760,000 tons came on six convoys to Murmansk that slipped through the Nazi blockade in the winter months when the Arctic route benefitted from almost total darkness. By July 31, 1943, 120,000 motor vehicles and 2,411 American tanks had been delivered by the three routes. Total Russian additions to their supply of motor vehicles in 1943 was 158,500, and losses were 67,000, leaving a total of 496,000 vehicles on hand at the end of the year. Russian official figures do not specify lend-lease contributions to their war effort, and actually the 158,500 additional trucks included lend-lease vehicles. The trucks and jeeps transformed Soviet logistics and increased the combat value of the artillery as the American 2.5-ton truck became the vehicle of choice to tow Soviet guns. At least one-quarter of the motor vehicles in use by mid-1943 were of American origin.

Other American supplies were arriving in substantial amounts by mid-1943. American boots and rations arrived in considerable numbers, improving the life of the individual soldier. Prisoners at Kursk frequently referred to American canned rations. Pictures of Russian soldiers generally show well-fed individuals from 1943 on. When deliveries were delayed in the early part of 1943, Stalin in his note to Churchill on April 2, 1943, stated that the cancellation of the northern convoys in March 1943 represented a catastrophic diminution of supplies and arms, indicating the value of the aid that had arrived.

In summary, the Red Army was rebuilt in the first half of 1943, restoring the combat value of the divisions that had been worn down at Stalingrad and in the offensives that followed. The number of units was increased with special emphasis on support units that could cope with the German panzers. These great strides were made possible by the 1.5 million new soldiers and millions of returning wounded. The outpouring of weapons from Soviet factories and the arrival of millions of tons of lend-lease material provided the trucks, weapons, and supplies for the new and renewed forces. Not the least of the improvements was the accumulated battle experience and gain in competence in the leadership of the Red Army, from the supreme commander to the platoon leaders. The Red Army had become a far more formidable foe than the army that melted before the Nazis in the summers of 1941 and 1942.

Chapter 8

The Death Blow: Belarus, 1944

IN DECEMBER 1943, Stalin met with Franklin Roosevelt and Winston Churchill at Tehran to make arrangements for postwar Europe. One of the crucial issues was Poland. The three leaders could not agree on a definitive plan, but agreed that eastern Poland would be transferred to the Soviet Union along with a portion of East Prussia. Poland would be compensated by moving the western border to the Oder River. Stalin did not agree that the Polish government-in-exile should be restored and suggested in March 1944 that there might well be a different government in Poland by the end of the war. Is it a coincidence that the Red Army waited at the gates of Warsaw while the Germans destroyed the Polish Home Army, which was allied to the London government?

The Warsaw situation was only one of many "coincidences" in 1944. In November 1943, Stalin was aware that the Red Army had the power to destroy the German Army with or without a second front. By waiting so long, Roosevelt and Churchill had lost their major bargaining point. After Tehran, Churchill changed his position on the second front and agreed to go along even though the conditions (a limited number of German divisions in France) were not met. In fact, the German position in France was far stronger in early 1944 than it had been at any time during the war.

In another related coincidence, British intelligence issued a book describing the German army to the units that took part in the Normandy landing to assist intelligence officers in questioning captured Germans. Rather than being a reasonably up-to-date description of the German Army in France, the book portrayed the position of November 1943, before the rapid growth of the force in France in early 1944 and the sudden stalemate in Hitler's Million Men to the Front program in the spring, as the German replacement army refused to release in excess of 600,000 men, many of whom had already been organized into shadow divisions and combat replacement battalions complete with weapons. These men should have been sent to France and Russia to form 60 new combat divisions in the three months preceding the invasion. Withholding the later data made the German Army look weaker than it actually was, therefore making it appear that Churchill's conditions that the German force in France be weak had been met.

Unfortunately, withholding this information had some bad results. For example, the German 91st Air Landing Division, formed in early 1944, was not included. This division was placed by Hitler's explicit order in the spring of 1944 behind the divisions guarding the beaches where the Americans would land. When American parachute troops dropped on Normandy behind the beaches expecting to find undefended towns, they ran into elite German troops, in sharp contrast to the inferior units on the beaches.

Another coincidence was the refusal of the replacement army to release the 600,000 men. The replacement army had carried out practice drills under the Walkure program, which was designed to restore order in Germany in the event of some emergency. One of these drills brought to Berlin on a few hours' notice the Gross Deutschland Panzer Brigade, the replacement unit for the Gross Deutschland Panzer Division. That same unit was ordered to Berlin hours after the generals attempted to kill Hitler, taking control of government buildings.

Was Churchill aware of the planned coup? If so, he did not discuss it with Roosevelt on the transatlantic telephone—otherwise Hitler would have been informed, as the cable was being tapped and translated transcripts were given to Hitler and a few other senior commanders.

Was Stalin aware of the planned coup? Although the plan for the Belarus offensive was well under way, in May he ordered the transfer of the 5th Guard Tank Army from the south, even though it delayed the opening of the attack. The army was of little use, as the heavy tanks needed 60-ton bridges, which could not be brought forward because of the poor roads in Belarus. However, Stalin wanted a strong force available to exploit an even greater victory than was achieved.

Was Poland the reason for selecting Belarus for the first major operation in 1944 rather than continuing the pressure in the south? Was Poland also the reason for the transfer of the 5th Guard Tank Army? Poland was the major thorn in discussions about postwar Europe. Stalin wanted to be in a position to take any necessary measures to ensure Soviet domination after the war, specifically to prevent the return of the anti-Soviet Polish government that was in exile in London.

The two strongest Russian fronts, the 1st Ukrainian and the 1st Belarusian, were focused on Belarus and Poland in 1944. Sweeping up the Balkans was left to a later date as a firm agreement had been reached at Tehran that all of the Balkans were to be in the Soviet sphere of influence except Greece.

The second front and the Belarus offensive were launched in June. Because of the missing 60 divisions, the German Army suffered more losses in July and

August than in any other period of the war. In those two months, the Germans lost 840,000 killed and missing, compared to a few hundred thousand at Stalingrad. Once the plot had failed and Hitler removed the generals, the German line stiffened in both east and west as 60 Volksgrenadier divisions were sent to the front. German losses dropped to about 100,000 per month. If the breakthroughs in France and Belarus marked the collapse of the German Army, then a sweeping series of attacks would have exploited the situation. Instead, the 60 divisions that were not formed in the spring of 1944 were put together in a matter of weeks, slowing the drives on both fronts in September. On both fronts, it was the re-inforced German Army and not logistics that slowed the advance to a grinding crawl, during which few Germans were captured.

The political events of the first half of 1944 had much more to do with Soviet strategy in 1944 than the availability of troops. Russia had ample forces to defeat the Germans when and where they chose, but the strategy was dictated by politics.

Bad weather and waiting for the second front to be launched delayed opera-tions on the eastern front in spring 1944 and gave both the Germans and the Russians an opportunity to rebuild in preparation for the summer offensives.

The German effort was divided between Russia and France because of the certainty of a second front in the summer of 1944, but the rebuilding ground to a halt in the spring when the replacement army ceased to form new divisions. In the east, the Germans did restore the existing divisions after heavy losses in late 1943 and early 1944, but the armies in the east were denied the necessary replacements to rebuild the corps detachments. These detachments combined remnants of two or three divisions into a division-sized force as a temporary measure until re-placements were available. Many of the corps detachments were reconstructed into two or more divisions after July 1944.

In the west, Hitler had planned to reinforce and make combat worthy two army groups after three years of occupation duty, but only a handful of new divisions arrived and none of the occupation divisions were rebuilt as field divisions. The Germans did increase the number of units in the west and rebuilt some divisions in the east. However, these accomplishments were far from what could have been achieved if they were not hindered by the refusal of the replacement army to release more than 600,000 men, which were held back in Germany to fight the SS and control Germany after the planned assassination of Hitler.

The Russians took advantage of the lull to rest their armies in the first half of 1944. They replaced losses in existing rifle divisions and invested most of their resources in creating new support units, mechanized corps, tank brigades, heavy tank regiments, and assault gun regiments, as well as all types of artillery units.

In December 1943, the Red Army had 480 divisions and their priority was providing replacements rather than creating additional divisions. All but 2 of the 18 new rifle divisions were created by upgrading rifle brigades and fortified sectors (table 8.1). Most of the activity was in the Far East. Three divisions were upgraded from fortified regions, brigade-sized units that had been used to defend quiet sectors. All of the divisions were immediately assigned to fronts, an

Table 8.1 New Rifle Divisions Formed in 1944

Division	Date Formed	Date Assigned	Front/Army	Cadre
342B	12/44	12/44	East 2	
355B	12/44	12/44	East 2	
361B	12/44	12/44	East 15	38B, 260rb
363B	12/44	12/44	East 35	95B, 246rb
365B	12/44	12/44	East 1	29Brb, 199 rifle reg
366B	12/44	12/44	East 25	21B, 247rb
384B	12/44	12/44	East 25	Rifle brigades
390B	11/44	11/44	East cog	Rifle brigades
335B	5/44	5/44	East cog	6, 23eastrb
83	2/44	2/44	Karelian 26	61mb, 85mb
176B	2/44	2/44	Karelian 32	65mb, 80mb
341B	6/44	6/44	Karelian 19	77mb
308C	6/44	7/44	2 Baltic 22	1 Ladoga rifle reg
321C	5/44	5/44	2 Baltic 1sh	137rb, 14rb
325B	5/44	5/44	2 Baltic 22	23rb, 54rb
327b	5/44	5/44	1UR 60	156 Fort Region
329B	4/44	4/44	1UR 3G	160 Fort Region
348B	6/44	6/44	2 Belarus	154 Fort Region

indication that they were already trained. Only three more divisions were created in 1945, two of them in the east (table 8.2).

The new Soviet divisions were given the numbers of divisions that had been designated as guards and renumbered. By June 1, 1944, there were only 17 independent rifle brigades in the Red Army. Rather than forming new rifle divisions, the Red Army was increasing the ratio of heavy weapons to riflemen to counter the German defenses and creating new armored and artillery brigades and regiments.

The number of other major formations remained stable as well. On July 1, 1944, tank and mechanized corps had increased from 35 to 37; independent tank brigades declined from 46 to 37; and artillery divisions increased from 80 to 83.

During the first half of 1944, the Red Army rapidly formed numerous assault gun regiments, providing three for each tank corps and many more to support attacking rifle divisions. The new units were formed by the Moscow Military District, which, along with the Stavka Reserve, commanded the enormous pool of

Table 8.2 Rifle Divisions Formed in 1945

Division	Date Assigned	Front/Army
345B	3/45	East 2
396B	1/45	East 35
32mtn	2/45	?

units that could be assigned to assault armies. On July 1, 1944, there were 6,400,000 Soviet troops in operational units on the eastern front, opposed by nearly 2,000,000 Germans and 1,100,000 Finns, Romanians, and Hungarians.

Soviet statistics show little change in the number of men in operational units. The low level of Russian losses permitted them to increase the size of the rifle divisions in this period. In January 1944, the strength of rifle divisions varied from 6,000 to 7,000. By June, the divisions assigned to the Belarus offensive were increased to a range of 6,900 to 7,200 men.

The Soviet Union was able to sustain this high level despite severe losses by inducting up to 2 million men per year. The class of 1926, those reaching age 18 during 1944, included at least 2,200,000 men as a result of a high birth rate of 43.6 children per thousand in 1926. Prior to 1942, the annual class had provided only 1,600,000 men because of the low birth rate in the Soviet Union caused by World War I and the Civil War. The New Economic Policy in the Soviet Union in 1924 led to better living conditions that were reflected in a higher birth rate beginning in 1924. The addition of a half million men to the annual class of recruits in 1942 and subsequent years was a determining factor in keeping the Red Army up to strength.

Because the Russians were able to replace men in the armaments industry and on the farms with women and teenagers, most 18-year-olds were available for the army. Over 1,400,000 Soviet women were in war production by 1942. Few men were excused from military service on the basis of physical fitness. The Germans estimated that 1.7 million Russians of the 2.2 million men drafted in 1943 were judged fit for service. In comparison, only 550,000 Germans fit for service reached military age each year.

An additional factor was the recruitment of men in the newly liberated Soviet territory in 1943. Despite the efforts of the Germans to evacuate men of military age before surrendering territory, the Red Army recruited hundreds of thousands of Soviet citizens, called booty troops by the Germans, as the Red Army advanced. From March 1 to May 20, 1944, the 2nd Ukrainian Front absorbed 265,000 men and the 3rd Ukrainian Front 79,000. In some units, more than half of the men were booty troops. The 54th and 55th Rifle Corps increased their rifle company strength to over 120 men by drafting civilians in liberated territory in the first half of 1944. Some of the men were former partisans and most had prior military service. After a few days of training, the booty troops were sent to the rifle companies.

Comparing two Soviet units provides an insight into the distribution of manpower by the Red Army. The 261st Heavy Antitank Battalion was a frontline unit performing an essential role. The battalion had 268 men: 15 who were 18 years old, 17 at age 19, 13 at age 20, 40 aged from 21 to 25, 139 aged 26 to 35, 30 aged 36 to 45, and 4 men over 45. Of all the men in the unit, only 34 were over age 36, which would be an acceptable age spread in the American army.

The 615th Artillery Regiment, positioned well behind the line, made fewer physical demands on its troops. One battery of the regiment had 71 men, of which

2 were age 19, 9 were 20, 44 were between 21 and 29, 8 were between 30 and 35, and 8 were over 35. In the artillery battery, 35 had only elementary schooling; 21 had attended but not graduated from elementary school; 9 were high school graduates; and 6 had attended high school but not graduated. Given the age structure of the Red Army, the age spread of the battery was surprisingly low, as was the level of education. However, the high number of men in the age group of 21 to 35 (52 out of 71) indicated the battery had more experienced soldiers, probably because the casualty rate in artillery units was far lower than in the infantry.

The Moscow Military District included the major share of the camps and schools that formed and rehabilitated new units. These units were held by the district until their training was complete. They were then sent to the Stavka Reserve or directly to the front. On June 1, 1944, the Moscow Military District held a large number of units, many of which would be transferred to the fronts involved in the offensive during June, July, and August. The Moscow District had 5 tank brigades, all of which remained in reserve; 23 tank regiments, 13 of which were sent to the front by the end of August; 14 artillery brigades, 5 of which were sent to the front; 24 assault gun regiments, 10 of which went to Belarus; 6 guard mortar regiments, 4 of which went to Belarus; 4 tank destroyer brigades, 2 of which went to the front; and 6 antiaircraft divisions, 2 of which went to Belarus.

The Stavka Reserve was the holding command for both the strategic reserve and armies employed in subsidiary operations, such as the Coastal Army in the Crimea after the Germans surrendered. The Stavka Reserve included the 2nd Guard Army, which was transferred to the 1st Baltic Front in July, and the 51st Army, which went to the 1st Baltic Front in June. Both of these armies had been with the 4th Ukrainian Front in the Crimea in April. The 5th Guard Tank Army was added to the 3rd Belarusian Front in June. The Coastal Army remained in the Crimea as part of the Stavka Reserve.

Tracking the movements of these reserve units was difficult for German intelligence. Located far from the fronts and in areas not easily photographed by German aircraft, Soviet units being reformed would disappear for weeks from the German intelligence unit cards. New units would not be identified until they appeared at the front. As a result, German intelligence consistently underestimated the number of Soviet reserves. Even the numbers that were identified were often challenged by Hitler as being the product of negative thinking. Historians also have been confused by the process in which a mass of relatively small units were concentrated to create an overwhelmingly powerful striking force in June 1944. The creation of the two horse mechanized groups that substituted for tank armies in spearheading two of the major thrusts was difficult to track because the groups were not formally part of the table of organization, but rather were an unofficial grouping of units assigned to front reserves.

Even after these many transfers had been made, the Moscow Military District and the Stavka Reserve had substantial numbers of armored units available to support ensuing operations. The cupboard was far from bare. For example, seven armored corps still remained in the Stavka Reserve on August 1, 1944. New units were continuously being formed, many with experienced cadres that quickly assembled the men from training schools into combat-ready units. Other military districts, Kharkov and Stalingrad for example, were also cranking out tank and assault gun regiments. The Red Army had staying power based on the steady flow of new units that would be needed in the face of stubborn German defense in the last year of the war.

Countering the enormous intake of new men each year were the horrendous losses suffered at the hands of the Germans. Permanent losses were nearly 3 million in both 1941 and 1942. In 1943, the Russians lost 1,977,000 killed, permanently disabled, or missing, and 5,500,000 wounded or sick who would later return to duty. Even in 1944, the Soviet infantry suffered heavy losses. One regiment from December 1, 1943, to February 23, 1944, had 222 killed, 967 wounded, 71 sick, 373 missing, and 5 lost due to other causes. Total losses in the regiment for the 12 weeks were a staggering 1,638 from a unit of about 2,000 men.

In the first half of 1944, 721,000 Soviet soldiers were permanently lost. On December 31, 1943, 6,387,000 men and women were in operational units of the Red Army. That number increased to 6,447,000 by June 30, 1944. The difference between the strength on December 31, 1943, and June 30, 1944 (60,000), plus the irrecoverable losses (721,000) indicates that there were 781,000 additions, which included returning wounded and sick and booty troops. Remarkably few new additions were made in these six months—781,000, compared to an average of more than 1 million new recruits every six months. Men went to new armored and artillery regiments forming in the military districts. Possibly some of the trainees were held in replacement regiments in anticipation of heavy casualties in the summer.

The temporary respite from heavy losses allowed the Russians to fill their existing rifle divisions just prior to the Belarus offensive. With an annual intake of nearly 2 million recruits and acquisition of booty troops from the liberated territory, the Red Army was in an excellent position to build its forces.

The Red Army embarked on a major program to upgrade its divisions in the first half of 1944. Because of a policy not to add replacements to a unit actively engaged in operations, the usual practice was to withdraw a division into reserve, fill the vacancies with replacements and supply new weapons, provide a period of training, and then return the division to active duty.

The new Russian recruit received considerable training. Private Baranov is an example. He was born in 1925 and drafted on August 30, 1943, at the age of 18. He was trained in the 72nd Replacement Regiment and on December 24, 1943 (four months after he was drafted), was assigned to the machine pistol company of the 508th Regiment of the 174th Rifle Division. After six months, the average period of survival, he was captured on April 5, 1944, a permanent loss to the Red Army. From this example, one can comprehend the incredible turnover in manpower experienced on the eastern front.

The Soviet 2nd Guard Army, which took part in the Belarus offensive, was ordered to bolster all of its divisions to 7,000 men and bring the rifle companies up to 104 men. Men over age 40 were to be transferred out of the rifle companies, although exceptional soldiers over 40 could be retained. In each of the divisions of the 2nd Guard Army, at least 400 men in service units were to be exchanged for the overage riflemen. All men over 50 years of age were formed into a special company and sent to the 9th Army Replacement Regiment, presumably for assignment to noncombat duty.

The Soviet 8th Guard Army, another army that would play a part in the Belarus offensive, was moved secretly beginning on June 12, 1944, from Ukraine to a position behind the 1st Belarusian Front. The divisions were brought up to a strength of 6,700 men before moving. After arrival, the army was concealed in a forest. More replacements came in to be trained by the veterans before the army moved to the front.

The Russian divisions used in the battle for Belarus were probably in better condition than those in Ukraine, which had fought almost continually since July 1943. The Germans in Army Group Center discovered the strength of the Russian infantry, who were more aggressive in offense and more tenacious in defense, often holding a position rather than withdrawing from a hopeless situation. The Germans believed that the morale of the Russian divisions was higher in Belarus because they had sustained fewer casualties in what had been a comparatively quiet sector. The Soviet divisions had more cohesion as the turnover had been lower and leaders were experienced in their positions.

The Red Army had all but ceased to create rifle divisions in 1944 and concentrated instead on the formation of new tank, assault gun, and artillery units. The replacement statistics indicate that the Soviet Union, rather than exhausting its resources, was controlling the flow of manpower into the operational forces to balance losses. The Russians used their temporary surplus to increase the number of men in the 476 rifle divisions and to create additional artillery and armored units to support the rifle divisions. In the second quarter of 1944, the Soviets routed about 25 percent of the new men to artillery and armored units being formed in the military districts. The result was that Soviet rifle divisions in 1944 were supported by far more tanks and artillery pieces than the German divisions. This growing disparity would have a profound impact on the battle for Belarus.

While the Russians continued to suffer heavy casualties at the hands of the Germans in 1944, the enormous reserve of Russian manpower allowed the replacement of losses in the divisions on an ongoing basis. The Red Army obligations were being reduced by the shortening of the eastern front and the launching of the second front.

An essential difference between the German Army and the Red Army in 1944 was the existence of a large Russian strategic reserve. The Red Army had enough divisions to allow the withdrawal of entire armies from the front for rehabilitation. Uncommitted divisions by the dozen, a strategic reserve, were available to reinforce a sector selected for an offensive operation. In the summer of 1944, the strategic reserve was at a high point because of a relatively low casualty rate in the spring as well as a contraction of the front as a result of successful operations south of Leningrad and in the Crimea that freed entire armies for deployment elsewhere. Most of the Soviet reserves were under the command of the Moscow Military District and the Stavka Reserve.

The weapons situation also improved in 1944. The supply of small arms to the Red Army was ample and production was reduced. In the armies of the Southern Front in 1944, the average army had 45,000 combat troops, 25,000 rifles, 10,000 machine pistols, 2,400 machine guns, and 800 antitank rifles. The machine pistols and machine guns were concentrated in the rifle companies, where most of the men were using automatic weapons. The plentiful supply of machine pistols was extended also to the support troops. In March 1944, the 615th Howitzer Regiment had 412 rifles and carbines, 62 pistols, 153 machine pistols, 1 light machine gun, and 1 antiaircraft machine gun in addition to twenty-eight 122 mm howitzers.

The Red Army grew even stronger in 1945. Russian small arms production was greater than losses, even though production had been reduced. The number of machine pistols in the rifle division increased from 727 in 1942 to 3,557 in 1945. The number of machine guns was reduced from 605 to 561 and that of antitank rifles from 212 to 11. By 1945, the supply of weapons exceeded need. Whenever a unit was short a weapon, the unit was probably short of men to carry it, or a better weapon had been substituted. In January 1945, the 3rd Guard Tank Army had 21,000 rifles versus an authorized 25,600, indicating a shortage of riflemen. The 9th Mechanized Corps was short 1,500 rifles, even though nearly 2,000 rifles were stored in the army depots. The army had 16,900 machine pistols, greater than the authorized 15,600. The 9th Mechanized Corps had an extra 830 men armed with machine pistols. The commander of the 9th Mechanized Corps was probably short about 700 men and had elected to arm 800 riflemen with machine pistols. The 3rd Guard Tank Army had more than the authorized numbers of light machine guns, heavy machine guns, and antiaircraft machine guns. The army was short of antitank rifles, but this weapon had outlived its usefulness. The army was short thirty-five 57 mm antitank guns but had substituted sixty-one 76 mm antitank guns.

Production of Russian tanks and SUs leveled off at about 24,000 per year in 1944, roughly equal to battlefield losses. The production of guns and mortars was almost equal to battlefield losses as well, about 126,000. The inventory of guns and mortars increased from 88,900 in January 1944 to 91,400 in January 1945. During 1944 the Russians upgraded the quality of weapons in the rifle division. The supply of 57 mm guns had improved and, although the shortage did not end, the 45 mm antitank guns in the divisional antitank battalion were being replaced by 57 mm guns. The 50 mm mortar was replaced by 82 mm mortars in the rifle divisions. The new M1944 100 mm antitank gun replaced the 57 mm gun in the tank destroyer brigades and the 76 mm gun in other units.

The Soviets had won the battle of production. On June 22, 1944, the German Army Group Center had far fewer tanks, assault guns, artillery pieces, heavy weapons, and even machine pistols than the attacking Russians. As the Belarus operation unfolded and the Germans lost many of their armored vehicles and weapons, there were few replacements. German battle groups had only a single artillery battalion and a handful of antitank guns to fend off Soviet armored corps equipped with new T-34/85 tanks with guns equal to the 88 mm gun on the German Tigers.

Soviet production far exceeded German production in 1944. By January 1944, Soviet stocks of most weapons were so great that production was cut back during the year. Delivery of rifles and carbines declined from 3,850,000 in 1943 to 2,060,000 in 1944, while machine pistols declined from 2,060,000 to 1,780,000. Delivery of machine guns was reduced from 355,100 in 1943 to 284,400 in 1944. Few mortars were received; only 2,000 were made in 1944, compared to 67,900 in 1943. Delivery of 76 mm guns remained constant, with 17,300 in 1944 compared to 16,600 in 1943, while medium and heavy artillery declined from 5,500 in 1943 to 4,300 in 1944. The 76 mm gun was also used in tank destroyer brigades as a heavy antitank weapon. Losses of 76 mm guns in 1943 were only 5,000 compared to production of 16,600, so no sizable increase in production was made in 1944 even though losses increased to 10,800.

Soviet stocks and production far exceeded even the dramatically increased German production in 1944, in spite of the German trade-off of military production for civilian goods. All Soviet production was concentrated on the eastern front, but the German defense in France and Italy made demands on German production even before the Allied landing in June 1944.

Lend-lease was important to the Soviet war effort. The number of weapons received by the Red Army includes both Soviet production and lend-lease deliveries. In 1944, lend-lease provided 151,700 small arms, 9,400 guns and mortars, 11,900 tanks and assault guns, more than 5,000 half-track personnel carriers, and 18,300 aircraft. Lend-lease made major contributions to other needs of the Red Army. For food, American canned meat became a common part of the army ration. For clothing, about half of the men in some units were issued British or American lend-lease boots, which the Russian troops did not favor because the boots were not waterproof.

Trucks that carried the infantry in the mechanized units and supplies from the railheads to the troops had a major influence on the conduct of the war. The German estimate of Soviet monthly truck production in mid-1944 was 2,700 1.5-ton GAZ trucks, 4,350 3-ton SIS trucks, 1,100 5-ton JaS trucks, 800 cross-country SIS trucks, and 550 small cars, for a total of 9,500 vehicles per month or 114,000 per year. Given the large number of lend-lease trucks, the estimate of Soviet production seems unusually high, unless many of the trucks were diverted to the civilian economy and not included in the deliveries to the army. The Soviet statistics indicate that 158,500 trucks were received by the armed forces (not produced) in 1943, and 157,900 trucks were received in 1944. There is no mention of the number of trucks from lend-lease in the Russian source.

The United States promised to send 159,000 motor vehicles to the Soviet Union between July 1943 and June 1944. A total of 427,386 trucks were shipped under lend-lease, and more than half of lend-lease shipments were made in 1943 and 1944. Therefore at least 100,000 trucks were delivered to the Soviet Union in 1943 and a similar number in 1944. Deliveries after January 1945 were much higher than average because the ships could unload in the Black Sea ports, and many trucks were sent to the Far East in preparation for the Manchurian campaign. Either Russian production was less than the Germans assumed or it included the assembly of American components in Russian truck factories. The truck factory at Gorki ceased production of Russian vehicles and assembled American trucks from subassemblies sent in crates to save shipping space, a very practical solution to the shortage of cargo ships.

The Russian soldiers liked the 2.5-ton trucks and the jeeps, which were considered much better than Russian trucks because of their ability to navigate cross-country. Therefore American vehicles became an integral part of many Soviet units. In 1944, the motorcycle regiment attached to a tank army consisted of three battalions of infantry on motorcycles, an armored car battalion, and a battalion of six 45 mm guns and six 76 mm guns, all towed by jeeps. The 615th Howitzer Regiment on March 11, 1944, had 7 GAZ-AA Russian trucks, a jeep, 21 International Harvester 2.5-ton trucks, and 14 Studebaker 2.5-ton trucks. Other German reports and photographs reflect a similar dependence on American made trucks.

Soviet tank and assault gun production continued at a high level in 1944 to replace losses. In 1944, 4,000 heavy, 17,000 medium, and 200 light tanks were received, including both lend-lease and Russian production, for a total of 21,200 tanks. Losses in 1944 were 16,900, including 900 heavy, 13,800 medium, and 2,200 light tanks. At the end of 1944, the Red Army had 4,700 heavy, 12,400 medium, and 8,300 light tanks, a total of 25,400, which was an increase of 4,300 from 1943. The number of light tanks was reduced by 2,000 while the number of heavy tanks increased by 3,100 and the number of medium tanks by 3,200.

The number of Soviet tanks and assault guns in the active fronts was only 5,800 out of a total of 24,400 at the end of 1943 and 8,300 of 35,400 at the end of 1944. The remaining tanks were in the Stavka Reserve, the military districts, the Far East, training units, or in depots in various states of repair. About 10 percent of the tanks were usually in transit from depots to the front or being returned for repair. The low figure of tanks in combat units for January 1944 is directly related to the large number of tank units being rehabilitated in the rear. Of those in stock on January 1, 1944, about 12,000 were available to fight the Germans, including those in combat units, the Stavka Reserve, and depots in the military districts.

Although the Soviet total includes obsolete tanks, tanks under long-term repair, or even abandoned heavily damaged tanks, still 35,400 was an impressive number of armored vehicles, even if more than half were not combat ready.

The new T-34/85s were armed with an 85 mm gun that was equal to the 88 mm gun on the early Tigers, giving the Russians an even greater superiority in tanks with 85 mm guns. The new JS tanks mounted an 85 mm gun with a longer range than the Tiger gun. The 11th Guard Heavy Tank Brigade took on the 503rd Tiger

Battalion at Korsun and was able to hit the Tigers beyond the effective range of the German 88 mm guns.

The Russian total includes tanks and assault guns received from Britain and the United States. Tank production in the Soviet Union in 1944 was 29,000. The remaining receipts, 5,700, represented the lend-lease tanks and assault guns. German estimates of both Soviet production and lend-lease arrivals were lower than the actual numbers. In 1944, the Germans identified 2 brigades with British tanks, 4 with American tanks, 5 with a combination of British and Russian tanks, and 8 with American and Russian tanks, a total of 19 out of 119 tank brigades identified. The United States sent the medium Grant M3, the light Stuart M3, and the medium Sherman M4A2.

The British sent Valentines, Matildas, and Churchills plus obsolescent American tanks from depots in Egypt. Many Valentines were produced in Canada specifically for export to Russia after the British army canceled their orders. During the war, the British sent a total of 5,218 tanks, including 1,388 from Canada. The United States sent 7,056 tanks (5,797 medium weight) and 4,158 miscellaneous armored vehicles.

Although the Russians liked the jeeps and 2.5-ton trucks, their opinions of lend-lease tanks were generally unfavorable. According to German intelligence reports, the Soviet tank drivers thought the Valentine was the best British tank, but that it could not compete with a Panther or Tiger. The Matilda could not move in bad weather because its tracks were too narrow. The armor was also too thin and the gun too small. The Russians replaced the British 2-pounder (40 mm) gun on the Matilda with a Russian 76 mm gun but could not replace the armor. Nevertheless, the engine was better than the engines in Russian tanks. The Matilda was used as an infantry support tank rather than against German tanks. The Russians did not like the Churchill either, although it was used widely in heavy tank regiments.

The Russian tank crews hated the Grant and the Stuart, and compared using them to sitting in a coffin. Both tanks used aviation gasoline for their engines that would explode if hit by German guns, unlike the diesel fuel used by British tanks and the special versions of the Sherman. The nickname for the Grant was a coffin for seven comrades, referring to the large crew and its tendency to burn. However, the Russians did like the later version of the Sherman with its diesel engine, improved armor, and smaller crew.

Russian assault gun production soared from 4,400 in 1943 to 13,600 in 1944. However, losses were much higher: only 1,100 in 1943 compared to 6,800 in 1944. Nevertheless, the Russians had 3,300 assault guns at the beginning of 1944 and 10,100 at the end.

In 1944, the Soviets had a wide range of assault gun types. In the heavy category were the JSU-152 with a 152 mm gun howitzer on a JS chassis, the JSU-122S with a high-velocity 122 mm gun on a JS chassis, and the JSU-122 with a standard 122 mm gun on a JS chassis. In 1944 a 100 mm gun was mounted on a T-34 chassis to make the SU-100. The SU-100 used a D-10S (antiaircraft designation) or BS-3 (antitank gun) 100 mm gun on a T-34 chassis. The BS-3 had a muzzle velocity of 900 meters per second, greater than the 85 mm, and fired a 15.6 kg shell, much heavier than the 85 mm that it replaced in the medium self-propelled tank destroyer battalions. The 100 mm gun pierced 150 mm armor at 1,000 meters, powerful enough to destroy any German tank at a range beyond the reach of the guns mounted on German tanks. The production of the SU-100 was under way at Sverdlovsk in September 1944. Guard mechanized artillery brigades were formed in December 1944 equipped with 65 SU-100s.

A new JSU122 using an A-19 Model 31/37 122 mm gun on a JS chassis was also developed in 1944, and production began that year at Chelyabinsk. The A-19 gun was far more powerful than the howitzer used on the SU-122 in 1942 and 1943. The A-19 gun had a muzzle velocity of 800 meters per second, compared to only 515 meters per second for the howitzer. The shell was also heavier (25 kg compared to 21.8 kg). The range of 122 mm gun was 20.4 km versus 11.8 km for the howitzer. Later models designated as the SU-249 used an even more powerful gun, the D-25C, the same gun used on the JS tank. Production began at Chelyabinsk, with eight made in August and seven in September 1944.

The JSU-152 was developed with the M1937 ML-20 gun howitzer, similar to the SU-152 but mounted on a JS chassis. The same gun was merely transferred to an improved chassis; the characteristics of the gun remained the same. The change was necessary because of the termination of KV chassis production at Chelyabinsk. The JSU-152 and JSU-122 were used by the heavy mechanized artillery regiments until the end of the war and in a heavy SU brigade formed in December 1944. The heavy brigade had 65 JSU-152s, 3 SU-76s, and 1,804 men.

In the medium class, using the T-34 chassis, the Russians had the SU-152 with a 152 mm gun howitzer, the SU-122 with a standard 122 mm gun, and the SU-85 with an 85 mm gun.

The SU-76 was the primary light assault gun, with a 76 mm gun on a light tank chassis. The American SU57s with 57 mm guns mounted on half-tracks entered combat in August 1944. In January 1945, the 3rd Guard Tank Army, with a light assault gun brigade equipped with American 57 mm guns on half-tracks, was short 13 vehicles, suggesting that the stock provided by the Americans was running low and replacements were no longer available. The United States had sent the entire stock to the Russians in 1943 and were no longer manufacturing the vehicle.

The Germans estimated monthly production of SUs in 1944 at 100 SU-76s at the Kirov plant, 100 SU-76s at Gorki, 200 SU-85s or SU-100s at Sverdlovsk, and 100 SU-152s at Chelyabinsk, for a total of 500 per month. The Germans estimated that 4,100 SUs were made by April 1944; the Soviets stated that 4,050 were made by January 1944. Total production in 1944 was 16,900, and monthly production was 1,400. By January 1945, the Red Army had 10,100 SUs.

The Germans determined the approximate level of SU-76 production at Gorki and Kirov by a study of the serial numbers of destroyed vehicles. Because of the small number destroyed at the front, the Germans believed correctly that the large number produced were used to form additional regiments to make the antitank gun line even more deadly behind advancing Red Army units. The production of SUs exceeded losses and made possible the expansion of the number of mechanized or self-propelled artillery units.

Another German study in July 1944 revealed that of 360 tanks and SUs destroyed in that month, 73 percent were T-34s and KV-1s, and only 6 percent were SUs. Of the remaining, 15 percent were obsolete tanks and 6 percent were miscellaneous types. The destruction ratio was at least 12 tanks to 1 SU, whereas production in 1944 was only 4 tanks to 3 SUs. The supply of SUs was so plentiful that battalions were assigned to some rifle divisions. The 252nd Rifle Division received the 110th SU Battalion, and the 62nd Guard Rifle Division received the 69th SU Battalion, apparently new formations added to the divisions. By the end of the war, 70 mechanized artillery battalions had been formed. The Germans attributed the replacement of antitank guns with SUs to increased production of the SU-76, then estimated at 500 per month.

The SU probably fired more rounds than a tank because of its multiplicity of roles. The lack of a turret allowed ample room for a large supply of shells and space for the gunners and loaders to work quickly. The number of rounds carried with the mechanized artillery guns was nearly identical for the same gun in a towed battalion. The SU-76 carried 60 rounds; the SU-85, 48; the SU-100, 34; the JSU-122, 30; and the JSU-152, 20.

In 1944 the Soviets developed the BS-3 100 mm gun with a 60-caliber barrel and a muzzle velocity of 887 meters per second, a powerful antitank gun. The 160 mm mortar M1943 MT-13 was introduced in January 1944. The heavy mortar was breech loaded and mounted on wheels. The mortar was designed for use against German fortifications from firing positions near the front. The shell had more explosive power than a 152 mm howitzer.

The 76 mm guns made up nearly half the guns of 76 mm or larger caliber used in 1944, followed by the 122 mm howitzer, which made up 31 percent. Together the two guns that made up the divisional artillery accounted for four-fifths of Soviet artillery.

Soviet arms production was providing the Red Army with an ample supply of weapons—in fact, so many that production was cut back in 1944. The German Army suffered catastrophic losses in men and weapons in June and July 1944, but recovered partially in the following months. The Red Army, on the other hand, had a declining rate of loss and therefore a surplus of men and weapons. Men were sent back into the civilian sector to begin rebuilding, and arms production was curtailed.

At the same time, lend-lease deliveries increased sharply and bottlenecks in the supply line were eliminated by the construction of railroads in Iran and the removal of the German threat to the convoys in the north. After the defeat in Belarus, Germany could only prolong its agony.

There remain some unanswered questions concerning the summer of 1944. Why did Churchill suddenly change his mind about the second front in the spring of 1944? Why did Stalin decide to attack Belarus in June 1944 after two or three futile attempts in the past, even though his generals told him he would have to shift an entire tank army from the south and delay the attack? And, of course, why did the German generals hold back 600,000 troops in the replacement army in 1944? The answers might be found in the transcripts of the trials of the German generals involved in the assassination plot. Because so many officers were brought to trial in the People's Court, it is clear that considerable effort was taken to find all the conspirators. The trials and the torture of some plotters were filmed for Hitler's viewing. If documentation exists, it may still be restricted.

Chapter 9

Conclusion

THE DISASTER experienced by the Red Army in 1941 was a direct result of earlier decisions made by Stalin. In 1938, he had purged the army of practically all officers from the level of division commanders upward and placed a Communist commissar in every unit to second-guess the commander. The atmosphere of fear created a philosophy of referring all decisions to higher authority and refusal to take responsibility. Inaction was preferable to any action that might be considered wrong in the future. Such a condition was suicidal in the face of the German blitzkrieg. The poor performance of the Red Army in the war with Finland was an early indication that it had serious problems. One of the reasons for the defeat at Izyum in the spring of 1942 was the interference of the commissars. In 1943, Stalin eliminated the commissars in the rifle companies and higher commands. Some of the commissars had sufficient military ability and became regular army officers.

A decision regarding the use of tanks rejected the advice of the veterans of the Spanish Civil War, many of whom were removed in the purge. The lesson of the Spanish Civil War was that tanks and infantry must work together to overcome a capable opponent. Because of the success of the German panzer corps in Poland and France against armies almost devoid of antitank weapons, Stalin's order to create 30 corps modeled on the German panzer corps left the conventional armies without tank support. The new corps, still in the forming stage and lacking modern tanks, were massacred by the Germans in the early months of the war.

In the introduction, eight questions were set forth concerning the success of the Red Army in World War II. The first was, where did the Russians find the manpower? Despite its horrible beginning, the Red Army was reborn. The total number of men at the front increased from 3 million in 1941 to 6.1 million in

1943 and 6.5 million in 1945, while the monthly permanent losses, and killed and missing soldiers, dropped steadily from 1941 until the final bitter battles of 1945. Women and children replaced men in the factories, farms, and mines. A continuous flow of new men and women replaced the losses. Women and children were as important to the Russian war effort as the men who served in the army.

A high percentage of the wounded and sick returned to duty within months. The proportion of missing was much higher in 1941 and 1942, when large numbers of divisions were surrounded and captured, and in the spring of of 1943 when the Red Army suffered a severe setback in Ukraine. The shifting results of the battles are clearly reflected in the ratio between permanent and temporary losses (table 9.1). In 1941 the ratio was 5:2; in 1942, 3:4; in 1943, 1:2.4; in 1944, 1:3; and in 1945, 1:2.5. Clearly after 1942 the Red Army was fighting a winning battle, taking heavy losses to be sure, but strengthened by recovering their wounded and nursing them back to health.

The losses for 1941 covered a period of six months and those for 1945 five months. The rate of loss per month was 745,000 in 1941 and 602,000 in 1945 compared to 573,000 in 1944. Despite the bitter battles in the spring of 1945, Red Army losses in 1945 were only slightly higher than the 1944 rate of 573,000 per month and far fewer than the 745,000 per month in 1941. The distribution of the losses indicates that the infantry took the brunt of it, 84 percent of those killed and 87 percent of those wounded. The armored forces suffered 7.7 percent of those killed and 5.5 percent of the wounded. The combat losses in other branches were minimal.

The average daily loss by divisions and tank corps engaged in offensives decreased from about 120 per day in 1943 to about 60 per day in 1944 and 1945. At the same time, the proportion of killed and missing compared to wounded and sick also decreased from 1:1.5 at Stalingrad and Kursk to about one killed for every three wounded in 1944 and 1945. In other words, permanent losses decreased from 60 per division and tank corps per day to only 15, as most of the wounded either returned to duty or replaced a fit man in a noncombat position.

The second question concerned the quantity of weapons needed to equip the new divisions. A vital key to Stalin's victory was the production of weapons.

Table 9.1   Red Army Losses

Year	Killed and Missing	Wounded and Sick	Total
1941	3,137,673	1,336,147	4,473,820
1942	3,258,216	4,111,062	7,369,278
1943	2,312,426	5,545,074	7,857,500
1944	1,763,891	5,114,750	6,878,641
1945	800,817	2,212,690	3,013,507
Total	11,273,026	18,344,148	29,617,174

President Franklin Roosevelt initiated the program of lend-lease in 1940 when it became obvious that Britain could not pay for the enormous stocks of weapons to replace those lost in France. Roosevelt also extended lend-lease to the Soviet Union in 1941 after the major loss of weapons and equipment in the first months of the war. Although lend-lease played a significant role in providing trucks, canned rations, boots, uniforms, radios, and other equipment, the Red Army fought with Russian-made weapons. The massive numbers of tanks came from factories built in the 1930s with the help of American engineers. Originally designed to mass produce automobiles and tractors, the huge factories, employing as many as 40,000 workers, were converted to manufacture tens of thousands of tanks. A photograph of a boy standing on a box in order to reach the controls of a drill press in a factory in Russia made a lasting impression on me, especially as I was learning to use a similar drill press in a shop class at the time. The classroom was used during the evening to train machinists for work in factories in Detroit.

In the 1930s, American engineers trained the Russians in the concept of mass production, which included planned obsolescence and making a product that was only as good as it needed to be for the task. Russian tanks lasted about six months before they were destroyed by German antitank fire, so there was no point in manufacturing an engine that would last five years. Russian weapons were not pretty, but they did the job.

The rate of loss of weapons reflected the changing nature of the battle against the Germans. In the last six months of 1941, the Red Army lost 5,500,000 rifles and 40,000 artillery pieces. In 1942, the Red Army lost 2,200,000 rifles and 25,000 artillery pieces in 12 months. These losses reflect the large number of divisions surrounded and captured. A real change came in 1943 when only 1,260,000 rifles and 12,000 artillery pieces were lost. The battles in 1944 resulted in the loss of 1,610,000 rifles and 21,700 artillery pieces, reflecting the bitterness of the fighting. The first five months of 1945 witnessed losses of 670,000 rifles and 7,800 guns as the Red Army broke down the last-ditch resistance of the Germans.

Tank losses also indicated the changing character of the war. In six months in 1941, 20,500 tanks, including 17,300 light tanks, were lost as the Germans destroyed the prewar tank divisions. In 1942 losses declined to 15,000 in 12 months, though still including 7,200 light tanks. In 1943 the battles became more intense and 22,400 tanks were lost, of which only 6,400 were light tanks. Medium tank losses soared from 6,600 in 1942 to 14,700 in 1943. In 1944 tank losses declined to only 17,000, but losses of the new SUs increased to 6,800, for a total loss of armored vehicles of 23,800 compared to 23,500 in 1943. The SUs were taking a much larger role in attacking the Germans. In the five months of battle in 1945, 8,700 tanks were lost, along with 5,000 SUs, a monthly average of 2,300 compared to less than 2,000 in 1944. Heavy tanks were becoming more readily available (1,500 were produced and 900 were lost), but the T-34 medium tank continued to be the workhorse, along with the SU-76.

Soviet tanks continued to improve in quality in 1945, as heavier tanks became available. The JS-3 appeared, weighing 47 tons with a speed of 40 km per hour. The guard heavy tank units were equipped with JS tanks. The purpose of the heavy tank was to destroy German tanks and antitank guns at long range from positions behind the advancing T-34s. At Korsun, the 2nd Guard Heavy Tank Brigade successfully engaged the German 503rd Heavy Panzer Battalion equipped with Tigers. The 122 mm guns on the JS tanks outranged the German 88 mm guns and destroyed them before the Germans could reach the JS tanks.

The Soviet figure for total tanks on hand on January 1, 1945, was 25,400. Fremde Heer Ost made similar estimates for other months, usually placing about 1,000 in the Far East, Iran, and the Caucasus; 2,800 in transit to the front; 1,000 in training units; and from 8,000 to 12,000 either in units at the front, in reserve, or not located. The Germans underestimated the extent of Soviet losses and the Soviet ability to repair damaged or worn-out tanks.

Many German Mark III and Mark IV tanks were captured and converted to light SUs. The Russians converted captured German Mark III tanks into the SU-76i at Zavod No. 38. More than 1,200 of the German chassis were rebuilt as fully armored self-propelled 76 mm guns and used as both tanks and SUs. The 1202th Mechanized Artillery Regiment was formed near Moscow on January 13, 1945, and equipped with 21 SU-76is. After enduring losses, the regiment received seven replacements, showing the continued availability of the type. The 438th Mechanized Artillery Regiment, formed in 1944, received rebuilt German assault guns. Later it received SU-85s made at Sverdlovsk. Use of the SU-76i in 1944 and early 1945 may have reflected a temporary shortage of SUs, as the number of regiments was rapidly expanded.

There was a steady increase in armored strength other than tanks. In the Belarus operation in 1944 there were 1,548 SUs; in East Prussia, 1,654; in the Vistula Oder operation, 2,479; and in Berlin in 1945, 2,701. By March 28, 1945, the Germans had identified 243 mechanized artillery regiments, including 49 with SU-76s, 36 with SU-85s, and 48 with heavy SUs. The SU regiments were acquiring better equipment. In January 1945, the 382nd Guard Heavy Regiment had JSU-122s with a more powerful model 249 gun. Of eight vehicles from the regiment destroyed by the Germans, all were made at the Kirov plant in Chelyabinsk in August and September 1944 and had a vehicle life of only five or six months. The JSU-122 had replaced the JSU-152 on the production lines at Chelyabinsk. The 1443rd regiment also had SU-122s with the type 249 gun produced at Sverdlovsk in November 1944.

The increasing supply of weapons changed the composition of the Red Army from 1942 to 1945. This shift in structure was made possible by the prodigious production of weapons. Firepower, not manpower, won the final battles. The number of weapons in the rifle divisions increased as the number of riflemen decreased. Recruits went to hundreds of new artillery, self-propelled artillery, and tank regiments. The number of guns in the self-propelled artillery regiments increased from 12 to 16 or 21. The fact that tank regiments had more tanks compensated for the abolition of some tank brigades. The total number of men at the front remained at about 6 million, but more were assigned to heavy weapons, guns, and armored vehicles, and fewer were serving in the rifle companies.

The third question was how the Russians were able to maintain the strength of the rifle divisions and tank units. An efficient training and replacement system not only replaced losses but continued to create new units. Despite the heavy losses inflicted by the Germans in the second half of 1941, the Soviets were able to mobilize divisions not only to replace those lost but also to add more than 60 to the total. A further 40 were formed in the first half of 1942 and another 40 again in the first half of 1943. Smaller increases occurred from that time to the end of the war. About 30 airborne divisions were added by the end of the war. Instead of being worn down by the Germans, the Red Army grew stronger as the war progressed (table 9.2).

The supporting arms, tanks, and artillery experienced the greatest growth in 1943. During that year, the tank forces grew to 5 armies, 37 corps, 80 dependent brigades, and 149 independent tank and mechanized artillery regiments. Artillery increased to 6 corps and 26 divisions.

For the remainder of the war, the Red Army concentrated on creating new armored and artillery units. Rifle brigades either formed rifle divisions or were abolished. The crossing of the old Soviet border later in 1944 ended the Red Army's bonus manpower of men drafted in liberated Soviet territory. The young men in the annual classes tended to be sent to the new armored artillery formations, which required longer training and greater skills. When manpower resources were not used to replace the losses in the divisions, the rifle strength of the divisions declined steadily. The 16 rifle divisions created in 1944 and 1945 were primarily new divisions formed in the Far East (9) and divisions formed from brigades (4).

Table 9.2　Numbers of Units, Troops, and Weapons, May 1942–January 1945

Type	May 1942	November 1942	July 1943	January 1945
Rifle divisions	442	436	471	529
Rifle brigades	139	172	99	36
Tank corps	24	27	29	27
Mechanized corps	11	12	14	14
Tank brigades	172	202	166	177
Tank regiments	81	170	222	60
Artillery divisions		7	27	35
Antiaircraft divisions		33	59	95
Tank destroyer regiments	110	351	353	367
Men	6,100,000	6,400,000	6,500,000	?
Tanks and SUs	6,900	9,900	12,900	?
Guns and mortars	77,700	103,100	108,000	?

The fourth question concerned the refusal of the Russians to give up. Stalin was tenacious and had powerful internal security forces to back him up. To maintain popular support, he launched a massive campaign stressing the need to defend Mother Russia rather than the Communist government. The people responded and willingly entered the army and the work force.

The Soviet Union had a prolific mobilization machine, far greater in capacity than the U.S. and German systems, both of which produced well-documented dramatic results in World War II. While the U.S. system raised 90 divisions (and countless other specialized units) and the Germans mobilized in excess of 400 divisions, the Soviet Union formed 700-plus divisions.

The more one studies the details of mobilization of the Red Army, the more impressive is the magnitude of the accomplishment. The Red Army in June 1941, in the midst of expansion, was poorly trained, equipped with obsolete weapons, and led by inexperienced commanders. The army, surprised in June 1941 despite the warnings, was destroyed at the frontiers. New armies were hastily but efficiently mobilized between July and December 1941. The new divisions, despite anecdotes of cavalry without saddles and shortages of all kinds, halted the vaunted Germany Army at the gates of Leningrad, Moscow, and Rostov. Most of these divisions had less than six months' training or had provided cadres for other divisions. The Red Army was able to switch from defense to offense in the winter offensive of 1941–42.

The generally accepted interpretation is that the Red Army defeated the Germans at great cost by simply throwing at German positions thousands of poorly trained and organized men armed only with antique rifles. This interpretation defines the Russian victories as the result of sheer weight of numbers overwhelming the defenders and that the strategy was possible because the leader, Stalin, had a complete disregard for human life. There is some truth to this interpretation in the fall of 1941, after the Nazis had destroyed the prewar Red Army, when desperate measures were required to delay the onslaught. Most of the German anecdotes relating to Soviet tactics refer to this period in 1941.

The usual interpretation of the success of the Russian offensive in December 1941 is that the severe winter worked in favor of the Soviets, who were better equipped for combat in a cold climate. In fact, the heavy snow was a major handicap for the attacking Russians. Movement was confined to the roads, so that German roadblocks could not be outflanked. Russian tanks and infantry could not move across the snow-covered fields, allowing the Germans to concentrate their efforts on blocking the roads. In addition, because of the severe weather the Germans established strong points in the villages, which offered shelter and warmth overnight. The advancing Soviets had to take each strong point by frontal assault before nightfall or retreat back to the nearest village in their control and begin all over again the next morning. Control of the roads and villages enabled the Germans to stand and hold as Hitler ordered. In the succeeding winters, the Red Army was not constrained by the milder weather and made enormous gains as the tanks and troops moved swiftly over the frozen but not snow-covered fields.

The fifth question concerned the failure at Izyum and the success at Stalingrad. Ground down by the winter offensive, the Red Army reformed a second time beginning in March 1942 but again suffered serious defeats during the German summer offensive of 1942, primarily as a result of poor leadership. The purge of officers in 1938 still had its consequences.

By November 1942, a third program developed a powerful force that defeated the Germans at Stalingrad and went on to victory. By mid-1943 the Red Army was well trained, well equipped, well supplied, and well led. In spite of Winston Churchill's belief that Gen. George Marshall could not create a 100-division U.S. army within 18 months after Pearl Harbor and train the force well enough to take on the Germans in France in 1943, with a much smaller industrial base, the Russians created more than 700 new divisions with far less time to train them (usually three to six months) and defeated the Germans in the bloodiest campaign in history.

The remaining three questions referring to the final years of the war are answered by the steady growth of the Red Army in numbers, training, weapons, and leadership. As early as December 1941, Russian training, weapons, and organization had improved. By the end of the war, they had reached a level that reduced the number of casualties substantially. By restoring the health of the wounded and reducing the number of casualties with the aid of better training, more weapons, and improved leadership, the Russians were able to maintain their superiority.

In May 1942, just before the German summer offensive; in November 1942, on the eve of the encirclement of Stalingrad; in July 1943, during the Battle of Kursk; and in January 1945, the beginning of the final offensives, there were significant increases in the numbers of tanks and guns supporting the infantry. The number of rifle formations (divisions and brigades) remained relatively stable during 1942. By July 1943, the number of rifle divisions increased as rifle brigades formed new divisions to replace those redesignated as guards.

For the remainder of the war, except in a few months, the Russians had a substantial reserve of men and weapons that could be used to obtain local superiority anywhere on the line. The Germans, on the other hand, seldom had many reserves and had to thin out less threatened sectors when troops were needed to counterattack. During the time required to accomplish the thinning process, the Russians made substantial gains.

This enviable position was made possible by the two keys to victory, mobilization and production. Despite the loss of 28 million people, the Soviets maintained an army of more than 10 million men and women, with 6 million on the eastern front. Millions of women and children replaced men in the factories and on the farms to produce the weapons and supplies for the army. Soviet sacrifices to defend their homeland ended Hitler's threat to the world.

Bibliography

Adair, Paul. *Hitler's Greatest Defeat: The Collapse of Army Group Centre, June 1944.* London: Arms and Armour Press, 1994.

Akalovich, N. *Osvobozhenie Belorussii.* Minsk: Nauka i Twxinka, 1989.

Akulov, P., and G. Tolokol'nikov, eds. *V Boiakh za Belorussiu.* Minsk: Belarus, 1970.

Anan'ev, I. M. *Tankovie Armii v Nastuplenii.* Moscow: Voenizdat, 1988.

Anaymanovich, M. A. *Voiska Protivovozdushnoi Oboroni Strani Istoricheskiy Ocherk.* Edited by P. Batitskiy. Moscow: Izdatelistvo, 1968.

Andronikov, Nikolaii, and W. D. Mostowenko. *Die Roten Panzer: Geschichte der Sowjetischen Panzertruppen 1920–1960.* Munich: J. F. Lehmann, 1963.

Anfilov, Viktor A. *Bessmertnii Podvig Issledovanie Kanuna i Pervogo Etapa Velikoi Otechestvennoi Voini.* Moscow: Nauka, 1971.

———. *Krushenie Pokhoda Gitlera na Moskvu, 1941.* Moscow: Nauka, 1989.

———. *Proval Blitskriga.* Moscow: Nauka, 1974.

Antipenko, N. A. *Na Glavnom Napravlenii.* Moscow: Nauka, 1967.

Babich, P., and A. G. Baier. *Razvitie Vooruzheniia i Organizatsii Sovetskix Suxoputnix Voisk v Godi Velikoi Otechestvennoi Voini.* Moscow: Izdanie Akademii, 1990.

Batov, P. I. *Pokhodkah.* Moscow: Voenizdat, 1966.

Beaumont, Joan. *Comrades in Arms: British Aid to Russia 1941–1945.* London: Davis-Poynter, 1980.

Bellamy, Chris. *Red God of War.* London: Brassy's Defence Publishers, 1986.

Bialer, Seweryn, ed. *Stalin and His Generals: Soviet Military Memoirs of World War II.* New York: Pegasus, 1969.

Biryukov, G. F., and G. Melnikov. *Antitank Warfare.* Moscow: Progress Publishers, 1972.

Blunt, Brian, and Tolley Taylor. *Brassey's Artillery of the World.* New York: Bonanza Books, 1979.

Bolotin, D. N. *Sovetskoe Strelkovoe Oruzie.* Moscow: Izdatelistvo, 1990.

Chistiakov, Ivan M. *Sluzhim Otchizne.* Moscow: Voenizdat, 1985.

Chuikov, V. I. *The End of the Third Reich*. Moscow: Progress Publishers, 1978.

Clark, Alan. *Barbarossa: The Russian-German Conflict 1941–45*. New York: New American Library, 1966.

Cole, John P., and F. C. German. *A Geography of the U.S.S.R.: The Background of a Planned Economy*. London: Butterworths, 1984.

Conquest, Robert. *The Great Terror: A Reassessment*. New York: Oxford University Press, 1990.

Dinardo, R. L. *Mechanized Juggernaut or Military Anachronism? Horses and the German Army in World War II*. New York: Greenwood, 1991.

Dunn, Walter S. Jr. *Heroes or Traitors: The German Replacement Army, the July Plot, and Adolf Hitler*. Westport, CT: Praeger, 2003.

———. *Hitler's Nemesis: The Red Army 1930–1945*. Westport, CT: Praeger, 1994.

———. *Kursk: Hitler's Gamble, 1943*. Westport, CT: Praeger, 1997.

———. *Second Front Now 1943*. University: University of Alabama Press, 1981.

———. *Soviet Blitzkrieg: The Battle for White Russia, 1944*. Boulder, CO: Lynne, 2000.

———. *The Soviet Economy and the Red Army, 1930–1945*. Westport, CT: Praeger, 1995.

Dunnigan, James F. *How to Make War*. New York: Morrow, 1988.

———, ed. *The Russian Front*. London: Arms and Armour Press, 1978.

Dupuy, Trevor N. *Understanding War*. New York: Paragon House, 1987.

Dupuy, Trevor N., and Paul Martell. *Great Battles on the Eastern Front: The Soviet-German War 1941–1945*. Indianapolis, IN: Bobbs-Merrill, 1982.

Ely, Louis B. *The Red Army Today*. Harrisburg: Military Services, 1953.

Eremenko, Andrei I. *Stalingrad, zapiski komanduyushchego Frontom*. Moscow: Voenizdat, 1961.

Erickson, John. *The Road to Berlin*. Boulder, CO: Westview Press, 1983.

———. *The Road to Stalingrad: Stalin's War with Germany*. New York: Harper & Row, 1975.

Fremde Heer Ost. *Truppen-Upersicht und Kriegsliederungen Rote Armee Stand August 1944*. Captured German Records. Washington, DC: National Archives.

Fugate, Bryan I. *Operation Barbarossa*. Novato, CA: Presidio Press, 1984.

Geschichte des Grossen Vaterlandischen Krieges der Sowjetunion. 8 vols. Berlin: Deutscher Militarverlag, 1964.

Glantz, David M. *August Storm: Soviet Tactical and Operational Combat in Manchuria 1945*. Combat Studies Institute. Fort Leavenworth, KS: U.S. Army Command and General Staff College, 1983.

———. *From the Don to the Dnieper: Soviet Offensive Operations, December 1942–August 1943*. London: F. Cass, 1991.

———. *Soviet Military Deception in the Second World War*. London: Frank Cass, 1989.

———, ed. *1985 Art of War Symposium, from the Dnieper to the Vistula: Soviet Offensive Operations, November 1943–August 1944*. Carlisle Barracks, PA: U.S. Army War College, 1985.

Glantz, David M., and Jonathan M. House. *When Titans Clashed: How the Red Army Stopped Hitler*. Lawrence: University Press of Kansas, 1995.

Glantz, David M., and Harold S. Orenstein, eds. *Belorussia 1944: The Soviet General Staff Study*. Carlisle, PA: David M. Glantz, 1998.

Golikov, Arseni. *With the Red Fleet*. London: Putnam, 1965.

Grabin, V. G. *Oruzie Pobedi*. Moscow: Izdatelistvo, 1989.

Grbasic, Z., and V. Vuksic. *The History of Cavalry*. New York: Facts on File, 1989.

Grechko, A. A. *Liberation Mission*. Moscow: Progress Publishers, 1975.

Grechko, A., et al., eds. *Soviet Studies on the Second World War*. Moscow: USSR Academy of Sciences, 1976.

Grove, Eric. *Russian Armor 1941–1943*. London: Almark, 1977.

Harrison, Mark. *Soviet Planning in Peace and War 1938–1945*. Cambridge: Cambridge University Press, 1985.

Haupt, Werner von. *Die 260. Infanterie-Division, 1939–1944*. Bad Nauheim and Dorheim: Verlag Hans-Henning Podzun, 1970.

———. *Geschichte der 134. Infanterie Division*. Weinsberg: Herausgegeben vom Kamardenkreis der Ehemaligen, 134. Inf.-Division, 1971.

———. *Heeresgruppe Mitte 1941–1945*. Dorheim: H. H. Podzun, 1968.

Heidkemper, O. *Witebsk*. Heidelberg: Vowinckel, 1954.

Hinze, Rolf. *East Front Drama—1944: The Withdrawal Battle of Army Group Center*. Winnipeg, Manitoba: J. J. Fedorowicz, 1996.

Hogg, Ian, and John Weeks. *Military Small Arms of the Twentieth Century*. Northfield, IL: Digest Books, 1973.

Hunter, Holland. *Soviet Transport Experience: Its Lessons for Other Countries*. Washington, DC: Brookings Institution, 1968.

Hunter, Holland, and Janusz M. Szyrmer. *Faulty Foundations: Soviet Economic Policies 1928–1940*. Princeton, NJ: Princeton University Press, 1992.

Illustrated Encyclopedia of 20th Century Weapons and Warfare. 24 vols. New York: Columbia House, 1969.

Istoriya Velikoy Otechestvennoy Voyny Sovetskogo Soyuza 1941–1945. 6 vols. Moscow: Voyennoye Izdatelistvo, 1960–63.

Istoriya Vtoroi Mirovoi Voyny 1939–1945. 12 vols. Moscow: Voyennoye Izdatelistvo, 1973–82.

Ivanov, S. P. *The Initial Period of the War: A Soviet View*. Soviet Military Thought Series, no. 20. Washington, DC: U.S. Government Printing Office, 1986.

Kazakov, Konstantin P., ed. *Artilleriia i Raketi*. Moscow: Voenizdat, 1968.

———. *Vsegda s Pekhotoi Vsegda s Tankami*. Moscow: Voenizdat, 1969.

Kazakov, Vasiliki I. *Artilleriia Ogono*. Moscow: Izd-vo, 1972.

Kehrig, Manfred. *Stalingrad: Analyse und Dokumentation Einer Schlacht*. Stuttgart: Deutsche Verlags-Anstalt, 1974.

Kennan, George F. *Russia and the West under Lenin and Stalin*. Boston: Little, Brown, 1961.

Kerr, Walter. *The Secret of Stalingrad*. New York: Playboy Press, 1979.

Klink, Ernst. *Das Gesetz des Handelns die Operation "Zitadelle," 1943*. Stuttgart: Deutsche Verlags-Anstalt, 1966.

Koltunov, G. A. *Kurskaia Bitva*. Moscow: Voenizdat, 1970.

Kotelnikov, Vladimir. "The Role of Soviet Science in the Great Patriotic War," in *Soviet Studies on the Second World War*, ed. A. Grechko et al. Moscow: USSR Academy of Sciences, 1976.

Krivosheev, G. F. *Poteri Vooruzhenikh sil SSSR v Voinakh Voevikh Deistviiakh i Voennikh Konflitakh Grif Sekretnosti Snyat*. Moscow: Izdatelistvo, 1993.

Kumanev, G. A. *Na Sluzhie Fronta i Tila 1938–1945*. Moscow: Izdatelistvo Nauka, 1976.

Liddell-Hart, Basil H. *The Red Army*. New York: Harcourt Brace, 1956.

Liudnikov, I. I. *Pod Vitebskom*. Moscow: Voenizdat, 1962.

Losik, O. A. "Primenie Bronetankovykh i Mekhaniziro Vannykh Voisk v Belorusskoi Operatsii." *Vizh* 6 (June 1984), 20–24.

———. *Stroitelistvo i Boyevoye Primeneniye Sovetskikh Tankovykh Voysk v Gody Velikoy Otechestvennoy Voyne*. Moscow: Voyenizdat, 1979.

Lucas, James. *War on the Eastern Front 1941–1945: The German Soldier in Russia*. New York: Bonanza Books, 1979.

Luchinsky, A. "28-ia Armiia v Bobruiskoi Operatsii." *Vizh* 2 (February 1969), 66–75.

Makhine, Theodore H. *L'Armee Rouge*. Paris: Payout, 1938.

Malanin, K. "Razvitie Organizatsionnik Form Sukoputhik Voisk v Velikoi Otechestvennoi Voine." *Vizh* 8 (August 1967), 28–39.

Manstein, Erich von. *Lost Victories*. Novato, CA: Presidio Press, 1982.

Mikhailkin, V. "Boevoe Primenenie Artillerii v Belorusskoi Operatsii." *Vizh* 6 (June 1984), 25–33.

Militarakademie M. W. Frunse. *Der Durchbruch der Schutzenverbande Durch eine Vorbereitete Verteidigung*. Berlin: Ministerium für Nationale Verteidigung, 1959.

Milward, Alan S. *War Economy and Society 1939–1945*. London: Lane, 1977.

Mitchell, B. R. *European Historical Statistics 1750–1970*. London: Macmillan, 1978.

Murmantseva, V. S. "Ratnii i Trudovoi Podvig Sovetskix Jenshin." *Vizh* 5 (May 1985), 73–81.

Niepold, Gerd. *Battle for White Russia: The Destruction of Army Group Centre June 1944*. London: Brassey's Defence Publishers, 1987.

Nove, Alec. *An Economic History of the USSR*. New York: Penguin, 1982.

Parotkin, Ivan, ed. *The Battle of Kursk*. Moscow: Progress Publishers, 1974.

Parrish, Michael, ed. *Battle for Moscow: The 1942 Soviet General Staff Study*. Washington, DC: Pergamon-Brassey's, 1989.

Pavlovskii, I. G. *Sukhoputniye Voyska SSSR*. Moscow: Voyenizdat, 1985.

Poirier, Robert G., and Albert C. Conner. *Red Army Order of Battle in the Great Patriotic War*. Novato, CA: Presidio Press, 1985.

Reinhardt, Klaus. *Die Wende vor Moskau*. Stuttgart: Deutsche Verlag-Anstalt, 1972.

Rokossovsky, Konstantin K. *Velikaia Pobdea Na Volga*. Moscow: Voennoe Izdatelistvo, 1965.

Rotundo, Louis C., ed. *Battle for Stalingrad: The Soviet General Staff Study*. Washington, DC: Pergamon-Brassey's, 1989.

Salisbury, Harrison E. *The 900 Days: The Siege of Leningrad*. New York: Avon, 1970.

Savushkin, R. A. *Razvitye Sovetskikh Vooruzhennykhj Sil i Voennogo Iskusstva y Mezhvoennyi Period 1921–1941*. Moscow: Lenin Military-Political Academy, 1989.

Schmidt, Paul K. *Hitler Moves East 1941–43*. New York: Bantam, 1966.

Schofield, Brian B. *The Arctic Convoys*. London: MacDonald and James, 1977.

———. *The Russian Convoys*. London: B. T. Batsford, 1964.

Seaton, Albert. *The Russo-German War, 1941–45*. New York: Praeger, 1970.

Seaton, Albert, and Joan Seaton. *The Soviet Army 1918 to the Present*. New York: New American Library, 1986.

Shtemenko, S. M. *The Last Six Months*. Garden City, NY: Doubleday, 1977.

———. *The Soviet General Staff at War 1941–1945*. Moscow: Progress Publishers, 1970.

Skorobogatkin, K. F., et al. *50 Let Voorezhennykh sil SSSR*. Moscow: Voyenizdat, 1968.

Stadler, Silvester. *Die Offensive Gegen Kursk*. Osnabruck: Munion, 1980.

Stoler, Mark A. *The Politics of the Second Front*. Westport, CT: Greenwood, 1977.

Stolfi, Russel H. S. *Hitler's Panzers East: World War II Reinterpreted*. Norman: University of Oklahoma Press, 1992.

Strana Sovetov za 50 let Sbornik Statisticheskikh Materialov. Moscow: Statistika, 1967.

Sutton, Antony C. *Western Technology and Soviet Economic Development*. 3 vols. Stanford: Hoover Institution Press, 1968–73.

Tiushkevich, Stepan A., ed. *Sovetskie Vooruzhennye Sily*. Moscow: Voenizdat, 1978.

———, ed. *The Soviet Armed Forces*. Washington, DC: U.S. Government Printing Office, 1985.

United States War Department, Military Intelligence Division. *German Military Intelligence 1939–1945*. Frederick, MD: University Publications of America, 1984.

———. *Handbook on USSR Military Forces. November 1945 Technical Manual 30–430*. Washington, DC: U.S. Government Printing Office, 1946.

U.S.S.R. Central Statistical Board of the USSR Council of Ministers. *National Economy of the U.S.S.R. Statistical Returns*. Moscow: Foreign Languages Publishing House, 1957.

U.S.S.R. Report: Military Affairs, June 12, 1986. Provisional Field Regulations for the Red Army (PU-36). Translated by Foreign Broadcast Information Service. Washington, DC: U.S. Government Printing Office, 1986.

Van Creveld, Martin. *Supplying War*. Cambridge: Cambridge University Press, 1977.

———. *Technology and War from 2000 BC to the Present*. New York: Free Press, 1989.

Van Tuyll, Hubert P. *Feeding the Bear: American Aid to the Soviet Union, 1941–1945*. New York: Greenwood, 1989.

Vassilevsky, A., et al. *Moscow Stalingrad 1941–1942: Recollections Stories Reports*. Moscow: Progress Publishers, 1974.

Velikai Otechestvennia Voina 1941–1945 Entsiklopediya. Moscow: Sovetskia Entsiklopediya, 1985.

Voenno Istoricheskii Zhurnal. JPRS Report, Foreign Military Review, Microfiche #5059. Moscow: Isdatellstvo ''Krachaia Zvezda.''

Volz, Arthur G. ''Soviet Artillery Weapons: I, The Imperial Heritage.'' *Soviet Armed Forces Review Annual* 10 (1985–86), 209–32.

———. ''Soviet Artillery Weapons: II, 1918–1941.'' *Soviet Armed Forces Review Annual* 11 (1987–88), 301–23.

———. ''Soviet Artillery Weapons: III, 1941–1945.'' *Soviet Armed Forces Review Annual* 12 (1988), 209–32.

Voronov, Nikolai N. *Na Sluzhbe Voyennoy*. Moscow: Voyenizdat, 1963.

Voznesenskii, Nikola A. *Soviet Economy during the Second World War*. New York: International Publishers, 1949.

Werth, Alexander. *Russia at War*. New York: Discus Books, 1970.

Westwood, J. N. *A History of Russian Railways*. London: George Allen and Unwin, 1964.

Wray, Timothy. *Standing Fast: German Defensive Doctrine on the Russian Front during World War II, Prewar to March 1943*. Combat Studies Institute Research Survey, no. 5. U.S. Army Command and General Staff College. Washington, DC: U.S. Government Printing Office, 1987.

Zaloga, Steven J., and James Grandsen. *Soviet Tanks and Combat Vehicles of World War Two*. London: Arms and Armour Press, 1984.

Zhukov, Georgi K. *Marshal Zhukov's Greatest Battles*. New York: Harper & Row, 1969.
Zhukov, G. K. *Reminiscences and Reflections.* Moscow: Progress Publishers, 1989.
Ziemke, Earl F. *The Soviet Juggernaut*. Morristown, NJ: Silver Burdett, 1988.
————. *Stalingrad to Berlin: The German Campaign in Russia, 1942–1945*. New York: Dorset, 1968.
Ziemke, Earl F., and Magna E. Bauer. *Moscow to Stalingrad: Decision in the East*. New York: Military Heritage Press, 1988.

Index

About the Author

WALTER S. DUNN, Jr. is an independent researcher and retired museum curator. He has published a dozen books on World War II and on colonial and local history.